JUST WORDS:
CONSTITUTIONAL RIGHTS AND
SOCIAL WRONGS

The Canadian Charter of Rights is composed of words that describe the foundations of a just society: equality, freedom, and democracy. These words of justice have inspired struggles for civil rights, self-determination, trade unionism, the right to vote, and social welfare. Why is it, then, that fifteen years after the entrenchment of the Charter, social injustice remains pervasive in Canada?

Joel Bakan explains why the Charter has failed to promote social justice, and why it may even impede it. He argues that the Charter's fine-sounding words of justice are 'just words.' The principles of equality, freedom, and democracy are interpreted and implemented by a fundamentally conservative institution – the legal system – within social and economic conditions that systematically frustrate their full realization.

Sophisticated in its analyses but clearly written and accessible, *Just Words* is cutting-edge commentary by one of Canada's rising intellectuals.

JOEL BAKAN is a professor of law at the University of British Columbia.

JOEL BAKAN

Just Words: Constitutional Rights and Social Wrongs

UNIVERSITY OF TORONTO PRESS
Toronto Buffalo London

© University of Toronto Press 2012
Toronto   Buffalo   London
www.utppublishing.com

Printed in the U.S.A.

Reprinted in Canada 150 Collection 2017

ISBN 978-1-4875-1655-0

Canadian Cataloguing in Publication Data

Bakan, Joel
Just words : constitutional rights and social wrongs

Includes bibliographical references and index.
ISBN 978-1-4875-1655-0 (pbk.)

1. Canada.   Canadian Charter of Rights and Freedoms.
2. Social justice.   I. Title.

KE4381.5B34 1997   342.71'085   C97-930672-8
KF4483.C519B34 1997

University of Toronto Press acknowledges the financial assistance to its publishing program of the Canada Council for the Arts and the Ontario Arts Council.

This book has been published with the help of a grant from the Canadian Federation for the Humanities and Social Sciences Federation of Canada, using funds provided by the Social Sciences and Humanities Research Council of Canada.

For my parents,
Rita and Paul Bakan

Contents

ACKNOWLEDGMENTS   ix

1 Introduction   3

Part I
2 Constitutional Interpretation and the Legitimacy of Judicial Review   15

Part II
3 Equality and the Liberal Form of Rights   45
4 Freedom of Expression and the Politics of Communication   63
5 Freedom of Association and the Dissociation of Workers   77
6 Power to the Powerful   87

Part III
7 Judges and Dominant Ideology   103

Part IV
8 Rights as Political Discourse: The Charter Meets the Charlottetown
  Accord   117
9 What's Wrong with Social Rights?   134

10 Conclusion   143

NOTES   153
REFERENCES   193
CASES CITED   219
INDEX   225

Acknowledgments

Above all, the person who has made the writing of this book possible is Marlee Kline. Words cannot express my gratitude to her for loving, caring for, and believing in me; for inspiring and challenging me intellectually; for reading and re-reading the countless drafts of this manuscript, always providing me with thoughtful and insightful comments and suggestions for improving it; and for her constant encouragement, especially when the dark cloud of self-doubt hovered over me.

To my parents, Rita and Paul Bakan, to whom this book is dedicated, I am grateful for the gifts of intellect, idealism, and compassion, and for teaching me to challenge convention, think critically, and care about the deeper things in life. They have been my most important and influential teachers. The animating idea of this book – that scepticism about the present is part of the struggle for a better future – is something I learned from them. I thank them as well for reading earlier drafts of this manuscript and for helping me improve it. Most of all, I thank them, as well as my sister and brother, Laura Bakan and Michael Bakan, for their constant love, support, and encouragement.

I owe great intellectual debts to Brian Dickson, Harry Glasbeek, Duncan Kennedy, and Joseph Raz, who were my teachers and mentors over the years. Andrew Petter deserves special thanks, not only as a friend, colleague, and source of intellectual inspiration, but also as the person with whom the idea for this book was first conceived. Many other friends and colleagues have helped me along the way, providing intellectual company, good-humoured criticism, comments on drafts, and numerous other kinds of support. I am especially grateful to Nick Blomley, John Borrows, Susan Boyd, Gwen Brodsky, Neil Brooks, Annie Bunting, Jamie Cassells, David Cohen, Davina Cooper, Brenda Cossman, Shelagh Day, Robin Elliot, Richard Ericson, John Fellas, Judy Fudge, Shelley Gavigan, Rob Grant, Mick Gzowski, Reuben Hasson, Douglas Hay, Didi Herman, Peter Hogg,

Allan Hutchinson, Nitya Iyer, Bernard Kalvin, Karl Klare, Roger Larry, Hester Lessard, Mark Lewis, Rod MacDonald, John McLaren, Patrick Macklem, Maureen Maloney, Michael Mandel, Lisa Philipps, Toni Pickard, Danielle Pinard, Wes Pue, Iain Ramsay, Bruce Ryder, David Schneiderman, J.C. Smith, Lynn Smith, Michael Smith, Sandy Tomc, Toni Williams, Claire Young, and Margot Young.

Osgoode Hall Law School and the University of British Columbia Faculty of Law have provided me supportive and stimulating environments in which to work. I would also like to thank the many students and research assistants I have worked with at these institutions over the years.

I am grateful to Virgil Duff, executive editor of the University of Toronto Press, who provided constant and enthusiastic support for this project. I also want to thank the anonymous reviewers of the manuscript, whose comments were very helpful.

I have attempted to write a book that will help people understand constitutional rights. To illustrate my arguments, I analyse the provisions of Canada's Charter of Rights and Freedoms, 1982, that guarantee rights of equality (section 15) and freedom (sections 2 and 7). Some key issues in constitutional law – Quebec, First Nations, language rights, and criminal procedure – though discussed at various points in the book, are not comprehensively dealt with. I believe that these issues require books of their own, and I judged at an early stage in the manuscript's development that a chapter or two examining each would not have done them justice. At the same time, I hope that the book's approach to analysing constitutional rights will be useful to those grappling with these important matters.

This book is the product of my thinking about constitutional rights over the last ten years. Chapters 1, 3–7, and 10 have not been previously published, though they draw on and develop ideas, occasionally reproducing actual passages, from papers that I published between 1989 and 1995 in the *Canadian Bar Review, McGill Law Journal, Public Law, University of Toronto Law Faculty's Legal Theory Workshop Series, University of Toronto Law Journal,* and *Constitutional Politics,* a collection of essays edited by Duncan Cameron and Miriam Smith. Chapter 2 is an abridged, updated, and amended version of an article that first appeared in the *Osgoode Hall Law Journal.* Chapter 8, which I originally wrote with Michael Smith, first appeared in *Social and Legal Studies* and is also included in *Charting the Consequences* (1997 forthcoming), a collection of essays edited by David Schneiderman and Kate Sutherland. Chapter 9 is based primarily on a piece that first appeared in *Social Justice and the Constitution,* a collection of essays that I edited with David Schneiderman, and its introductory paragraphs are drawn from the Introduction to that collection, which I wrote with David Schneiderman.

JUST WORDS

1

Introduction

One cannot combat the real existing world by merely combating the phrases of this world.
Karl Marx (1981, 41)[1]

The Canadian Charter of Rights and Freedoms, 1982, is composed of words that describe the foundations of a just society: equality, freedom, and democracy. These words of justice, or just words, state the highest ideals of progressive social movements and have inspired struggles for social justice throughout history. People have fought for civil rights, self-determination, trade unionism, the right to vote, and social equality in their name. The Charter has become a symbol of hope for social justice advocates because of its powerful words. A decade and a half after its constitutional entrenchment, however, social injustice remains pervasive in Canada. Why has the Charter failed to protect or advance social justice in Canada? Recasting the 'living tree' metaphor so often used to describe it, I argue that the Charter is only paper, dead tree, with ink on it. Its fine-sounding words of justice are only words, just words. They can do nothing on their own, and the social processes that give them effect tend to thwart whatever progressive promise they might hold. The Charter's potentially radical and liberatory principles of equality, freedom, and democracy are administered by a fundamentally conservative institution – the legal system – and operate in social conditions that routinely undermine their realization. That is why, I argue below, the Charter has done little to promote social justice in Canada despite its just words. The present chapter briefly describes my arguments, locates them within the literature on rights and on the Charter, and explains the book's normative foundations.

This book is about the relationship between Charter law and the social forces that shape its interpretation and effects. I explore that relationship by analysing the Supreme Court of Canada's Charter jurisprudence and asking why the court has done what it has under the Charter, what the real effects are of its decisions, and what it and other courts are likely to do with the Charter in the future.[2] Charter law, I argue, is constituted by discourses about law, rights, and society that are *ideological* – a term I use to indicate that they are anchored in and help sustain specific patterns of social relations and political order (Eagleton 1991, 8). To begin with, law, particularly constitutional law, is represented in judicial decisions and mainstream scholarship on the Charter as separate from politics – as a search for objective truth, a matter of trust in impartial processes, or some combination of the two. This is the basis – a tenuous one, I argue in part I – for claims that judicial review of parliamentary institutions under the Charter is principled, as opposed to political, and therefore legitimate, even though judges are not democratically representative or accountable.

Part II examines the ideological conception of rights that informs Charter law. Courts tend to rely on liberal rights discourse when interpreting the Charter, presenting government regulation as the primary threat to human liberty and equality, and individuals as abstract equals unaffected by structural forms of domination and exploitation. These ideas and images (discussed at length in chapter 3) are firmly anchored in Charter law and contribute substantially to the Charter's incapacity to redress most areas of social injustice. The Charter's equality rights, for example, are largely ineffective because the causes and symptoms of social inequality generally lie beyond their judicially determined scope (chapter 3); the right to freedom of expression protects people only from discrete governmental restrictions on their speech and thus does not affect the social processes that restrict people's ability to communicate effectively (chapter 4); and freedom of association cannot protect workers from unemployment and the increasing mobility of capital, which are the real threats to their rights to organize, bargain collectively, and strike (chapter 5). I argue further that social injustice is actually worsened by the Charter in some areas. There is an unfortunate symbiosis between the anti-government ideology of neo-liberal right-wing politics and the deregulatory form of Charter rights. Individuals, groups, and corporations are able to use the Charter to avoid legislative restrictions designed to prevent them from harming and exploiting others – a point I illustrate in chapter 6 by examining Charter victories of business corporations and individuals accused of sexual assault and hate crimes.

I discuss again the liberal form of rights in part IV (chapters 8 and 9) to help explain the effects of rights discourse in political contexts beyond the courts. Chapter 8 analyses the uses and effects of rights discourse, around issues of women's equality, First Nations, and Quebec, during the lead-up to the referendum on the Charlottetown Accord.[3] Chapter 9 criticizes the argument that the Charter's failure to achieve social justice can be remedied by entrenching another Charter, a 'social charter,' which explicitly protects social (positive) rights.

Part III (chapter 7) examines the effects of ideological discourses about society on Charter adjudication. I argue that judges, because of their education, socialization, and the processes through which they are appointed, tend to stay within the bounds of conservative discourses, about work, family, sexuality, race, and other social phenomena, when deciding Charter cases. Because claims for social justice under the Charter often must draw on oppositional and alternative ideas, this conservative disposition is a limit, further to that of rights' liberal form, on the progressive potential of Charter litigation – a point that I illustrate by examining how members of the court have dealt with Charter challenges to legislation regulating labour relations, commercial advertising, and benefits for gays and lesbians.

There are important differences between the arguments of this book and those of other progressive scholars of the Charter. To begin with, I analyse Charter law from an external perspective, focusing on its social and ideological dimensions. As social theorists of law have long insisted, strictly internal legal analysis cannot lead to understanding of how law actually works.[4] Weber (1954, 11–12), one of the first modern sociologists of law, noted that law can be studied from two different perspectives – the 'juridical point of view' and the perspective of 'sociological economics.' The former is concerned with 'the correct meaning of propositions the content of which constitutes an order supposedly determinative for the conduct of a defined group of persons'; the latter, with 'the interconnections of human activities as they actually take place.' According to Weber, the juridical point of view (which I call the 'internal perspective') is deficient because it focuses only on normative questions within the legal system and thus generates knowledge about law that 'has nothing to do with the world of real economic content' (12). Understanding law fully, in his view, requires analysing it from a standpoint outside the legal system.

Following Weber on this point, I am interested in the social and ideological dimensions of Charter law, not questions about its validity or soundness as judged by the internal conventions of legal method. This does not mean that the internal perspective on law is irrelevant; rejecting it as a standpoint for studying law does not deny its relevance as an object of inquiry (Hunt 1993; Sargent 1991). Scholars must intelligibly construe law from the perspective of those who create and use it, before they can identify and analyse its social and ideological dimensions. In the following chapters I thus examine in detail the contents and conventions of Charter law as a necessary step before analysing, from an external perspective, their limits, contradictions, effects, and determinants.

The emphasis on external analysis distinguishes my work from most other Charter scholarship, the bulk of which assumes an internal perspective and considers primarily normative questions: what should courts do? what should the law be? how should this or that legal provision or decision be interpreted?[5] Progressive internal analysis usually presumes that the purpose of the Charter is to advance social justice, and then it interprets and evaluates Charter law from this perspective. Analysts argue, for example, that Charter rights guarantee adequate standards of social and economic welfare (Jackman 1988; 1993), legal aid (Mossman 1988; Hughes 1995), shelter (Parkdale Community Legal Services 1987) and workers' rights (Beatty 1987; 1991). At a more philosophical level, some scholars argue that rights litigation has progressive potential because it is principled, as opposed to political (Beatty 1987; Dyzenhaus 1989), while others claim that it can be made progressive by rooting out its conservative foundations through interpretation (Minow 1990; Trakman 1991; 1994; Nedelsky 1993) (I examine both schools in chapter 2). There is thus a wealth of insight into what the Charter should or might do, but little about 'where we *already* are and ... what we *already* do' (Fischl 1993, 783).

I do not want to deny, however, that internal analysis of the Charter and law is intellectually rigorous. E.P. Thompson has noted, for example, that 'Blackstone's *Commentaries* [a paradigmatic example of internal legal analysis] represent an intellectual exercise far more rigorous than could have come from an apologist's pen' (1975, 263). Thompson is right about the intellectual rigour. He is wrong, however, to imply that apologetics cannot take an intellectually rigorous form. Internal legal thought is rigorous, and elegant on occasion, but it implicitly defends a method that presumes, rather than questions, law's autonomy from politics and society.[6] Most legal scholars acknowledge the gap between the ideal of law and its practice, expose and correct mistakes and inconsistencies in legal doctrine, criticize corruption and incompetence, and see a place for values and policies, sometimes even progressive or radical ones, in legal reasoning.[7] All of this, however, only reinforces a more general faith in law by implying the plausibility of aspiring to achieve its ideal form. Law is presumed to be, '[like] religion,' as Marx characterized Hegel's understanding of the state, 'beyond the limitation of the profane world' (Marx 1967, 225).[8]

The work in this book differs as well from that of other external Charter analysts.[9] In particular, I reject the argument put forward by some (but certainly not all) of these scholars that the Charter and rights discourse are inherently flawed as forms of progressive politics. Progressive scholars offer two versions of this argument. First, they criticize constitutional rights litigation for being 'inherently antidemocratic' because it enables judges to override decisions of elected representatives (Mandel 1994, 70; see also Ely 1980; Monahan 1987).[10] The flaw in this hypothesis, as I argue more fully in chapter 2, is its presumption that decisions of legislatures or governments are necessarily more democratic than those of courts. Because of unequal political resources, the existence of multiple parties, and numerous imperfections in extant democratic institutions, electoral processes cannot always produce governments, and certainly not particular policies, that have majority support. Theoretically, then, a Charter decision can actually serve the principle of majoritarianism by striking down legislation not supported by a majority. Arguably, the court's decision to strike down unpopular criminal prohibitions on abortions is an example of this (*Morgentaler* 1988). A Charter decision might also support majoritarianism by making elections fairer and thus improving the representativeness of governments, as in *Dixon* (1989), where a court ordered the redrawing of electoral riding boundaries. Moreover, majoritarianism can itself be blatantly inegalitarian and thus undemocratic. Though it often serves egalitarian ends in capitalist systems because it grants political power to the majority as a hedge against the private economic power of the minority, majority rule can also reinforce domination. History is replete with examples of minorities, defined by race, religion, sexuality, disability, and other social and personal characteristics, being oppressed, exploited, and excluded from key areas of economic and social life by majorities. Unjust treatment of minorities by a majority is anathema to the participatory ideals underlying notions of democratic citizenship, and constitutional rights litigation is one strategy that might be used against such injustices (more about which in chapter 4).

In theory, then, formally countermajoritarian restraints on representative institutions – such as those imposed by the Charter – might advance democracy and equality. I am not arguing that the Charter is likely to have such effects. As I demonstrate below, in current social and political conditions, the Charter does not further democratic and egalitarian values, except in narrow and exceptional circumstances (namely, where majority power has been used to entrench oppression), and, even then, not substantially; moreover, it often serves to undermine these values. Despite the imperfections of representative institutions in Canada, and the numerous examples of abusive and oppressive exercises of governmental and legislative power (against First Nations, workers, women, immigrants, lesbians and gays, and others), the historical record, at least of the period since the Second World War, arguably demonstrates that they have wider progressive potential and capacity than courts in many areas of social policy.[11] I base this assessment, however, on what legislatures and courts have actually done, not on a comparison of their ideal forms. In contrast, anti-democracy critiques of constitutional rights tend to emphasize comparisons of institutional forms, without considering how varying social and political circumstances might shape the relative effects of legislative and judicial actions in different times, places, and contexts. The resulting presumption against constitutional rights can both exaggerate the democratic potential of representative institutions and categorically deny the possibility that, in some circumstances, constitutional rights can advance democratic values.[12]

Next, I want to distinguish my approach from the claim, characteristic of much work in the critical legal studies school, that rights discourse is inherently regressive because it imposes an 'impoverished and partial notion of social life' on society (Hutchinson 1995, 25). Hutchinson is one of the leading advocates of this view in relation to the Charter (see more generally Gabel 1984). Rights discourse, he argues, is individualistic and formalistic and 'has hijacked citizenship and made it subservient to its own civic ambitions' (Hutchinson 1995, 214). The project for progressive politics is to replace rights discourse with new discourses, described variously as 'democratic conversation' and 'radical' or 'unmodified' democracy (207, 223), which would serve to reconstitute community through people's 'experience of interpersonal relations and its [the community's] ties' (187). Within his self-consciously 'postmodern critique' (225), Hutchinson constructs and reconstructs discourse in a social vacuum, free of material constraints, thus implying that its qualities are intrinsic rather than a product of social forces. He evaluates the limits of rights discourse, and the emancipatory potentials of other modes of discourse, in the abstract, apart from the specific social forces that shape their nature and effects and the actual opportunities and capacities of those who use them in political struggle. Political discourses thus appear as autonomous, having profound effects on social relations but being curiously unaffected by them. Hutchinson offers no systematic analysis of the multiple social and economic forces that undermine democratic citizenship today, nor of how these shape the nature and power of various political discourses.

Hutchinson's inattention to the effects of underlying social and economic forces on discursive practice is not a mere oversight, but rather a reflection of the deep scepticism about claims to understand the empirical dimensions of history and society that is currently fashionable in postmodern social theory. This is a major distinction between my work and his (and other postmodern rights theorists). Explaining the 'reality' of constitutional rights is this book's goal. My aim is to understand the wider social processes that shape, sustain, and determine the effects and nature of discursive practices under the Charter. Though postmodern theorists are correct in their view that unmediated access to final truths about the world is impossible – we can, after all, know and explain the world only through language, a social construct – that does not preclude our understanding 'how things work, how our world is put together, how things happen to us as they do' (D. Smith 1990, 34–5). I agree with Hunt (1992) that the process of gaining knowledge about the world is one of 'successive approximation to reality' (58); we can try to come 'to grips with empirical reality in order to engage politically in its transformation' (62), while still avoiding the dangers and pretensions of positivist and empiricist social science (see also Barrett 1991, 167; Eagleton 1991, 1–32).

A fundamental feature of empirical reality in Canada today is the fact that we live in a capitalist system of social relations. Class analysis – examination of the relationships and processes of economic production, particularly property and ownership, that establish unequal patterns of power and dependence among people (Meikins Wood 1995) – is thus necessary (albeit not sufficient) for critical theory and practice (Fudge and Glasbeek 1992b; Harvey 1993; Frankel 1994), as should become apparent in the chapters that follow, particularly 3–6, 9, and 10. Postmodern analysts, such as Hutchinson (1995), tend to be sceptical of class analysis, partly because it posits a 'reality' beyond discursive practice (174; see also Laclau and Mouffe 1985, 58). Such scepticism may explain Hutchinson's failure to consider fully the inevitable constraints of capitalist social relations on discursive strategies surrounding struggles for social change.

My differences with Mandel, Hutchinson, and other external critics of the Charter who take similar approaches, as well as with the progressive internal scholars discussed above, are primarily analytical; we share a general conception of social justice (described below) but differ on how to assess the role of constitutional rights in the struggle to achieve it. My concern is with the tendency in their analyses, whether in favour of the Charter or against it, to pay insufficient attention to the constraining influences of economic, social, and political conditions on the operation and effects of the Charter. That is what I try to avoid here. I argue throughout this book that the Charter, and particularly its failure to advance social justice, must be explained in relation to the specific conditions in which it operates. All political institutions, including the Charter and rights, are necessarily constrained in their operation by the wider social system that they are established to govern. That is why it is necessary to be sceptical of both Charter optimism and pessimism when they are based on allegedly essential features of the Charter or rights. The emancipatory and egalitarian potential of the Charter ultimately depends on the social and historical circumstances surrounding its use (D. Herman 1994; Brown 1995, 100).

It is necessary for me to explain the normative foundations of the book. To this point, I have been using value-laden terms such as 'social justice' and 'progressive' to describe the standards against which I am evaluating the Charter's operation. In analysing Charter law from outside the internal norms of legal discourse I do not mean to imply that the analysis lacks a normative dimension. On the contrary, the book's central question – 'Why has the Charter failed to advance a progressive vision of social justice?' – presumes a normative standpoint. Its basic elements are co-terminous with the Charter's 'just words' – equality, freedom, and democracy – but defined much more broadly than the limits of Charter discourse would allow.

Equality entails elimination of major disparities in people's material resources, well-being, opportunities, and political and social power, and an absence of economic, social, and cultural oppression and exploitation. Perfect social equality may be impossible, but the aspiration to rid society of oppressive and exploitative disparities, based on unequal social relations – such as those of class, gender, and race – is realistic and worth fighting for.

Freedom involves the ability of people to develop their capacities; to determine, through deliberation, choice, and action, how to live their lives; and to participate in the democratic governance of social, economic, and political life. This conception of freedom encompasses negative freedom, or the protection of people from aribitrary uses of official authority and coercive power, but it also includes a positive dimension: the capacity – the resources, abilities, and opportunities – to exercise freedom and avoid coercion by others. Freedom thus requires a measure of social equality.

Democracy means active participation of people in determining the conditions of their existence and association. Extant institutions of Canadian government manifest only a thin version of democracy. Most people do not participate in self-government, except in a rudimentary and formalistic fashion: they vote for representatives every few years on the basis of platforms formulated by parties to which they do not belong, and they have little access to the government of the day unless they are part of an organized lobby group. The active exercise of rights to form and join political parties, and to lobby representatives and governments, not to mention run for election, requires time, energy, information, and resources not available to most people, especially those struggling just to make ends meet. In contrast, powerful economic actors and wealthy individuals have a disproportionate influence on the political process. They support the campaigns of politicians who protect their interests and dictate government policy through decisions to invest (or not) in a region or country, while the media wage ideological war against governments perceived to be hostile to business, and bond-rating agencies press such governments with the threat of low ratings.

In addition, the actual scope of democracy in most putatively democratic states, including Canada, is narrow, limited to the selection of governments and legislators, occasional referenda, and certain non-governmental institutions (unions, clubs, shareholders' meetings, and so on). Most decisions affecting people's daily lives are beyond direct democatic control. Allocation of resources, the nature and amount of economic investment, and modes and locations of production are primarily governed by private economic decisions (Schiller 1995, 21). Major industrial, resource, service, agricultural, media, entertainment, and real estate enterprises determine whether and under what conditions people work; what they read, hear, and see; where and how they are sheltered; what they eat; and the state of their environments. The power of private economic actors over people's lives is further strengthened by evisceration of governmental (and thus democratic) authority through privatization, deregulation, liberalized international trade regimes, and new communications technologies.

The powerful ideals of equality, freedom, and democracy are, in short, only partly realized in Canada today. That is better than nothing – a point underlined by the fact that throughout history, and in many contemporary societies, these ideals are not even legitimate aspirations. The Charter, however, cannot protect and advance a progressive conception of social justice, despite its just words; it cannot compensate for the systematic undermining of ideals of social justice by the routine operation of society's structures and institutions. That is this book's central argument.

Constitutional rights strategies share with all other forms of political action some potential and some dangers, yet they cannot substantially redress social injustice because it is produced by a multitude of factors beyond their reach. What, then, should be done to bring about progressive social change? Though I do not pretend to have an answer to this question, the arguments of this book draw on two presumptions about social change: first, class analysis and politics are essential, though not sufficient, for understanding and working to ameliorate social injustice; and second, progressive social change can be facilitated by an activist state. I defend these presumptions in the last chapter.

One final word is in order. External analysis of law, such as that of this book, is often criticized for being 'cynical' – in addition to 'nihilistic' (Fiss 1981–2), 'pointless' and 'perverse' (Dworkin 1986, 11–16),[13] and 'irrational, if not explicitly insane' (Goodrich 1992, 16) – because it seeks to define the limits of law rather than reveal its alleged potential (Weiler 1990, 41). I reject this characterization and want to emphasize that this volume is an exercise in scepticism, not cynicism. Scepticism, at least mine, about existing institutions, such as the Charter and the courts, is driven by a hopeful (perhaps naïvely so) belief that criticism of extant social and political conditions can help create a better future. The real cynics, in my view, are those who shun scepticism as either dangerous or futile and defend the status quo as the best that we can aspire to. Scepticism about the Charter may turn out to be misguided, but I would rather err on its side than on that of the flag wavers – even at the risk of having my work characterized as 'self-loathing' because it implicitly 'denies [lawyers'] own civic agency and political efficacy' (A. Fraser 1993, 71–4). The Charter has ample defenders in the legal profession, judiciary, media, and academy. Criticism of it at least provokes reflection, asking people to question what they might otherwise take for granted. The purpose of criticism is not to prove that nothing is possible, but rather to understand what is.

PART I

2

Constitutional Interpretation and the Legitimacy of Judicial Review

There are two, and in the end only two, types of faith. To be sure there are very many contents of faith, but we only know faith itself in two basic forms. Both can be understood from the simple data of our life: the one from the fact that I trust someone, without being able to offer sufficient reasons for my trust in him; the other from the fact that, likewise, without being able to give a sufficient reason, I acknowledge a thing to be true.
Martin Buber (1951)

Throughout history even the most despotic regimes have sought to justify their power. Rulers recognize that while coercive force is the ultimate guarantor of their authority, a social order is best preserved through a population's acquiescence. Thus where power is found, so too are discourses and institutional arrangements that seek to establish its legitimacy. In this chapter I analyse and criticize the types of argument that constitutional jurists make to legitimate the authority of judges in constitutional cases. Judicial review under the constitution requires judges to determine the legal validity of actions by the legislative and executive branches of the state. The principles usually advanced in a liberal democracy to legitimate the exercise of state power are not available for judicial review; these principles are, indeed, contradicted by the practice. Judges, who are neither responsible to nor representative of the electorate, scrutinize the power of institutions that are thought to be both. Constitutional jurisprudence and scholarship are concerned to a large degree with constructing arguments aimed at mediating the apparent contradiction between judicial review and the principles of democracy. Such arguments have in common an emphasis on formal reasons for legitimacy – ones related to the processes and methods through which judicial decisions are made.[1] The central idea in all these arguments is that constitutional law is separate from politics. Judicial decisions are legitimate, despite the absence of democratic accountability, because they are principled and thus fundamentally different from the partisan and interest-driven world of politics.

Two basic types of argument for formal legitimation – one based on truth and the other on trust – are standard in Canadian constitutional discourse. The first holds that the constitution compels judges to reach legally correct answers to particular constitutional questions. Judges do not, therefore, substitute their policy choices and preferences for those of elected officials. The position acknowledges that when judges make decisions under the constitution they exercise power – they use the authority of the court, and therefore the state, to condone or rearrange existing social and legal relations – but portrays the exercise of such power as legitimate because it is required by the constitution. Legitimacy thus depends on the tenability of a unique link between the constitutional prescription in question and the result reached by the court in its name. The difficulty with this type of reasoning is that many, indeed most, of the provisions of the constitutional text are couched in language so general as to allow for numerous plausible meanings. Constitutional concepts such as 'liberty,' 'equality,' 'freedom of expression,' and 'property and civil rights' are indeterminate: they have no fixed or intrinsic meaning and cannot therefore direct judges to specific results in constitutional cases. Thus, while in theory judges must be constrained by constitutionally prescribed concepts when deciding cases, such constraint is absent in practice. Judges and constitutional scholars construct interpretive methods that allegedly resolve the ambiguities of constitutional provisions and point interpreters towards their true meanings.

The second type of argument – based on trust in judges – contrasts sharply with the first. It rejects the notion that judges can be constrained by the constitution to reach particular decisions, postulating instead that constitutional provisions are vague and general standards that provide some structure for the adjudicative process but do not determine unique and uncontroversial solutions to disputes. Hence it openly acknowledges constitutional decisions as resting on judicial choice and discretion. Judges, like other policy makers, are expected to balance competing interests and consider the probable consequences of deciding one way or another. This account legitimates judicial review on the basis that judges can be trusted, because of their personal qualities and institutional role, to balance competing interests fairly and reasonably; their alleged professionalism, impartiality, moral acumen, and general sense of fairness and decency legitimate the decisions they make. It rejects abstract and general reasoning, deduction from allegedly determinate norms, conceptualization, adherence to precedent, and the other trappings of constraint-based legal reasoning, which are seen as impediments to, not requirements of, rational and honest decision making.

In the first section of this chapter, I hypothesize that the two types of legitimation argument shaped constitutional reasoning in Canada prior to entrenchment of the Charter. The rest of the chapter concentrates on legitimation arguments used under the Charter. In section II, I examine the predominant truth-based method of interpretation developed by courts in Charter adjudication – namely, purposive reasoning – and seek to show that, because of the indeterminacy of constitutional norms, it does not satisfy the criterion of legitimacy that it is designed to realize. Section III analyses trust-based arguments in the Supreme Court's Charter adjudication. There I suggest that there are insufficient grounds for trusting judicial choice and discretion and, accordingly, that trust is not a satisfactory basis of legitimacy. In section IV, I analyse the hypothesis, articulated in various and often quite elaborate ways by many scholars, that constitutional decision making is constrained and objective, even though there are not always constitutionally determined answers to constitutional questions. I examine both mainstream and progressive versions of this position. Finally, in section V, I look critically at the claim often understood to follow from the insufficiency of truth and trust as formal grounds of legitimacy – namely, that the only legitimate response of the court in constitutional cases is judicial restraint.

I

The legitimacy of judicial review under the constitution has been a problem in Canadian legal thought for more than a century. Throughout its tenure as the final court of appeal for Canadian constitutional cases,[2] the Judicial Committee of the Privy Council (hereinafter the Judicial Committee) approached constitutional adjudication as a technical and legalistic exercise, reasoning in its decisions as though the broad concepts elaborated in the British North America (BNA) Act, 1867, could determine particular meanings and results through judges' deductive analysis of the constitutional text and doctrine. While the Judicial Committee acknowledged that ambiguous phrases required resort to various techniques and rules of statutory construction, as well as consideration of their textual context, it assumed that determinate meaning could always be found within the text. The BNA Act was to be treated 'by the same methods of construction and exposition which [courts] apply to other statutes' (*Lambe v. Bank of Toronto et al.* 1887, 579): '... If the text is explicit the text is conclusive ... when the text is ambiguous ... recourse must be had to the context and scheme of the Act' (*A.G. Ontario v. A.G. Canada* 1911, 583).[3] Underlying this approach to interpretation was a presumption that the Law Lords of the Judicial Committee were constrained by the text of the BNA Act, 1867, and therefore required by the act to reach the results that they did. At least in theory, then, the intervention of judicial choice and discretion was avoided.[4]

The Judicial Committee's interpretive method attracted two types of criticism in

Canada. Cairns (1971) characterizes these as 'fundamentalist' and 'constitutionalist.' The fundamentalists believed that the original intention of the constitutional framers was to establish a centralized federal system, as embodied in the BNA Act, 1867, and evident in the materials surrounding its inception. The fault of the Judicial Committee, according to them, was its radical deviation from the framers' purposes and intentions. Constitutionalists, in contrast, 'asserted that the Judicial Committee should have been an agent for constitutional flexibility, concerned with the policy consequences of their decisions' (Cairns 1971, 307). They called for liberal and flexible interpretation, open acknowledgement of the policy role of judges, and consideration of social and economic facts in constitutional adjudication.

The two modes of critique identified by Cairns correspond to the two types of legitimation argument outlined above. The fundamentalists attacked the legitimacy of the Judicial Committee's constitutional decisions on the ground that they did not reflect the true meaning of the constitution. The judges of the Judicial Committee were, according to this reasoning, substituting their views (and biases) for the allegedly uncontroversial requirements of the constitution. Implicit in the critique is an understanding of the legitimacy of judicial outcomes that required that they be determined by constitutional norms: judges were to serve not as policy makers, but rather as humble servants of constitutional law and the purposes and intentions underlying it. The constitutionalist stance, in contrast, presumed that legitimacy could be based on trust in judicial policy making. It saw the judge as an enlightened policy maker, whose job it was to keep the constitution current with changing times through careful and impartial consideration of the social and economic consequences of his[5] decisions. He was not to posture as a mechanical administrator of allegedly determinate constitutional norms.

The two positions, with their different assumptions about the legitimacy of judicial review, are evident in constitutional scholarship of the 1930s. For instance, Vincent MacDonald (1937), W.P.M. Kennedy (1937), and F.R. Scott (1937), three of Canada's most respected constitutional scholars, relied on them in responding to the Judicial Committee's 1937 decisions on the federal government's 'new deal.'[6] That program, like its U.S. counterpart, legislated protection for workers and farmers, and general social security, in the wake of the Depression. In its decisions, the Judicial Committee struck down the program as an incursion on provincial jurisdiction. MacDonald, Kennedy, and Scott developed both fundamentalist and constitutionalist criticisms of the decisions.[7] In a fundamentalist vein, they insisted that the Judicial Committee had misinterpreted the constitution, substituting its own pro-provincial predilections for the constitution's requirements. Scott (1937), for example, noted that its pro-provincial bias represented a 'constitutional revolution' and 'had the effect of giving us a constitution exactly the opposite, in one vital respect, of that which we actually adopted in 1867' (488). Similarly, Kennedy

(1937) argued that the decisions had frustrated the centralist intentions of the founders of Canada (400), while MacDonald (1937) was sure that the decisions depicted 'a constitution of a character the complete reverse of that intended; for the result is a decentralized federalism with the effective residue of legislative power in the province' (424). Implicit with each author is the view that the decisions were illegitimate because the Judicial Committee had refused to follow the true goal of the constitution – namely, strong centralism.[8]

The three authors, in the constitutionalist strand in these articles, criticized the Judicial Committee for its narrow and technical reasoning and its unwillingness to consider openly the probable policy consequences of deciding constitutional disputes one way or the other. Kennedy (1937), for example, complained that the judges had neglected major 'questions of expediency or of political exigency,' (393) and MacDonald (1937) noted that while 'purely legal interpretation' might have been fitting in other areas of law, in constitutional law 'interpretation [turned] on consideration of policy ... to a large degree' (426) and should not seek to avoid policy considerations. The critics' acknowledgment of the need for more open policy making in constitutional adjudication implied an understanding of legitimacy based on trust in judges rather than on constraint by the constitution. However, because there was little reason to trust a judicial body located across the Atlantic, and staffed by British Law Lords, to make sound policy decisions for Canada, they argued that the Judicial Committee's jurisdiction in Canadian constitutional cases was illegitimate and should be abolished.

The themes of truth and trust continued to inform constitutional thought through the 1940s and 1950s. Like the three authors just discussed, leading scholars postulated that constitutional law is different from other types of law because of its close connection to the central political, social, and economic issues of the day. They also embraced the view that narrow and legalistic constitutional interpretation masked the political character of constitutional decisions. Bora Laskin (1955), for example, argued that constitutional adjudication inevitably requires choice 'according to social and economic preferences' and that such choice is 'concealed in constitutional interpretation,' not avoided by it (126). 'The constitution,' according to him, 'is as open as the minds of those called upon to interpret it; it is as closed as their minds are closed' (127). In Laskin's view, on the basis of text and doctrine alone, most constitutional cases 'could just as well have been decided the other way' (124). Similarly, Friedmann (1951) found 'two opposing viewpoints' (812) on adjudication. The first, reflecting the Judicial Committee's dominant approach, required judges 'to ignore political and social issues' and decide disputes on 'technical legal grounds,' though, in reality, it usually involved substitution of the judiciary's 'political philosophy' for that of the legislature (812). The opposing view, endorsed by Friedmann, 'though not without some reservations' (813), rejected as a 'delusion' the first view's 'unpolitical treatment of predominantly political and social issues clothed in legal form.' LaBrie (1949) shared Friedmann's evaluation of the competing approaches, noting 'the very wide degree of judicial discretion' (340) exercised 'behind the façade of statutory interpretation' (310).[9]

Laskin, Friedmann, and LaBrie, while concurring in their diagnoses of the Judicial Committee's difficulties, differed on the cure, and the contrast between truth and trust arguments is at the core of their disagreement. Friedmann (1951) and LaBrie (1949), having rejected the idea that narrow and legalistic methods could constrain constitutional interpretation, still believed that constraint was necessary to legitimacy and that it was possible if judges relied on the deeper principles of the constitutional order to guide their decisions. Friedmann (1951) located these principles in contemporary social consensus (822),[10] and LaBrie (1949), in the historical foundations of the constitution (319).[11] Laskin (1955), by contrast, had few qualms about judges making political choices but sharply criticized the Judicial Committee for refusing to acknowledge this unavoidable reality. Rather, judges making constitutional decisions should openly take account of social and economic facts and policies and thus provide an honest and rational basis for decisions that are inevitably political. Implicit in Laskin's (1955) ideas is the grounding of judicial authority in trust. 'The course [of constitutional decisions] must be set by the light of the particular judge's mind' (127), which could be trusted because of the judiciary's 'tradition of impartiality and security of tenure which mirrors their independence' (1947, 1087).[12]

Constitutional appeals to the Judicial Committee were abolished in 1949, and the Supreme Court of Canada became the highest arbiter for Canadian constitutional cases. The court's record on interpretive methods is more complicated than that of the Judicial Committee, which, despite its critics' protests, departed only very rarely from a narrow and legalistic approach.[13] During the 1950s the court showed some signs of moving away from such a stance in its constitutional decisions (Weiler 1974, 227).[14] In the 1960s, however, and most notoriously in its decisions under the Canadian Bill of Rights, it returned to a legalistic and formal style.[15] Perhaps it was this reversion that led to a resurgence of calls by constitutional jurists in the 1970s that it abandon narrow, technical reasoning and embrace a purposive approach. Like Friedmann (1951) and LaBrie (1949), leading jurists of the 1970s, such as Weiler (1970; 1973; 1974), Hogg (1979), and Laskin (1973), now a judge, believed that narrow and technical reasoning did not sufficiently constrain judicial choice and discretion, that constitutional adjudication was, in the absence of constraint, 'political,' and that the purposes and principles underlying constitutional prescriptions should constrain justices in constitutional cases.

Weiler, for example, attacked the Supreme Court of Canada for its narrow legalism (1974, 229), which, rather than constraining judicial choice and discretion, cloaked them in 'very abstract formulae' (1973, 364). He advised judges to let themselves be guided by the impersonal principles, policies, and purposes underlying legal norms. Once a judge had elaborated these foundational elements, he or she could follow their 'probable implications ... even when they [were] in opposition to his [or her] own personal values and policy preferences' (Weiler 1970, 19, 23, and 26). Hogg (1979) also advocated purposive reasoning in constitutional adjudication as a satisfactory compromise between implausible formalism and unfettered judicial choice and discretion (72–3). Finally, Laskin (1973) considered it the most appropriate method for constitutional cases (a pronounced departure from his earlier advocacy of trust), as it required judges to understand constitutional law as 'serving ends that express the character of our organized society,' with the content of these ends determined by 'the development of a consensus' within it (119).[16]

Purposive reasoning thus seemed, to these commentators, to meet the objections to formal reasoning while avoiding the view that the constitution was as open as the minds of those who interpreted it. They saw the purposive approach as a more developed and sophisticated scheme for constraining judicial choice and believed that it infused with meaning often vague and indeterminate constitutional texts and doctrine. It acknowledged the implausibility of textual determinism while maintaining that judicial interpretation of the constitution is bound by objective norms (N.C. Sheppard 1986, 206).[17]

Purposive reasoning, however, did not remain restricted to legal academic discourse; soon after the Charter's entrenchment, the Supreme Court of Canada explicitly adopted it as its primary method for deciding cases under the Charter. In the next section, I analyse and criticize the court's purposive reasoning in its Charter decisions as being an inadequate solution to the insuperable problem of legitimacy in constitutional adjudication.

II

The legitimacy of judicial review became a matter of urgent concern with entrenchment of the Charter in 1982. From that time, judicial review has necessarily involved judges in scrutinizing the substance of legislative and governmental initiatives for their compliance with vague and open-ended articulations of rights and freedoms. Not surprisingly, the corresponding expansion of the scope of judicial activity has intensified concerns about judicial power in constitutional adjudication. Academic and judicial constitutional discourse on the Charter has focused on defining and prescribing methods of interpretation that can legitimate the exercise of judicial authority in such cases. As we see below, truth and trust strongly inform this discourse, as they did in pre-Charter constitutional thought.

In the present section I examine critically the predominant truth-based method of interpretation used by the Court in Charter adjudication. This method involves, first, purposive interpretation of the Charter's guarantees of rights and freedoms, and, second, use of a four-part set of criteria for applying the open-ended standards of section 1 of the Charter.[18] In describing and analysing each of these two steps, I demonstrate that neither serves to limit judicial choice and discretion and therefore that neither meets truth-based criteria of legitimacy in Charter adjudication.

At the time of the Charter's entrenchment, and before the Supreme Court had decided any cases under it, constitutional scholars expressed concern that the Court might resort to narrow and legalistic techniques of interpretation in Charter adjudication. They implored the Court to adopt a purposive approach, elaborating and applying the purposes and principles underlying and informing the various rights and freedoms articulated in the Charter. Otherwise, they argued, the Court would simply impose its conservative views on the Charter under the guise of narrow legalism, as it had done with the Canadian Bill of Rights. The provisions of the Charter were, according to these scholars, too vague and open-ended to avoid such judicial politicking; constraint of judicial choice and discretion in Charter adjudication was possible only through techniques of interpretation designed to uncover and apply the purposes and principles underlying the Charter's rights and freedoms.[19]

The Court used purposive reasoning in its first decision under the Charter (*Skapinker* 1984, 366). It insisted in its early cases that the constitution could not be interpreted 'by reference to rules of statutory construction' (*Hunter v. Southam* 1984, 155) and that the 'austerity of tabulated legalism' (156[20]) and 'narrow and technical' construction should be avoided (*Skapinker* 1984, 366).[21] 'Broad, liberal and purposive' interpretation was to be the Court's method, as supported by its pervasiveness in Canadian constitutional jurisprudence (it was 'applied in countless cases': *Skapinker* 1984, 365[22]) and by its consistency 'with the classical principles of American constitutional construction' and with contemporary (non-Canadian) cases decided by the Judicial Committee of the Privy Council (*Hunter v. Southam* 1984, 156). The purposive approach to the Charter requires interpreters to uncover the interests and values that a right or freedom is meant to protect (*Big M Drug Mart* 1985, 344; *Oakes* 1986, 119). Because many of the Charter's provisions are vague and open-ended, unlikely to be clarified by reference to the text alone (*Hunter v. Southam* 1984; *Big M Drug Mart* 1985), the Court supplements textual analysis with examination of Canada's history, traditions, and fundamental values (*Big M* 1985, 359–60) to determine a right or freedom's purpose. '[A Charter guarantee] which by itself does not in any way define [its scope] must be construed,' according to Justice McIntyre, 'with reference to the constitutional text and to the nature, history, traditions, and social philosophies of our society' (*Alberta Reference* 1987, 403–4); only such a method can give meaningful content to the 'protean' concepts of the Charter – for example, equality (*Andrews* 1989, 164–9).

Purposive reasoning, as used by the Court, presumes that each right or freedom has a distinct, uncontroversial, and discernible purpose, which can define its scope. Such purposive reasoning is presented by the Court as limiting judicial choice; where the constitutional text is vague, indeterminate, and therefore incapable of constraining judicial choice, its underlying purposes and principles constrain the judges (Hogg 1987, 87). The law of the constitution, rather than the predilections of judges, thus still apparently rules.

Members of the Supreme Court have insisted on numerous occasions that the Court's only legitimate role is to apply constitutional law, not to question the wisdom and policies of the legislature (*Hunter* 1984, 659–60; *Operation Dismantle* 1985, 503, 494; *Motor Vehicle Act Reference* 1985, 496; *Alberta Reference* 1987; *Egan* 1995; *McKinney* 1990). They see purposive reasoning not only as consistent with this understanding but as allowing for its realization. On several occasions, they have explicitly linked purposive reasoning and constraint. In the *Motor Vehicle Act Reference* (1985), for example, Justice Lamer states that the task of securing the full benefits of the Charter for individuals while 'avoiding adjudication of the merits of public policy' can 'only be accomplished by a purposive analysis' (499). Similarly, in *Morgentaler* (1988), Justice McIntyre notes that the purposive approach requires courts to 'interpret the *Charter* in a manner calculated to give effect to its provisions, not to the idiosyncratic view of the judge who is writing,' and that purposive reasoning 'prevents the Court from abandoning its traditional adjudicatory function in order to formulate its own conclusions on questions of public policy, a step which this Court has said on numerous occasions it must not take' (140). Thus the Court, like the constitutional jurists discussed above, understands purposive reasoning as a compromise between the implausible view that judges are constrained by constitutional text and doctrine alone and the unacceptable position that their decisions reflect nothing more than political choices.

The burden of the argument in favour of this compromise is that purposive reasoning does constrain judicial choice and discretion – a burden that cannot, in my view, be satisfied. The view that constitutional texts and doctrine cannot constrain judicial choice, but that constitutional purposes and principles can, proposes an untenable solution to an insoluble problem. Peller (1985) puts the point well: 'The demonstration of the inherent indeterminacy of legal rules would at first glance seem to apply just as easily to attempts to ground legal decision-making in the identification and application of purposes, policies and principles' (1152–3).

The same holds true at second glance. The belief that purposive reasoning constrains decisions sufficiently to avoid concerns about legitimacy raised by judicial choice and discretion assumes both that the purpose of a constitutional provision can be identified without the intervention of judicial subjectivity and that the purpose, once identified, can be applied to determine uncontroversially the results of particular disputes. Both assumptions seem highly unlikely.

The first assumption underlies the pre-Charter discussions of purposive reasoning analysed in section I. The jurists there believed that the principle or policy identified as the purpose of a constitutional provision, or of the constitution as a whole, could be rooted in a consensus about history, the fundamental values of society, or the conventional sources of constitutional law. Thus they thought it possible to identify a purpose that was constitutionally 'true,' rather than a product of choice and a subject of dissension. Kennedy (1937), MacDonald (1937), Scott (1937), and LaBrie (1949), for example, supported their views by referring to the 'uncontroversial' intentions of the constitutional framers. Friedmann (1951), and later Laskin (1973), believed that the purposes of constitutional norms could be found in a consensus of public opinion about shared goals and values – principles that would, in Friedmann's words, 'find acceptance by all major political parties' (1951, 822). For Weiler (1970) and Hogg (1979) the relevant principles were those that could be identified incontestably as underlying the conventional sources of constitutional law.

The Court has adopted all of these sources – history, fundamental principles of society, and underlying principles of constitutional law – as appropriate places to find the purposes of Charter rights and freedoms. According to the Court, the purpose of a right or freedom should be determined through analysis of its 'historical origins,' the 'values that underlie our political and philosophic traditions,' the 'larger objects of the Charter itself,' and the language and textual context of the right or freedom (*Big M* 1985, 346). Through analysis of these sources judges and other constitutional interpreters can decide the purpose of a given right or freedom, apparently without making controversial or value-laden choices along the way. The judicial responsibility is simply to identify the principles and purposes that everyone would agree informed the right or freedom being interpreted.[23] This is, of course, an impossible task. The question 'What is the purpose of a right or freedom?' is not one that yields an incontrovertibly correct answer. Questions about the history of a right or freedom, or the political and philosophical values that it supposedly embodies, are themselves charged with politics and values; they are not matters of legal right and wrong.[24]

The Court's interpretation of the Charter's guarantee of freedom of association illustrates this point. In the *Alberta Reference* (1987), the Court held that freedom of association does not include the right to strike. Writing as part of the majority,

Justice McIntyre argued that the purpose of the Charter as a whole is to protect individual rights, not group rights. Freedom of association, it followed, is 'a freedom belonging to the individual and not to the group formed through its exercise' (397). Its purpose is to protect the 'attainment of individual goals' through group activity (395) – more specifically, to protect the rights of individuals to form and join groups, to exercise their individual constitutional rights in groups, and to do in association what they are lawfully entitled to do as individuals. By definition, then, any understanding of freedom of association that 'accord[s] an independent constitutional status to the aims, purposes and activities of the association' is wrong (404).

In contrast, Chief Justice Dickson, writing in partial dissent, understood the purpose of freedom of association as including protection of the activities of groups qua groups. He pointed to 'our constitution's history of giving special recognition to collectivities or communities of interest other than the government and political parties' (364) and emphasized that 'association ha[s] always been the means through which political, cultural and racial minorities, religious groups and workers have sought to attain their purposes and fulfil their aspirations' (365–6). Freedom of association does not, therefore, find its only point of reference in the individual (366–7). It belongs to groups, such as trade unions, not only to their individual members, and its purpose is to protect the essential activities of these groups – in this case, strikes and collective bargaining.

The conflicting approaches to freedom of association – individualist versus collectivist – in the two judgments illustrate just how untenable is the belief that purposive reasoning obviates the need for judicial choice and discretion. If judges must choose from among different and often conflicting formulations of the purpose of a right or freedom, purposive reasoning involves judicial subjectivity. It is in fact impossible to discover the unique and uncontroversial purpose of any of the Charter's rights and freedoms. Is the purpose of freedom of expression to protect the operation of democratic institutions, and is it thus confined to political speech? Or does it aim to provide a forum for ideas in all sectors, and thus include commercial and artistic speech? Is freedom of religion confined to ensuring that people are free to engage in religious exercises and practices? Or must the state be neutral in all matters of religion and thus also not support any religion? Is equality intended to ensure similar treatment of all groups? Or does it require differential treatment to ameliorate existing, unequal distributions of power? Courts have addressed these and other questions over the past decade and a half,[25] but their answers are products of interpretation, not legal necessity.

In general, the ideals articulated in Charter rights and freedoms are highly contentious and political. They are contested concepts that generate disagreement in the judicial and legal communities, and even more pronounced controversy in the larger society. Yet purposive reasoning presumes that it is possible to identify a principle or policy that everyone agrees is the purpose of a particular right or freedom. Such accord is highly unlikely in a country, such as Canada, where contradictory, conflicting, and even diametrically opposed interests constitute the social and economic order. The idea of social consensus is based on a purely hypothetical and highly unlikely convergence of interests among individuals and groups. It is therefore wise to remain sceptical of claims that a controversial position, such as a claim about the meaning of a Charter right or freedom, is supported by consensus. On this point, I agree with American constitutional scholar John Ely (1980, 63) that 'there is no consensus to be discovered ... and to the extent that one may seem to exist, that is likely to reflect only the domination of some groups by others.'[26]

None of this is to deny the possible appearance of consensus, even in a divided and diverse society such as Canada, if principles and policies are defined so abstractly as to mean anything to anybody. Where, however, the purpose of a right or freedom is so defined, purposive reasoning does little to constrain judicial choice.[27] As Chief Justice Dickson notes in another context, judicially created definitions of a constitutional provision are unhelpful when they are 'hardly ... narrower than ... a literal reading of the words ... [of the provision] alone' (*A.-G. Canada v. Canadian National* 1983, 262). The same can be said of definitions of rights and freedoms reached by the Court through purposive reasoning. To take an example, in *Hunter v. Southam* (1984), the Court interpreted the 'right to be secure against unreasonable search or seizure' (section 8) with the aid of purposive analysis. The word 'unreasonable,' the Court noted, was 'vague and open' and could not be defined by 'recourse to a dictionary, nor for that matter by reference to rules of statutory construction' (144–5). None the less, it would be 'possible to assess the reasonableness or unreasonableness of the impact of a search' by relying on the purpose underlying section 8 (157), which the Court identified as 'protect[ion of] individuals from unjustified State intrusions upon their privacy' (160). This definition, however, is itself 'vague and open,' with little more capacity to constrain judicial discretion than the provision itself. It does not indicate what circumstances must be present and what procedures must be followed before state interference with privacy is justified, nor the interests included in the concept of privacy. While the definition derived through purposive analysis is narrower than the term 'unreasonable,' it is still far too broad to determine 'right answers' in search and seizure cases.

We might look at many more examples to see that purposive reasoning does not avoid difficulties raised by a vague and indeterminate text. The Charter's rights and freedoms invite discord when questions are raised about their purpose, and if judges articulate the purpose at a high level of abstraction, disagreement simply re-emerges in arguments about what the purpose of a right or freedom means when applied to a particular constitutional dispute. For these reasons, purposive reasoning does little to constrain judicial interpretation. It does not inhibit judicial subjectivity and cannot therefore sustain the burden of the argument that the constitution determines adjudicative outcomes. As we see below in sections III and V, we might offer two responses to this criticism, both defending judicial review, but each of them flawed. Before analysing these two arguments, however, I next examine truth-based approaches to section 1 of the Charter.

As noted above, the Supreme Court's Charter jurisprudence usually involves two steps. First, the Court defines the content of a right or freedom through ascertaining of its purpose (the process just reviewed). Second, if it finds a limit on the right or freedom, the Court asks, under section 1, whether the limit is 'reasonable' and 'demonstrably justified in a free and democratic society.' It will uphold the impugned government action if it meets these standards, despite its limiting a right or freedom. Section 1 poses a significant problem for proponents of constitutional constraint. One would be hard pressed to come up with standards any more openended than those that it sets out. Whether a governmental action is 'reasonable' and 'demonstrably justified in a free and democratic society' is a matter of opinion and political choice, not a technical legal question.

In a number of its decisions, the Court has attempted to mediate the contradiction between its commitment to constraint and the political questions that arise under section 1. The leading case is *Regina v. Oakes* (1986). Chief Justice Dickson, writing for the majority, established a set of criteria to structure the section 1 analysis in all Charter cases. The Court will uphold legislation under section 1 only if its purpose is 'of sufficient importance to warrant overriding a constitutionally protected right or freedom'; the measures adopted are 'rationally connected to the objective'; the measures, 'even if rationally connected to the objective in the first sense, ... impair as little as possible the right or freedom in question'; and the 'deleterious effects' of the measures 'are outweighed by the importance of the objective' (138–40) (and, as a result of the Court's gloss on *Oakes* in *Dagenais* 1994, by their 'salutary effects').

The translation by the Court of section 1's ambiguous and general language into a neat, four-step test was clearly an attempt to avoid case-by-case evaluations of legislation under vague standards such as 'reasonable' and 'demonstrably justified in a free and democratic society,' which unavoidably would appear to require questioning the wisdom and political desirability of particular laws. The *Oakes* (1986) criteria, taken together with the Court's precise specifications concerning the onus and standard of proof (136–8),[28] serve to make the section 1 inquiry look legal rather than political. This appearance of legalistic constraint is, however, an illusion. As I argued above, attempts to inject content into vague textual provisions cannot get around their indeterminacy. Such efforts inevitably raise two questions: first, why is one definition of a vague standard necessarily better than another; and, second, how can the vagueness and indeterminacy of the definitions themselves be avoided by judges when deciding constitutional cases? Both questions are raised by the Court's interpretation and application of section 1 in *Oakes* (1986) and the cases following it.

First, it is not clear why the four criteria in the *Oakes* (1986) test constitute a uniquely correct interpretation of section 1. The words 'reasonable limit' and 'demonstrably justified in a free and democratic society' do not necessarily, or even obviously, translate into the Court's four-step test. The argument that the test was determined by the text of section 1 and the purposes that supposedly underlie it is simply implausible. According to the Court, the test follows from the need for a 'stringent' (difficult for the government to meet) standard of justification under section 1, which in turn follows from the Charter's purpose of protecting rights and freedoms and from 'the fundamental principles of a free and democratic society.' This chain of reasoning may be appealing, but it is hardly one that would qualify as uniquely determined.[29]

Second, the criteria identified in *Oakes* (1986) are themselves indeterminate and do not preclude the influence of judicial proclivity in section 1 analyses. The first and fourth criteria, for example, do not avoid judicial choice and discretion: indeed, they invite it. Whether or not the purpose of legislation is 'sufficiently significant to warrant overriding a constitutionally guaranteed right,' and whether its importance outweighs the 'deleterious effects' of a particular measure, are matters of opinion, not legal necessity. The explicit policy orientation of these questions is probably responsible for the Court's reluctance to rely on them as justifications for not upholding legislation under section 1. With respect to the first criterion, the Court has confidently found in most – though not all – cases that the 'sufficient importance' of the legislation in question is 'self-evident.'[30] Similarly, it has generally avoided the balancing of legislative objective against effects contemplated by the fourth criterion as a ground for not upholding legislation under section 1.[31]

The second and third criteria in the *Oakes* (1986) test, in contrast, have played a central role in the Court's striking down of legislation in a number of cases. Both concern the relationship between the means chosen by the legislature and the objective of the legislation. The requirement of means/ends proportionality creates an impression of technicality and scientific objectivity. The question is simply one of fit: is there a sufficiently tight 'fit' between the means and the end? Accordingly, these criteria are more able to sustain the appearance of constraint than the first and fourth. Once again, however, the appearance of constraint is illusory. In determining whether or not a legislative measure fits the purpose that it was designed to achieve, the courts cannot avoid making controversial choices concerning the wisdom and desirability of the legislation. The terms of the criteria – 'rationally connected' and 'impair as little as possible' – are indeterminate. Clearly, people will differ on how connected the means and the ends must be to qualify as a 'rational connection,' or on how little a legislative measure must impair a right or freedom before it is said to impair that right or freedom 'as little as possible.'[32]

Moreover, the way the Court characterizes the purpose of a legislative provision will tilt the argument about proportionality of means and end in one direction or the other. The tightness of the fit will inevitably depend on the level of generality at which the purpose is defined. If the purpose is characterized in terms tautologically equivalent to the legislative provision, then there will be an absolute fit – no other provision would be capable of achieving the purpose. If the purpose is defined in general and abstract terms, while the legislative provision is very specific, the fit will appear much looser. None of this would be a problem if there were some determinative source for identifying the purpose of a given legislative provision. However, characterization of such purpose is itself a discretionary exercise. The Court might refer to any number of sources in support of a particular characterization – legislative records, counsel for the government, pre-legislative reports, the preamble to the act, a construction of the whole act or a particular part of it, and so on. Within and among each of these it will be possible to find support for many characterizations of legislative objective, and there is no source or method for deciding which is correct.

In *Edwards Books and Art* (1986), for example, the Court decided that a legislative scheme in Ontario requiring Sunday closing of all retail businesses, except those with fewer than eight employees and less than five thousand square feet of floorspace, violated freedom of religion but could be upheld under section 1. In its section 1 analysis, the Court determined that the law impaired religious freedom 'as little as possible.' While acknowledging that an alternative bill proposed by the appellant was less restrictive of religious freedom and would have protected Sunday holidays for some retail workers, the Court believed that the scheme would not have protected Sundays off for retail workers protected by the law already in place. 'What concerns me,' wrote Chief Justice Dickson on behalf of the majority, 'is the limitation of [the alternatives'] *scope* in terms of the employees who would be denied the benefit which the Act was designed to provide them' (777). In other words, the alternatives did not do exactly what the current scheme did – namely, enforce a uniform day of rest for all retail employees and firms, save firms with fewer than eight employees and less than five thousand square feet of floorspace. This reasoning characterizes the provision's purpose in terms identical to those of the provision itself. By so doing, the Court created not only a perfect fit between legislative means and ends but ruled out the possibility of any alternative's achieving the purpose.[32]

Let me sum up a long and complex argument about constraint-based approaches to interpretation and legitimacy in the Court's Charter jurisprudence. In interpreting the Charter, the Supreme Court usually follows two steps – first, purposive analysis of a right or freedom, and second, application of section 1 criteria laid out in *Oakes* (1986). The presumption underlying each step is that the Court can give the admittedly indeterminate provisions of the constitutional text sufficient meaning to constrain judicial choice and discretion. This approach then legitimates judicial review because it requires judges only to give effect to constitutional prescriptions, not to substitute their views and values for those of democratic bodies. I have argued that there are two fundamental flaws in this scenario. First, nobody, including judges, can define the purpose of a right or freedom, or the criteria to be relied on in applying section 1, without making controversial value choices. Second, the purposes identified in the cases and the section 1 criteria established in *Oakes* (1986) are, like the constitution itself, vague and general, to the point of being indeterminate.

III

My analysis to this point has concentrated on attempts by scholars and judges to anchor the legitimacy of judicial review in constraint of judges by constitutional law. I would now like to return to the other type of legitimation identified at the outset of this chapter, and reflected in the early writings of Bora Laskin – namely, trust in judges. Trust-based arguments reject the possibility of legally determined answers to constitutional questions and accept judicial policy making as necessary and desirable. The judge's role is to identify competing interests, balance these one against the other, and determine which ought to prevail through impartial evaluation of the potential consequences of available outcomes. The legitimacy of judicial review is based on trust in, rather than denial of, judicial choice – a point illustrated by the Court's decision in *Jones* (1986).[33]

In *Jones* (1986) the Court upheld a legislative provision requiring parents to send their children to public school unless they obtained a certificate from the education authorities certifying that their children were receiving sufficient education at home or elsewhere. Mr Jones educated his children, along with a number of others, in the basement of a fundamentalist church of which he was the pastor. The legislative provision violated his freedom of religion, he argued, because by requiring him to apply to a secular school board for certification it effectively compelled him to recognize that his authority over his children, and implied duty to teach them, came from the state and not from God. The Court dismissed his appeal. Consistent with the trust approach, its reasons for doing so are remarkably unconcerned with demonstrating constraint by constitutional norms. It all but abandons the purposive approach, and it does not apply the *Oakes* (1986) test. It proceeds instead by 'weigh[ing] the competing interests,' finding that the 'minimal' and 'peripheral' (255) 'interference [by the legislation] with [Mr. Jones'] freedom of religion' is outweighed by the state's 'compelling' (253) interest 'in the education of its citizens' (252).

When, as in *Jones* (1986), courts abandon constraint-based reasoning and engage in open balancing of interests, they rely implicitly on trust in judges as a basis of legitimacy for judicial decisions. I want to argue, however, that there is little reason to trust judges as arbiters of controversial political issues. As Hogg (1985) notes: '[The judiciary's] background is not broadly representative of the population: [judges] are recruited exclusively from the small class of successful, middle-aged lawyers; they do not necessarily have much knowledge of or expertise in public affairs, and after appointment they are expected to remain aloof from most public issues' (98). Judges also operate at or near the centres of social, economic, and political power and within an institutional framework committed to perpetuating the existing social order. The perspective that they bring to decision making, no matter how sincere their efforts to be neutral and impartial, is inevitably shaped by their social and institutional location. They will generally interpret law and facts from the standpoint of dominant groups in society, with which their professional discipline has historically been allied.[34] In this sense, the judiciary is presumptively conservative, despite genuine attempts by particular judges to be otherwise. As a whole the judiciary cannot, in Miliband's (1973) words, 'be independent of the multitude of influences, notably of class origin, education, class situation and professional tendency [and other attributes, one should add, such as race and gender], which contribute as much to the formation of [a judge's] view of the world as they do in the case of other [people]' (124). It is unclear why we should trust the value judgments of an elite group of predominantly white, upper-middle-class, male lawyers, let alone privilege them over all others.

The Court's majority judgment in *Dolphin Delivery* (1986) provides a good illustration of the problem. In that case, as in *Jones*, the majority relied on balancing arguments to reach its decision. A union had challenged an injunction against picketing, arguing that the injunction infringed its freedom of expression. The Court held against the union, balancing the 'public interest' in labour peace against the union's interest in freedom of expression, concluding that the former outweighed the latter. Implicit, and sometimes explicit, in its reasons is the view that industrial action is illegitimate when it extends beyond the primary parties in a labour dispute, a position that effectively prevents attaching much importance to secondary picketing. Such a narrow conception of legitimate union activity is not surprising in light of the judiciary's antipathy, both historical and contemporary, towards trade unions, but it is unclear why people who do not share that view, such as those in the labour movement, should trust judges. The point is further illustrated by the Court's assumption that there is a conflict between secondary picketing and the public interest. The majority of the public are workers, not owners and managers, and it is arguable that the expansion, not restriction, of unions' capacity to engage in measures designed to advance employees' interests – such as secondary picketing – advances the public interest rather than detracts from it. Needless to say, the Court did not see things this way, but that fact only underlines the partial nature of its perspective and helps show why trust is an implausible basis for the legitimacy of judicial review.

Despite the weaknesses of the trust-based approach, it is often argued that there are good reasons for preferring it to truth-based ones. Open balancing of interests is understood by some commentators to promote honest and open adjudication, as well as judicial results that are more in tune with social and economic reality (Cohen 1935; Laskin 1955; Lederman 1964; Michelman 1986). Judicial balancing of interests, however, can be just as obfuscating as more traditional forms of legal decision making. Before two interests can be compared, they must be identified, and judgments about the value of an interest can be hidden within this allegedly neutral process. For example, competing interests can be made to look more or less important in relative terms by manipulating the levels of generality at which each is articulated (Fried 1963). One interest can be portrayed as 'highly generalized and obviously crucial,' and the other as a 'rather particular and narrowly conceived claim' (763).

In *Jones* (1986), for example, the court articulated the interests of the complainant and of the government at markedly different levels of generality. It characterized the government's interest as the 'efficient education of the young' (299), the complainant's as a personal desire to refrain from acknowledging 'that the government, rather than God, [had] the final authority over the education of his children' (295). In other words, it saw the government's interest as education in general, rather than enforcement of a particular policy within the education system, and Mr Jones's interest as a mere individual claim of freedom of religion rather than freedom of religion in general. Thus, even before it weighed and balanced the respective interests, it effectively placed one in a more favourable position, facilitating its reaching the conclusion it did.[35]

The second argument in favour of explicit interest balancing – that it ensures that judicial decisions are grounded in social reality – assumes that judges using this technique will consider all relevant facts and interests raised by a dispute. However, a court will never have a complete picture of the facts and interests at stake, because many of these will simply be beyond its comprehension (Tushnet 1985). In *Dolphin Delivery* (1986), for example, the Court, in balancing competing interests, assumed that permitting courts to enjoin secondary picketing would promote industrial peace. It had no evidence to support this assumption, and the judges appear to have thought such evidence unnecessary. Yet it is arguable that in many circumstances labour injunctions directly and indirectly threaten, rather than promote, industrial peace. Their use may exacerbate tensions between unions and employers, prolong strikes, and even incite violence.[36] Admittedly, this is a speculative argument, but no more so than that advanced by the Court. There is little reason, in short, to assume along with the Court that upholding judicial authority to block secondary picketing promotes labour peace. The Court's speculative approach to the relationship between such injunctions and labour peace illustrates how interest balancing does not necessarily put courts in touch with social reality. Judges must still make assumptions about how the world works, and these are not necessarily better informed, more sophisticated, or less value-laden than those made by judges using more traditional judicial techniques.

Some constitutional scholars rely on a version of the trust approach to argue that constitutional litigation has progressive potential. They urge judges to free themselves of law's conservative constraints and embrace alternative and oppositional perspectives in making their decisions.[37] According to these scholars, judges must 'reach beyond [their own viewpoints]' (Minow 1987, 95), look at what is 'outside [themselves] and [their] representational schema' (Cornell 1988, 1198), adopt 'the standpoint of ... historically denigrated group[s],' and take account of these groups' subordination and suffering (Cornell 1988, 1172; see also Conklin 1989, 267). 'Inauthentic' perspectives (DeCoste 1993, 274) should be challenged and replaced by 'representative' perspectives of oppressed people (Minow 1987), ones that are 'transformative' of existing principles (Cornell 1988, 1220) and directed towards social justice (Conklin 1989, 267). Through 'emotional maturity,' 'exploring [their] own stereotypes,' and 'self-confrontation and confirmation' (DeCoste 1993, 275), judges should be able to 'glimpse the perspectives of others,' 'cherish difference and welcome anomaly' (Minow 1987, 79).

   Underlying these prescriptions is profound faith in the capacity of judges to act as agents of progressive social change – it is as though judicial consciousness is simply there for the raising. This unexamined trust represents startling disregard of the social constraints on adjudication (see chapter 7 for further discussion of this point).[38] Though asking judges to reject dominant conceptions, and to consider facts about the world and oppression within it, may help dereify rights discourse, it also risks deifying the judiciary, at least to the extent that it presumes that judges can embrace the perspectives of non-dominant groups. There is nothing I can see in the social constitution of the judiciary that warrants such faith, and viewing the judiciary through rose-tinted glasses contributes to understanding neither the limits nor the potential of adjudication.

IV

In the second section of this chapter I challenged the view that the outcomes of constitutional adjudication are determined by constitutional law. I argued that we cannot rely on the constitutional text, and the purposes and principles supposedly informing it, to constrain judicial choice and discretion, because they are insufficiently precise to answer constitutional questions definitively. A number of legal theorists have rejected this critique, arguing that it wrongly denies the possibility of objectivity and constraint in the absence of logical determinacy (for example, Fiss 1981–2; Dworkin 1986; Stick 1986; J. Williams 1987; Langille 1988). Such determinacy may be a formalist's dream, they point out, but notwithstanding its absence, constitutional adjudication is still objective – judges are neutral, impartial, and required to defend their decisions with reference to external norms. I call this the weak constraint thesis to distinguish it from the strong constraint thesis (logical determinacy) examined above, in section II. The weak constraint thesis attempts to establish a middle ground between judges as mere agents of constitutional truths and judges as deciding cases on the basis of choice and discretion. In so doing it relies on themes of both truth and trust.

Writers who argue for weak constraint usually make three points. First, they concede that law is logically indeterminate; that there is often no uncontroversial link between a legal prescription and a judicial result. Legal reason, they argue, is a matter of interpretation, not logical deduction, and it therefore 'necessarily entail[s] strong personal elements' (Fiss 1981–2, 232). Various interpreters will have different understandings of the same legal materials, reflecting, at least in part, their moral and political convictions (Dworkin 1986, 256). Second, adjudication is none the less objective, constrained, and rational. Proponents point out that judges generally internalize, and experience as constraining, a set of values, attitudes, conventions, and procedures. These are, according to Langille (1988), the 'structural conditions' or 'social rules' or 'rules of the game' accepted by judges as a group; Fiss (1981–2) calls them 'disciplining rules' and finds their source in the 'interpretive community' of judges (234); and Dworkin (1986) speaks of the judge's 'interpretive attitude' – her internalization of a duty to reach legal decisions on the basis of principle rather than desired outcomes (47, 52). Judges approach their task with an attitude that enables them to transcend personal interest and decide cases neutrally and impartially. Third, weak constraint theorists argue that, while legal materials may often allow for multiple, competing, and equally reasonable interpretations, the range is not infinite. Unique 'right answers' to legal questions may not exist, but wrong answers do, because legal doctrine limits interpretive possibilities. Langille (1988), for example, argues that concepts such as contract and property can no more be rejected by a lawyer than can the second law of thermodynamics by a physicist (503–4). Similarly, Dworkin (1986) states that neither a Marxist nor a fascist interpretation of the law could satisfy the requirement of doctrinal justification in a liberal democratic legal system (408). In short, radical interpretations are impossible.

In a sense, the weak constraint thesis represents a hybrid of the truth and trust approaches. Like the former, it sees judges as constrained by something other than their own subjective desires; like the latter, it adopts the view that legal norms, and even the principles underlying them, are often logically indeterminate. While law is not logically determinate, adjudication is constrained by the institutional and doctrinal structure in which it takes place. Therefore it is rational and constrained, even though interpreters may differ a great deal in their understandings of indeterminate legal prescriptions.

What is perplexing about this stance, however, is its claim to legitimate constitutional adjudication. Constraint-based legitimacy requires that constitutional provisions dictate a single and uniquely correct result in each case; otherwise judges are making choices, and hence exercising political power, without electoral approval or accountability. The logical determinacy argument, though unbelievable as a description of adjudication, at least answers the normative question of why, in a putative democracy, judicial decisions should be authoritative and obeyed – they are determined by the constitution. Weak constraint arguments more accurately describe the adjudicative process, by rejecting logical determinacy, but do little to legitimate its outcomes. Instead, they effectively redefine what has traditionally been at stake in the question of legitimacy – the undemocratic character of judicial power – by shifting the terms of debate from the substantive results of constitutional decisions to the purely procedural norms of adjudication.

Paramount among the latter norms are the prescriptions that judges base their decisions on relevant and applicable law and decide like cases alike (Fiss 1981–2; Dworkin 1986). Judicial internalization of these is thought to ensure a 'phenomenology of considered decision: its felt involuntary or even inevitable character' (Hart 1977, 146) preventing judges from consciously relying on their moral and political beliefs. As psychology, this is perhaps an accurate description for many judges. It also supports at some level the integrity of judicial process while remaining realistic about logical determinacy. However, it fails to address democratic legitimacy; indeed, it merely obscures the fact that, however they make decisions, judges exercise unaccountable political power.

By neatly sidestepping that fundamental issue, weak constraint theorists implicitly invite us to trust judges. They do not deny that judges make politically and morally controversial choices in giving content to admittedly indeterminate norms, but they seek to assuage concerns about this fact by arguing that judges, because they internalize a particular set of 'how to' rules about judging, feel constrained by the law and therefore do not consciously try to advance their own moral or political views when deciding constitutional cases. However, this reasoning only brings us back to the trust approach, while ignoring its difficulties. As I argued in section III, there are not good reasons, especially for non-dominant groups in society, to trust judicial choices, regardless of the procedural norms that judges feel bound by when deciding constitutional cases. Nothing in the weak constraint approach meets this concern. In conceding that often there are not right answers to legal questions and that judicial subjectivity inevitably affects adjudication (even if judges act as if it does not), it begs the question of why judicial authority should be considered legitimate.

Underlying the weak constraint approach is an appeal to the inherently principled, as opposed to political, nature of judicial reason. Judges' experience of law as constraining supposedly ensures that their decisions are not arbitrary, capricious, or driven by personal views and interests. Weak constraint theorists are heirs to the likes of Blackstone and Coke in their endeavour to demonstrate that the rule of law can impose principle on power.

The latter notion underlies the work of contemporary analysts who claim that constitutional adjudication can advance social justice because of its principled form. Charter constraints on political institutions, they argue, effectively harness power to principle and thus protect non-dominant groups from oppression and exploitation. Beatty (1987), for example, hypothesizes that judicial review under the Charter provides a 'forum of principle' – the courts – where disputes are decided 'much more as a matter of reason and right than on the possession of material and political influence.'[39] Those disadvantaged by lack of political and economic power are offered by the Charter '[a] new opportunity to participate in the process of government' in a 'much fairer and more neutral forum for citizen participation' than the legislature. In the courts, Beatty argues, one can expect impartial and principled deliberation, as compared to the 'pleas of passion and panderings to prejudice by [legislators] whose understanding of issues may be marginal at best' (181). Similarly, Dyzenhaus (1989) notes that law 'requires of judges that they attempt to show that their decisions are justified by a coherent scheme of principle (375)' and argues that this quality of law allows judicial review under the Charter to enhance participatory democracy and help 'bring the law more into line with citizens' needs' (374).

The presumption that law is principled tends to override concerns about law's actual operation in these arguments. Beatty, for example, concedes that, in historical terms, the performance of judges and the common law has been less than ideal from a progressive perspective. The 'predominant value system of the court' in relation to labour, he argues, reveals 'a persistent pattern of favouring the interests of business and commerce' (1987a, 191). Beatty is less concerned, however, about the actual effects of law than its conceptual potential. In 1988, after the Court had handed down its fifth ruling against unions, Beatty suggested that one way to 'allay the doubts of those who are instinctively suspicious of judicial review' is 'to portray constitutional review in its best light' (Beatty and Kennet 1988, 574). In other words, look at law for what it might be, not what it is: if the labour cases had been 'decided properly,' then they would have shown that the Charter protects the interests of working people.

Dyzenhaus similarly tends to gloss over the issue of reality. In his work on South African administrative law (a precursor to his work on the Charter), for example, he acknowledges that the common law has historically served as a 'bed of morally repugnant values' but argues that its concepts do not require such values (1990). Concepts, in other words, can transcend their historical context. It is therefore not surprising that when he turns to the Charter, Dyzenhaus prescribes judicial activism unqualifiedly as a strategy for progressive change, without any analysis, and only thin speculation, about whether such activism will actually serve progressive ends (1989).[40]

Though Beatty and Dyzenhaus's scepticism about political institutions is commendable, its coupling with idealized presentations of law lead their analyses astray. Beatty and Dyzenhaus analyse legislatures from an external perspective. They focus on the undue influence exerted in politics by socially powerful groups, a fact that would not be apparent if, in accordance with the ideals that justify legislative power, these authors simply accepted that legislatures are representative and accountable. Why, however, is the scepticism of external analysis not applied equally by Beatty and Dyzenhaus to courts: why do they portray courts in their 'best light' and all other institutions in the harshest light?[41] They effectively rig the game: they take at face value the legitimating principles of the legal system, presuming that 'law offers us truth ... impartiality and merit whilst denying the filthy side of politics' (Sumner 1979, 276), when this is exactly what they should be trying to prove. Hence their negative characterization of politics, combined with veneration of courts and individual rights, is analytically wanting.

V

The above analyses suggest that judges inevitably make controversial policy decisions in constitutional adjudication and that there is little reason to trust them to do so. The two arguments most often relied on to support the legitimacy of judicial review – truth and trust – do not hold up to close scrutiny, nor does the hybrid embodied in the weak constraint thesis. It is now necessary to deal with a fourth argument for legitimacy, which follows from the critiques of the other three:

namely, because judges are neither constrained by constitutional law nor worthy of trust, their proper role in constitutional cases is to defer to the decisions of democratic institutions. Obviously, this argument serves only to legitimate judicial decisions that uphold legislation, not ones that strike it down.

Numerous variations of the deference argument have been advanced by commentators,[42] and it has also been used by the Supreme Court to justify upholding legislation in several cases. In the *Alberta Reference* (1987), for example, the majority opinions argued that labour relations is a 'delicate,' 'dynamic and unstable' 'field' in which the 'balance of competing interests' (391) should be left to the 'freely elected legislature and to Parliament' (420). Similarly, in *Edwards Books and Art* (1986), Chief Justice Dickson, writing for the majority, noted that balancing of competing interests in relation to Sunday closing policy is a task beyond the Court's legitimate authority and competence (776–7). Striking down the legislation would have involved 'substitut[ing] judicial opinion[s] for legislative ones as to the place at which to draw a precise line [between competing interests]' (782). Justice LaForest supported this view in concurring reasons, noting that the area of Sunday closing, constituted by 'sociological and economic forces' (796) and 'many competing pressures' (795), raised issues requiring 'choices the Court is not in a position to make' (796) (see also Justice LaForest in *McKinney* 1990; *Egan* 1995; and *RJR-MacDonald* 1995). Justice Sopinka picks up on this theme in *Egan* (1995) to explain why a law excluding lesbians and gays from pension benefits that are provided to legally married and common law couples, though a limit on section 15, should be upheld under section 1 (574–6).

While nobody is willing to claim that courts should defer to legislative judgment in all cases, there is no uncontroversial way to differentiate between cases where deference is and is not appropriate. Deciding whether an area is 'political,' and hence one calling for judicial restraint, is itself a political matter. As one commentator has aptly observed: 'Self-restraint is easily turned on or off' (Braden 1948, 48). Looking at recent reliance on deference arguments by the Court, one wonders why restrictions on workers' rights (*Alberta Reference* 1987), lesbian and gay pension benefits (*Egan* 1995), and child-support payments under the Income Tax Act (*Thibodeau* 1995) are seen as 'political,' while those on corporate crime (*Hunter v. Southam* 1984), cigarette advertising (*RJR-MacDonald* 1995), and regulatory offences (*Wholesale Travel* 1991) are not.[43] Commentators are no more consistent. Weiler (1984), for example, argues that federalism issues are 'political' and therefore require a deferential approach by the Court, while suggesting that it is proper for the Court to play an activist role under the Charter. Monahan (1987), in contrast, understands adjudication on federalism as relatively devoid of political content but urges that in Charter cases the Court should develop 'techniques of judicial deference precisely so [it] might avoid being faced with ... essentially legislative determinations' (98). In general, prescriptions of deference allow judicial activism in some areas but call for deference in others, yet there is no 'right answer' to the question of where the line should be drawn.

The deference argument also presumes that priority should be given to the democratic process over all other values. The moral and political value of any given judicial outcome that requires striking down legislation is automatically overridden by the perceived need to protect the democratic process from judicial scrutiny. Deference as a 'theory of judicial review' requires its advocates to condemn decisions striking down legislation and applaud ones upholding it, regardless of their views on the substance of the legislation. For example, a deference advocate would have to disagree with the Court's decision in *Morgentaler* (1988) to nullify a restrictive abortion law and agree with its decision in the *Alberta Reference* (1987) to uphold legislative restrictions on strikes and collective bargaining, even if her own political orientations are pro-choice and pro-labour. In so doing, she would implicitly elevate democratic process over values represented by the potential outcomes of the cases. The deference argument necessarily encodes a commitment to democratic process over all other values, and when people, including judges, invoke the argument they unavoidably make a political choice in favour of the former.

As well, the deference argument assumes that governmental institutions are democratic. Advocating deference to these institutions in the name of democracy implies as much and in so doing makes a controversial and value-laden judgment. People disagree about the extent to which democratic ideals must be reflected in the actual practices of a political system before the system is in fact democratic. As I argued in the previous chapter, because of the unequal distribution of wealth and power endemic to putatively democratic social systems, the ideal of democracy is more a resource for rhetorical posturing than a reflection of political realities. The Canadian electoral process, like that of most advanced capitalist states, requires money, and lots of it, to support candidates, organize pressure groups, campaign, and advertise. Wealthy individuals and groups therefore enjoy significant, and perhaps insurmountable, advantages. They are able to exert a disproportionate influence on determining who runs for election and which issues become the focus of debate. Moreover, it is arguable that democracy cannot be fully realized in the absence of social and economic equality, and there may be cases where judicial activism can advance such equality, even if at the expense of democratic process.[44] Those who argue for restraint often suggest that judicial review is undemocratic and illegitimate even when aimed at securing social conditions that advance democratic values (Monahan 1987, 126–7), once again indicating the implicit elevation of democratic process values over all else.

In criticizing arguments for deference I do not mean to endorse judicial activism under the Charter. I agree with Monahan and Petter's (1987) historical observation that 'where there has been progress towards [social justice] ... the impetus has, with few exceptions, come in the democratic rather than the judicial arena' (124). Moreover, as they and others (including me) argue, courts have tended to use their authority against the interests of disempowered groups and individuals. There are, as earlier sections of this chapter and the following parts of the book make apparent, good grounds for scepticism about judicial activism under the Charter. However, it does not follow that, because courts are unlikely to make progressive decisions under the Charter, they act illegitimately when, and if, they do.[45] A normative prescription of deference as the only legitimate judicial action under the Charter cannot be derived from a set of empirical observations about courts' historical (and current) tendencies (though a strategic prescription can be so derived). In short, I am not prescribing activism or deference in the abstract. My point is that such abstract prescriptions usually serve to mask substantive political and moral positions.

This is a good place to correct the common misconception in constitutional theory that the gist of left critiques of the Charter is to prescribe judicial deference under the Charter. 'For [the left external critics of judicial review],' Dyzenhaus states, 'a judicial decision is legitimate only when it reflects the decision that the representatives of the majority have in fact made' (1989, 377) (and, in his view, these critics therefore unwittingly embrace the authoritarian qualities of positivism). Brock (1993) argues that external critics (of both the right and the left) reflect the 'communitarian tory' tradition in their prescription of a limited role for judicial review under the Charter (268). Another commentator notes: 'Both left- and right-wing Charterphobes assail the Charter in the way best calculated to evoke shock and horror in a society like ours – that is, they accuse it of generating anti-democratic political consequences' (as cited by L. Smith 1994, 64–5). Thus Charter supporters characterize external critiques of the Charter as concerned primarily with prescribing that judges defer to democratically elected officials and then chastise their 'regrettable tendency' to accept 'an idealized vision of what goes on in our legislatures' (L. Smith 1994, 61). However, many external critiques of the Charter (albeit not all: see chapter 1), including the analyses in this book, argue not that legislatures should be free of judicial scrutiny because their decisions are inherently more democratic and progressive, but ask what real effect the Charter is likely to have, given the social forces informing its operation.[46]

VI

I have argued that attempts by constitutional jurists to establish formal grounds for the legitimacy of judicial review are ultimately rooted in hypotheses about constraint by constitutional truths or about trust in the judiciary. Those relying on constraint disagree on the correct sources of constitutional truth. Some find it within the text; others, in the alleged purposes of particular constitutional provisions. The latter group is, in turn, divided on the question of where to look to discover the purpose of the provision: the intentions of the framers, traditional principles of society, current normative consensus, the principles underlying conventional constitutional law, or some combination of these. Other scholars believe this search to be futile. For them, judges are not, and cannot be, constrained by constitutional norms; the legitimacy of judicial review must therefore be based on trust in judges.

In the first three sections of this chapter I attempted to demonstrate the role played by arguments premised on truth and trust in constitutional discourse before and after the enactment of the Charter. In sections IV and V, I examined two types of argument related to these themes. First, I discussed in section IV the weak constraint theory as an attempt to meet the indeterminacy critique developed in section II. Weak constraint theory accepts that the constitution is indeterminate but invokes in defence of judicial review the particular style of decision making engaged in by judges. I argued that the hypothesis ultimately relies on trust, because it requires unquestioning acceptance of the shared values and assumptions that constitute the judicial perspective. Second, I analysed critically the deference argument, according to which neither constraint nor trust can legitimate judicial interference with legislative decisions. According to it, there are no constitutional truths to constrain judges, and no reasons to trust them; therefore in constitutional cases the only legitimate judicial action is inaction.

My aim throughout this chapter was to demonstrate that none of these four arguments establishes the legitimacy of judicial review. The idea of constraint by constitutional truth is unbelievable. The questions that arise in constitutional argument are controversial, and the materials relied on to answer them indeterminate. Interpreters of the constitution, whether judges or not, must make choices and exercise discretion; and the idea of trusting judges to make such choices and exercise discretion is problematic. Notwithstanding sincere attempts by judges to be impartial, principled, and professional, they cannot escape the personal and structural conditions that determine a partial and elite perspective. It is not clear why oppressed and marginalized groups that do not share that perspective should trust and obey decisions that reflect it, particularly when all too often those decisions simply reinforce the very structures of domination, oppression, and exploitation that affect them. Deference arguments and the weak constraint thesis appear to offer ways around the impasse created by the unlikelihood of constitutional truths and the unacceptability of trust in judges. As I demonstrated above, however, they raise similar difficulties, as well as some new ones.

To conclude, the project of constructing formal grounds to legitimate judicial review has been a failure. Critical analysis of the arguments advanced by constitutional jurists in Canada inevitably reveals premises that are either unbelievable or unacceptable when viewed in light of the actual workings of judicial review. Such arguments may be sensible and coherent in the abstract – that is, in the absence of any facts about the practice of judicial review – but they do not legitimate the concrete results of that practice. In the end, constitutional argument may best be understood as a call to faith rather than persuasion by reason. Within constitutional reasoning we see appeals both to truth and to trust, without sufficient reason for either. Constitutional arguments do not even attempt to address the realities of the practice they seek to legitimate. Quite the contrary, they proceed by obscuring and marginalizing concerns – such as the indeterminacy of purposive reasoning and the partiality of judicial perspective – that should be central to their analyses. Notwithstanding their patina of intellectual rigour and analytical depth, they are really just appeals for faith in the institution of judicial review and, correspondingly, obedience to the outcomes that it produces.

PART II

3

Equality and the Liberal Form of Rights

Instead of attempting to classify, measure and then arithmetically equalize different groups' ability to deploy power, a preferable approach ... is to consider how diverse ... sites of power (combine to) produce asymmetries.
Davina Cooper (1995, 48)

In part I, I argued that constitutional adjudication is political, in the sense that it requires judges to determine how power should be exercised on the basis of inde-terminate legal norms. This part examines a question raised by that argument: what are the politics of Charter adjudication? The fact that judges are not fully constrained by legal texts does not mean they are free of all constraints. This and the following three chapters demonstrate that judges are constrained in Charter adjudication by the basic tenets of liberal discourse: suspicion of state power (anti-statism) and atomism. I argue in this part that this ideological form of rights nar-rows substantially the progressive possibilities of Charter litigation. It does so in relation to equality rights (this chapter) and the freedoms of expression (chapter 4) and of association (chapter 5). It also creates a potential for thwarting governmen-tal initiatives aimed at promoting social justice (chapter 6).

This chapter focuses on the Charter's equality rights provision – section 15. That provision, I claim, has not had, and is unlikely to have, a substantial effect on social inequality in Canada because the Supreme Court of Canada's interpre-tation of it, though presented explicitly in broad and substantive terms, embodies anti-statism and atomism. This chapter, however, does not only analyse equality rights. It also provides a foundation for the rest of part II by introducing issues relevant to all Charter rights. In section II, for example, I look at the general structure of Charter rights discourse; and in section III I make two general arguments about rights: first, that, even within the limits of liberal ideol-ogy, they can sometimes be effective tools in progressive social struggle; and second, that the ideological character of those limits makes rights resistant to reinterpretive strategies.

I

Equality is a cherished ideal in democratic societies but there is little consensus on what it means or requires. Several conceptions of it occur in Canadian political and legal culture. The narrowest – administrative equality – requires only that existing laws be administered equally to everyone. It relates to the processes involved in applying laws, not to their content. Its requirements would be met, for example, even in a legal system composed of blatantly racist laws (such as formerly apartheid South Africa's) so long as the laws are equally applied to all members of the oppressed race. The same would not be true of a second conception – formal equality – which prevents laws, not just processes for implementing them, from drawing distinctions between people on the basis of personal characteristics such as race and sex. The celebrated decision of the U.S. Supreme Court ending official racial segregation in southern schools is a good example of the progressive potential of formal equality where the state has explicitly singled out one group for harsher treatment than others (*Brown* 1954). The concept, however, focuses exclusively on whether a law draws formal distinctions between groups, ignoring laws that appear to be neutral yet may have unequal effects on particular groups. Moreover, laws that explicitly treat one group differently from others as a way of promoting equality – progressive income tax, employment equity, affirmative action, and social welfare programs for poor people, for example – run afoul of formal equality, a point underlined by attacks on such programs as violating equality and by section 15 cases, where courts have struck down affirmative-action schemes (*Apsit* 1988) and legislation designed to benefit women (Fudge 1987; also see chapter 6).[1]

Because of the limitations of both administrative and formal equality, progressive activists, and especially feminists, lobbied hard around the time of the Charter's entrenchment for the text of section 15 to go beyond these concepts (Fudge 1987). They got the final text to include rights to equal protection and benefit of the law, in addition to equality before the law (administrative equality) and under the law (formal equality). Soon after section 15 came into effect, the Supreme Court of Canada accepted the arguments of feminist lawyers[2] that section 15 protected 'substantive equality': analysis of whether or not a law complies with the equality provisions, the Court held, must go beyond its legislative form and consider 'its impact upon those to whom it applies, and also upon those whom it excludes from its application' (*Andrews* 1989, 168). Thus, according to the Court, '[a] bad law will not be saved merely because it operates equally upon those to whom it has application nor will a law necessarily be bad because it makes distinctions' (168).

The Court has expressed high hopes for its approach to equality, noting that it will serve to remedy or prevent 'discrimination against groups subject to stereotyping, historical disadvantage and political and social prejudice in Canadian society' (*Swain* 1991, 992).[3] This fine ambition will undoubtedly be realized on occasion, but it is unlikely that any meaningful movement towards *social* equality will result from the Court's apparently progressive approach.[4]

Social equality is an absence of major disparities in people's resources, political and social power, well-being and of exploitation and oppression.[5] Though perhaps ultimately unattainable, full social equality is a worthy aspiration, long a goal for progressive activism. Social inequality is pervasive in Canadian society: its symptoms have been well documented in an endless stream of reports and analyses on (to name a few) women, poverty, First Nations, income and wealth, unemployment, health care, disability, and immigration. Social inequality is not inevitable. That is why the struggle against it is worthwhile. Transformation of the causes of social inequality is possible: the question is how to achieve it. I believe that litigation on equality rights is unlikely to challenge significantly the causes and effects of social inequality. This is so despite the Court's 'substantive equality' approach and the admirable commitment of progressive lawyers to working with advocacy groups and victims of social inequality to mount challenges under section 15. The limitations of equality litigation and the reasons for its ineffectiveness in relation to social inequality lie in the ideological form of rights, a point I elaborate in the next section.

II

The ideological form of rights is composed of the basic tenets of liberal discourse: anti-statism and atomism. Anti-statism is manifest in the traditional conception of rights as protecting individuals from public (state) interference in their private affairs but not requiring positive assistance by the state. The presumption is that state power, not the oppressive and exploitative social relations that typify civil society, is the primary threat to human liberty and equality. Atomism represents rights as belonging to individuals (or groups), with other individuals (or groups), institutions, or state agencies having corresponding duties. It constructs social conflict in dyadic terms, as an accumulation of discrete clashes between rights-bearers and duty-holders, each clash potentially resolved by adjusting the relationship between the two disputants. Power relations and social conditions beyond the rights/duty dyad are irrelevant; disputes are considered and resolved outside the multi-layered and complex social realities in which they arise. Historically rooted and structural forms of domination and subordination – between men and women, capital and labour, heterosexuals and gays and lesbians, whites and people of colour – are thus erased. Atomism contemplates more than simple individualism, as its dyadic (and thus abstract and ahistorical) construction of social conflict underlies claims to group and collective rights as well as those of individuals (I. Young 1990, 30–1).

Three analytically distinct elements of the Court's Charter jurisprudence reflect the dominant ideological form of rights. First, only state action is caught by the Charter's rights. The Charter differs in this way from most regulatory legislation, including human rights legislation, which imposes legal obligations on non-governmental actors. Second, because only state action, not inaction, triggers rights, they limit what the state can do but do not require that the state do anything. Third, a rights claim must be framed in dyadic terms (a feature that follows from rights' atomistic form), as a challenge to a discrete state action with specific effects on a particular individual or group: the right of an individual or group (to do, not do, or have something) imposes a specific correlative duty (to allow, not require, or give something) on the state. These three limitations, separately and together, prevent litigation on equality rights from making substantial inroads on social inequality.

First, the Supreme Court has interpreted the Charter to impose obligations only on state (primarily governmental) bodies.[6] Though this interpretation is not dictated by the text of the Charter (which can sustain broader readings: Hogg 1986–7; Beatty 1987; Elliot and Grant 1989), it does reflect classical liberalism's concern with protecting individuals from the coercive power of the state. Justice LaForest explains the rationale thus: 'This Court has repeatedly drawn attention to the fact that the Charter is essentially an instrument for checking the powers of government over the individual ... Historically, bills of rights ... have been directed at government. Government is the body that can enact and enforce rules and authoritatively impinge on individual freedom. Only government requires to be constitutionally shackled to preserve the rights of the individual' (*McKinney* 1990, 261–2). The Charter, including its equality rights, therefore imposes no obligations on actors defined by the Court as 'private.' Employers, corporations, landlords, non-governmental institutions (such as hospitals and universities), and sexual assaulters and abusers, to cite a few examples, are immune to its prescriptions.[7] Because most day-to-day coercion, need, want, and discrimination in people's lives result from their relations with private actors, the Charter's equality rights are close to useless for combating major areas of social inequality (Hutchinson and Petter 1988). Moreover, the Court defines 'government actors' narrowly, as entities that have governmental 'authority to coerce' and those directly controlled by government (*McKinney* 1990). Courts have found that legislative, executive, administrative, and bureaucratic institutions meet these criteria, as do municipalities (*McKinney* 1990, 270), colleges (*Douglas College* 1991), Canada Post Corporation (*Rural Dignity of Canada* 1992), legal aid societies (*Schiewe* 1992), and government-appointed adjudicators (*Slaight* 1989). Other institutions, such as universities and hospitals, fall outside the Charter's scope, despite being created by government, heavily regulated, publicly funded, and responsible for public functions (*McKinney* 1990; *Stoffman* 1990). Increasing privatization of government services and operations means that in future fewer and fewer agencies will be subject to the Charter.

Second, equality rights are triggered only by government action, not inaction. Consistent with its view that the Charter protects individuals only from state action, the Court has refused to interpret the equality and other rights of the Charter as requiring the state to protect individuals through its action.[8] The Charter creates a metaphorical fence around individuals that is enforced by the courts through nullification of trespasses by the state.[9] Laws are struck down, and other state acts (such as arrests, collection of physical evidence, criminal charges and convictions, and sentences) are invalidated, if found by a court to violate a right. Such scenarios, where rights require the state not to act in a particular way, manifest a negative conception of rights. Positive rights claims, in contrast, require the state to act by providing some benefit to rights-holders, either directly, through a social program (health care, social assistance, unemployment benefits), or indirectly, through social legislation that imposes obligations on private actors (rent control, minimum wages, pay equity).

Such claims do not fit within the state-as-Leviathan conception imbedded in the Court's jurisprudence. 'It would be a very big step,' observed Chief Justice Lamer, 'for this court to interpret the Charter in a manner which imposes a positive *constitutional* obligation on governments' (*Prosper* 1994). The Court has not taken that step in relation to the equality or any other of the Charter's rights, despite the urging of progressive lawyers.[10] Equality rights are negative in the Court's jurisprudence. 'Section 15 is not a general guarantee of equality,' according to Justice McIntyre, writing for a majority of the Court in *Andrews* (1989): 'It does not provide for equality between individuals or groups within society in a general or abstract sense, nor does it impose on individuals or groups an obligation to accord equal treatment to others. It is concerned with the application of the law' (163–4). Section 15 is thus triggered by state action – 'the application of law' – but not by the state's unwillingness to act to promote 'equality between individuals or groups within society.' This logic is played out in a decision of the BC Court of Appeal (*Eldridge* 1995).[11] The Court stated: '*Andrews* emphasized that in addressing the question as to whether legislation creates a distinction the focus must be on the "impact of the law on the individual or group concerned"' (18–19). Further, 'section 15 [should not] be interpreted in such a manner as to effectively impose on government a positive duty to address all inequalities when legislating benefits in the area of medical services. That [would be] equivalent to imposing an obligation on government of ensuring absolute equality' (26). The clear signal from cases such as this and *Andrews* is that section 15(1) is not a vehicle for requiring positive governmental action to redress social inequality.[12]

The Court's unwillingness to interpret Charter rights positively is belied at first glance by its statement in *Schacter* (1992) that the right in section 15(1) to equal benefit of the law is a 'positive right,' requiring 'special considerations in the remedial context' (721). A closer look, however, reveals that the negative character of equality-rights doctrine remains largely unaltered after *Schacter*. The Court held in *Schacter* that unemployment-insurance child-care benefits had to be provided equally to biological and to adoptive parents (721–2) and therefore that the Unemployment Insurance Act's provision of such benefits to the latter but not to the former was unconstitutional. Though the Court could have remedied the constitutional breach by striking down the benefit for adoptive parents (and thus creating equality between the two types of parents), it rejected this option on the ground that such a 'remedy' would have 'deprive[d] eligible persons of a benefit without providing any relief to the [biological parents]' (722). The Court held also that extending the benefit to biological parents was inappropriate because such a solution would have required it to override Parliament's judgment on a fiscal matter.[13] The Court opted for a third approach: it ordered the government and Parliament to go back to the drawing board and construct a scheme that provided equal benefits to natural and to adoptive parents.[14] In other cases, the Court stated, it might be appropriate for a court to take a bolder approach and order that the actual benefit being received by one group be extended to the other. The Ontario Court of Appeal followed this suggestion in *Haig* (1992) in extending human rights protection under the Canadian Human Rights Act to lesbians and gays, even though 'sexual orientation' is not an explicit ground of prohibited discrimination in the act.[15]

The *Schacter* (1992) case undoubtedly opens the door for courts to compel governments to act affirmatively, either in the weak sense of politely asking them to equalize benefits, as in *Schacter* (1992), or in the strong sense of compelling them to extend a benefit or protection enjoyed by some groups to some other groups, as in *Haig* (1992). In both instances, however, the Court is concerned only with imposing limits on how the state can act if it decides to act: there is no requirement that the state act in the first place. If the state decides to confer a benefit – be it parental leave or protection from discrimination – then it must do so in compliance with the Charter. The issue, as pointed out in *Haig*, is 'choosing the appropriate remedy for a benefit-conferring, underinclusive *statutory provision* that violates a Charter right' (520). In *Schacter* (1992) itself, the Court explicitly stated that Parliament was not constitutionally required to provide unemployment benefits, only to equalize legislative provision of those benefits (721–2). Thus the Charter is still triggered only by operation of a law, not by general conditions of social inequality that might require state redress. There is no indication in *Schacter* that the Court will depart from its predominantly negative understanding of the Charter's equality rights and interpret them as imposing obligations on government to create regulatory and spending regimes designed to remedy social inequality.[16]

Third, and in my view most limiting, equality rights are atomistic. Even if the Court reversed its previous rulings and developed a positive jurisprudence on equality rights that imposed obligations on private actors, the rights would remain atomistic and thus incapable of substantially redressing social inequality. Atomistic rights, whether positive or negative, and regardless of the scope of their application, can contemplate only dyadic relationships.[17] If an individual or group has a right to x, then some legally identified entity has a duty to ensure that individual or group gets x. Where x is a benefit, the duty is positive: the duty-bearer must do something to ensure that the rights-bearer gets x. Where x is a liberty, the duty is negative: the duty-bearer must not do anything that constrains the rights-bearer from doing x. What all rights claims have in common is the demand that one actor give, do, or not do, some specified thing to another.

This exclusive focus on the actions of two actors in relation to one another (whether individual/state, individual/private organization, or individual/individual) leaves out the complicated and ongoing processes through which relations among multiple actors and actions combine to construct people's actual life conditions and shape their choices, capacities, identities, and desires (I. Young 1990, 27). Equality rights claims are thus unable to get at the causes of inequality and other social ills; they deal only with discrete symptoms, leaving underlying social structures untouched. That is why, as Russell (1994) observes, 'the Charter has done little to alter power relations, redistribute wealth, or promote social welfare within the Canadian version of welfare capitalism' (40).

To take one example, the economic dimensions of social inequality, and poverty in particular, are beyond the reach of the Charter, and this would be true even were its rights interpreted to impose positive obligations on both governmental and private actors. Poverty and economic inequality are rooted in intersecting relations of class, gender and race, not in particular acts of government or private actors. In most capitalist societies, for example, a minority of people owns the bulk of productive property – factories, agricultural land, commercial real estate, and natural resources – while the majority depends on that minority for goods and services (including necessities such as food and shelter) and employment. Lacking sufficient property to sustain themselves, most people 'pay ... others for it,' according to Macpherson (1985), thus engendering 'a continuous net transfer of part of the powers of the non-owners to the owners' (79). Property relations necessarily create dependence of non-owners on owners, and thus power of the former over the latter (Macpherson 1985; Morris Cohen 1978), a point graphically illustrated by George Bernard Shaw (1929): 'If you own an English or Scottish county you may drive the inhabitants off it into the sea if they have nowhere else to go. You may drag a sick woman with a newly born baby in her arms out of her house and dump her in the snow on the public road for no better reason than that you can make more money out of sheep and deer than out of women and men' (102). The power of property owners to exclude people from the means necessary for their existence is at the root of poverty's presence in capitalist societies (E.O. Wright 1994). Most people do not have direct access to the resources necessary for human survival, let alone a decent life; and if they, or those who support them, cannot earn an income to buy those resources (because of insufficient employment, lack of marketable skills, ill-health, child-care obligations, and so on) they will probably be poor.[18]

It would be artificial, however, to draw a sharp distinction between poor people and the majority of the so-called middle class.[19] Poverty is only the worst expression of the economic inequalities endemic to capitalism. Most people, to survive, must either work for business enterprises (capitalists) or be supported by someone who does.[20] Enterprises in turn extract as profit the difference between their production costs (primarily workers' wages) and the revenue generated by selling their product or service. Social insecurity and other deprivations are not mere by-products of this system, nor random events, but inevitable results. Profit and worker's wages are inversely related: lower wages mean higher profits. Profit in turn is the accepted goal of business enterprises: business is expected, indeed often legally obligated (to shareholders), to do whatever is necessary to increase profit. That is why many businesspeople vociferously oppose policies that increase labour costs – such as minimum wages, collective bargaining rights, and strong health and safety standards – and welcome high unemployment, which creates a surplus of labour, thus reducing workers' bargaining power.

More generally, much of business has a positive interest in the existence of economic insecurity and poverty, which serves to mute workers' demands. People might be less likely to 'choose' to devote the bulk of their time to the monotonous, unhealthy, and dangerous tasks often required of low-paying jobs if poverty were not the likely consequence of not working. It is well accepted among many in the business elite that 'a capitalist society is by its nature unequal and so faces a trade-off: the more unequal it is, the more economically efficient it becomes. Without the incentives offered by inequality ... a capitalist society simply loses its dynamism ... Unless there is a penalty for being out of work, workers will not seek employment. There needs to be fear and greed in the system in order to make it tick' (Hutton 1996, 172–3).[21] We can best understand business opposition to government programs aimed at promoting economic security as an expression of this logic, though it is usually more palatably articulated as reflecting concerns about debt, deficits, or inflation. The more general point is that economic insecurity and poverty are products of the normal, accepted, and prescribed operation of capitalist social relations (Wright 1994).[22]

The inherent inequalities of capitalist social relations are in turn structured by gender and race relations, as well as factors such as disability, age, and region. Women[23] and racialized groups,[24] for example, are often paid less than white men for similar work; they are also discriminated against in hiring and promotion and over-represented in low-paying, insecure, and non-union jobs, which fact contributes to higher rates of poverty and economic security among them. Women face a matrix of social obligations – primary obligations for child care, care of sick and elderly relatives, and housework (Gavigan 1993; Kline 1993; Boyd 1994) – which, when combined with the absence of affordable child care, makes full-time work outside the home impossible for many of them, thus increasing their financial dependence on male earners.[25]

Race relations, in addition to and overlapping with those of gender, also intersect with capitalist economic structures, and in numerous different ways (Manning 1983; Anthias and Yuval-Davis 1992; Gabriel 1994; Small 1994). For example, there is a long and horrible history of capitalist exploitation combining with racist oppression of First Nations in Canada. In nineteenth-century British Columbia, the crown asserted underlying title to all land and then proceeded to sell, lease, and give away large tracts to private individuals and resource companies, who excluded First Nations from the land and destroyed its capacity to sustain their societies. Governments and settlers' original assertion of property rights over these lands illustrates the combined operation of economic ambitions and racism. The claim to crown title in British Columbia was founded on a belief, still prevalent in some quarters, that First Nations are uncivilized and their societies unworthy of respect. In other parts of Canada, similar beliefs underlay the making and breaking of land treaties (Macklem 1991; Borrows 1992a; 1992b). In short, First Nations have been denied an economic base by dominant interests taking and destroying their lands, and this has resulted in severe poverty among their peoples (Statistics Canada 1993).

My purpose in examining (albeit briefly) relationships among poverty, economic insecurity, capitalism, gender, and race is to give some sense of the complexity of social inequality. Poverty and economic insecurity result from the convergence of numerous structural and institutional processes. The Charter's equality rights, because of their atomistic form, cannot address these processes; only discrete injustices are within its scope, yet social inequality is more than an accumulation of discrete injustices.[26] Despite these limitations, progressive lawyers have used the

Charter in attempts to fight poverty in the courts, arguing that sections 7 and 15(1) require stronger legislative protection of poor people. Martha Jackman (1992) sums up the anti-poverty position on the Charter this way: 'In principle, the Canadian Charter of Rights and Freedoms, and in particular the right to life, liberty and security of the person under section 7, and the right to equal protection and equal benefit of the law under section 15, provide a solid basis for challenges to inadequacies and inequities in social welfare legislation' (61). Supreme Court decisions on equality such as *Andrews* (1989) and *Turpin* (1989) bolster this position because of their substantive equality approach to section 15 (Jackman 1992; Brodsky 1992a). On these legal bases, activist academics and lawyers have made numerous arguments interpreting the Charter as imposing obligations on governments to provide poor people with social benefits, in relation to housing, income assistance, health care, child care, and employment.[27] Some arguments only challenge discriminatory aspects of program administration, and more ambitious ones claim that the Charter requires governments to provide certain benefits and at particular levels of sufficiency.[28]

Social welfare claims under the Charter generally get a chilly reception in court because they rely on a positive conception of equality rights which, as noted above, has not been embraced by the courts. I want, however, to put aside that difficulty and argue that even if anti-poverty advocates succeed in persuading courts to accept their claims to positive rights, which is at least a theoretical possibility, this would have little effect on the nature and scope of poverty in Canada. Though equality rights may be capable of accommodating claims for more and better social welfare programs, it cannot recognize, nor be used to remedy, the conditions that cause poverty and thus make those programs necessary.[29] Anti-poverty arguments under the Charter tend to assume rights' dyadic form (though see Nedelsky and Scott 1992). They interpret the Charter as imposing an obligation on government to give, do, or not do something to a particular individual or group of individuals and ask the Court to enforce that obligation. While I do not want to deny the significance of such claims (especially to the complainants), or even their capacity to cause or facilitate substantial change in some contexts, on their own they do little more than address some of the symptoms of poverty.[30] They do not touch the background causes, in particular the constellation of social and legal relations through which wealth and resources are created and distributed in society. Charter arguments against poverty, if accepted by the courts, would only impose obligations on governments to provide groups with particular remedies; they would not affect the social and economic conditions that produce poverty.

Significant social change requires work at the structural and institutional levels of society, not just patching up of the most egregious and visible effects of exploitative and oppressive social processes.[31] Though social welfare rights are necessary and important, they are only a safety net in a social system whose normal and accepted modes of operation knock some people off the ledge and keep most others precariously balanced on it (I. Young 1990, 69–70). State power can be used to promote genuine social security, but it must be aimed at the conditions and processes that cause insecurity, in addition to treating the symptoms of those processes through social welfare rights (see chapter 9).

In the last two decades states and governments have done exactly the opposite, persistently pursuing macroeconomic policies that exacerbate the exploitative and oppresive dynamics of capitalist social relations. In North America trade deals have enabled Canadian business to shop around in the United States and Mexico for cheap labour and lower regulatory standards; interest rates have been high, and corporate and wealth taxes low; there has been no systematic attempt to move away from export-led growth; deregulation, privatization, and technological innovation have affected large sectors of economic and social activities; and collective bargaining, unemployment insurance, and social spending have been rolled back. These developments have resulted in high unemployment, deeper and wider poverty, and pervasive economic insecurity even among those who are employed.

Attacking poverty and economic insecurity requires state policy that ameliorates the inherent inequalities of capitalism manifest in these symptoms. The dyadic form of rights (especially when combined with their negative and anti-statist features) makes the Charter particularly ill-suited for achieving this goal. The Charter contemplates only particular instances of state regulation and spending; at best, it can require the state to provide remedies for poverty's ill effects. In the meantime, however, national and international political economic developments, far beyond the scope of the Charter, increasingly intensify social inequality and injustice (Laxer 1993; Bakker 1994; A. Johnson, McBride, and Smith 1994; Brodie 1995).

III

Taking together the various formal features of equality rights in the Court's jurisprudence – exclusion of non-state actors, negative orientation, and dyadic structure – it is difficult to avoid the conclusion that most areas of social inequality lie beyond the reach of section 15. Yet I do not deny certain positive features of Charter equality rights. I readily concede that the Supreme Court considers social context in its equality decisions, that litigation over equality rights may in specific contexts achieve progressive results, and that rights can be reinterpreted in ways that avoid the formal limits discussed above. While each point is true, none is an answer to the arguments that I make above.

First, I agree that the Court does in fact deal with social context in its equality decisions, holding that claims of equality rights must be evaluated in terms of the actual effect of a law in its social context (*Andrews* 1989; *Turpin* 1989). In *Weatherall* (1993), for example, it recognized that, given the reality of pervasive sexual violence against women in society, frisk searches of women prisoners by male prison guards are qualitatively different than similar searches of male prisoners by female guards; therefore it held a policy prohibiting the former but allowing the latter to be non-discriminatory. Similarly, in *Symes* (1993), the Court stated that if the operation of a provision of the Income Tax Act could be shown to place a greater financial burden on women than on men in relation to child care because of the social fact that women assume the burden of child care, then the provision would have to be altered (though in the end the Court was not satisfied that such linkage existed). These cases and others suggest that the Court considers the wider social conditions that cause laws to have unequal effects. Nowhere, however, does the Court suggest that equality rights require such conditions to be changed. It considers social inequality only as a context for determining whether a law violates a Charter right, but not as a source of a Charter violation; only inequality caused by a law will be scrutinized and remedied under section 15 (*Andrews* 1989; *Symes* 1993).

Second, I agree with those who argue that rights, even within the limitations of liberal ideology, can be an effective strategy in progressive social struggle. Liberal discourse on rights promises ideals with great resonance among progressive people. The participatory and other rights that people enjoy today in liberal democracies were secured through protracted historical struggles and offer tangible protections (Meikins Wood 1986, 149). They articulate deep-felt human needs for security, autonomy, and community. Civil rights and liberties are essential components of a just society, and with the increasing influence of conservative ideas in mainstream politics, we should not take for granted protection from arbitrary, capricious, and discriminatory state action (Bartholemew and Hunt 1990, 1). This is especially true for historically exploited and oppressed groups. 'Where one's experience is rooted ... in *being* illegitimate, in being raped, and in the fear of being murdered,' notes Patricia Williams (1993) in relation to the experience of African Americans, 'then ... adherence to a scheme of negative rights – to the self, to the sanctity of one's personal boundaries – makes sense' (502). Protecting people from coercive and discriminatory state action is undoubtedly important, and the Charter can provide immediate relief from direct state coercion or discrimination.

Lesbian and gay activism under the Charter provides a good example. Many laws directly subject lesbians and gays to harsher treatment than heterosexuals.[32] To take a few examples, only heterosexual couples can be legally recognized as married; most legislative and contractual employment-benefit schemes provide benefits only to spouses of employees, thereby excluding partners of lesbian or gay employees; adoption laws preclude lesbian and gay couples from adopting children; and human rights legislation does not, in some jurisdictions, include sexual orientation as a protected ground. All these measures assume the form of direct legislative discrimination against lesbians and gays, and the Charter's equality rights have thus been useful in challenging them. The case law in this area is based on a recognition by governments (which have conceded the point in litigation[33]) and courts[34] that section 15 protects lesbians and gays, even though sexual orientation is not an explicitly enumerated ground of protection. This recognition has opened the door to using the Charter in lesbian and gay struggles for equality, though it is still unclear how far the courts will go in dismantling existing legal inequalities. Positive results include judicial extension of legislative protection of human rights (*Haig* 1992), 'spousal' benefits (medicare: *Knodel* 1991; pension-plan survivor benefits: *Leschner* 1992), and adoption privileges (*G.[C.E.]* 1995; *K. and B.* 1995). On the negative side is a recent Supreme Court decision, *Egan* (1995), which potentially undermines some of these gains.[35] Overall, however, the experience of lesbians and gays with the Charter indicates that progressive victories are possible, at least where there is a congruence between the liberal form of equality rights and the remedy sought.[36]

There are, however, three major caveats to my acknowledgment that Charter litigation can sometimes yield progressive results. The first caveat is that Charter victories do not necessarily translate into positive effects in people's daily lives. Social circumstances often make it impossible for people to exercise the rights created by successful cases. Particular lesbian and gay employees, for example, may be unable to claim spousal benefits for their partners, even if such benefits are won under the Charter, because of legitimate fears about the consequences of 'coming out' to their employers. *Morgentaler* (1988), though not technically an equality rights case, provides a further example. In that case, the Court struck down criminal prohibitions on abortion and thus removed a legal barrier to women's access to abortion. *Morgentaler* does not, however, necessarily advance the reproductive freedom and choice of most women. Access to abortion services is restricted by numerous social constraints that continue to exist even in the absence of criminal prohibitions: lack of funds to pay for the service or travel to a place where it is available; censure from family, partners, doctors, communities; unavailability of doctors to perform abortions; and so on (Lessard 1991). In short, for many people, winning a right does not automatically mean that it can be exercised.

The second caveat restates earlier arguments: because of the atomistic form of rights, Charter victories are necessarily narrow and unlikely to have much effect on wider aspects of the issues they address. In addition to the barriers preventing women from exercising their legal rights to abortion, for example, genuine reproductive choice for women requires more than abortion services: it requires that women be able to have children if they choose to. Neither positive nor negative Charter rights to abortion services help here. Many women do not have children, or must give up their children for adoption, because they cannot afford to raise them.[37] Other women are forcibly deprived of their children: First Nations women, for example, have their children taken away by state agencies at substantially higher rates than non-First Nations women (Kline 1992; 1994). Womens' reproductive choice to have or keep children is thus heavily circumscribed by class and race, along with other factors such as disability (Mosoff 1995) and sexual orientation (Millbank 1994). Litigation over Charter rights, such as that which led to *Morgentaler* (1988), cannot begin to deal with the wide array of social and economic constraints on womens' reproductive choices, whether to have, not have, or keep children. It contemplates only discrete state acts and lacks the capacity to do anything about the social and institutional forces that determine the degree to which women have genuine reproductive freedom and choice.

The Aboriginal right to fish provides further illustration of the second caveat. The court has held that Aboriginal rights in the west coast salmon fishery are protected under section 35 of the Constitution Act, 1982 (*Sparrow* 1990; *N.T.C. Smokehouse* 1996; *Van der Peet* 1996). The scope of this protection, however, is narrowly defined by the Court: to receive constitutional protection, an Aboriginal right must have existed in 1982 (when section 35 was entrenched in the constitution) (*Sparrow* 1990), and it must relate to Aboriginal practices that existed at the time of contact between First Nations and Europeans (meaning, for example, that commercial fishing for salmon is not protected: *N.T.C. Smokehouse* 1996; *Van der Peet* 1996). Moreover, even if an Aboriginal right meets these criteria, a court can still find that government restrictions of it are justified (*Sparrow* 1990). These limitations on the constitutional protection of Aboriginal rights have drawn criticism from advocates of First Nations rights (Asch and Macklem 1991; Borrows 1996).

Though I am sympathetic to these criticisms, I want to make a different point here: namely, no matter how broadly consitutional protection of Aboriginal rights is defined, its effects are still entirely dependent on there being salmon to fish. The west coast salmon fishery is currently in crisis as a result of deep drops in salmon stock. The fishery, which had for thousands of years provided a social and economic base for many First Nations in what is now British Columbia, is on the brink of collapse. The crisis is a result of overfishing and government mismanagement since the end of the nineteenth century when the non–First Nations commercial fishery began in earnest (Cernetig 1996; Glavin 1996). The current conditions of the salmon fishery seriously threaten the capacity of First Nations people to exercise constitutionally protected Aboriginal rights to fish salmon, regardless of how broadly those rights are interpreted by the courts. The Aboriginal right to fish can protect First Nations only from discrete restrictions on their ability to fish for salmon, but not from related structures of political economy and colonialism that are destroying the fishery.

The third caveat is that a Charter victory for one group may have regressive effects on others. Because Charter claims take the form of demands by particular individuals or groups for remedies that address their specific concerns, there is little room within them for considering effects on other groups. The Federal Court's decisions under section 15 (affirmed by the Supreme Court of Canada) requiring that certain unemployment insurance (UI) benefits be equally available to biological and to adoptive parents (*Schacter* 1992), and to people over and under sixty-five (*Tetreault-Gadoury* 1991), appear progressive. They resulted in $500 million of UI funds being directed to improvements in parental and maternal benefits (including extension of sickness benefits to women who have difficult pregnancies) and extension of UI benefits to people who are sixty-five and over.[38] For many workers and unemployed people, however, these new amendments represented a legislative assault. The government raised the revenue for these extensions by increasing the number of weeks that a person must work before being eligible for UI benefits, reducing the number of weeks a person can receive benefits, and stiffening penalties for workers who quit work without just cause or refuse to take suitable jobs or are fired for misconduct. The government estimated that these changes would lead to thirty thousand fewer people receiving UI benefits (the Canadian Labour Congress put the figure at 130,000: Cameron 1989). Women workers, along with immigrant, older, and disabled workers, were hit particularly hard by these changes as they are overrepresented in unstable, part-time, and seasonal jobs, where longer eligibility requirements are most difficult to meet and shorter benefit periods have the harshest effects (*Globe and Mail* 1989; End Legislated Poverty 1990; Mandel 1994, 396).[39] Thus the Charter-induced expansion of UI benefits and benefits to all new parents, and to people who are sixty-five or older, though progressive when viewed in isolation, were effectively paid for by the most vulnerable and oppressed groups among working people, a regressive result in the larger picture.

A similar example is Elizabeth Symes's Charter challenge (ultimately unsuccessful) to provisions of the Income Tax Act (*Symes* 1993). Symes was a partner in a law firm and practised law full time. She claimed that the Act discriminated against her as a woman because it did not allow her to deduct child-care costs as a business expense. Had her claim succeeded, it would have been a victory for one particular group of women – self-employed businesswomen, such as Symes (and, incidentally, self-employed businessmen); it would have had no 'general application to the issue of accesible, affordable, quality child care for women who wish to work outside the home' (Young 1994b, 29). Indeed, success for Symes would heve effectively been paid for by other women, less well off than she. Governments' fiscal commitments to child care, like those to UI benefits, are usually fixed, and the child-care benefits (in the form of tax expenditures) that business women (and men) would have been entitled to if Symes had won her case would probably have been diverted from other child-care funds or social services or recouped through increased taxes on employed women (and men) (Fudge 1989; Iyer 1992, 201–2; Mandel 1994, 450; C. Young 1994a, 558, 589). A victory for Symes would also have reinforced the trend towards privatization of child-care and other social services (C. Young 1994a, 564) and divided the child-care lobby by 'demobiliz[ing] a powerful section of that lobby – upper income self-employed professional parents – who stand to benefit from the business expense deduction' (Cossman, as cited in C. Young 1994a, 566).

Finally, I agree with those scholars who argue that the liberal form of equality and other rights is neither logically nor conceptually necessary. They[40] concur with me on the limits imposed by that form, and I agree with them that it is possible to conceive of rights as assuming different, and less limiting, forms. It is conceptually possible to shift 'the interpretive emphasis of a right to ... patterns of relationships' in place of 'formal, individualistic equality' (Nedelsky and Scott 1992, 60); or to reconceive social rights in terms that go beyond provision of state benefits to ones that can 'attack the causes of poverty at the source, namely seriously unequal distribution of wealth, income and control of the conditions of work' (71–2). Rights need not be 'quasi absolute, debate stopping conclusions,' 'defined pervasively in the image of a single and determinative moral "good"' (Trakman 1994) that serve as 'trumps' over other claims (Nedelsky and Scott 1992, 62). But they can be reconceived as 'sites of dialogue, metaphorical forums in which members of society converse about different claims regarding basic values and relationships,' a 'language of a continuing process rather than the fixed rules' (62–3), a 'mediatory discourse' (Trakman 1994).

The concept of rights, in short, can be reinterpreted to avoid the regressive limitations of currently dominant conceptions; a new, non-liberal language of rights can accommodate demands for structural change and attacks on the causes of social inequality. The mere existence of a new language, however, is no guarantee that it will be heard, listened to, or acted on by those who have social and political power.[41] This takes us back to an issue addressed in the first chapter: the significance of calling dominant rights discourse ideological. The liberal limits of rights are not purely discursive but are anchored in historical forces and extant social structures and institutions. Though avoidance of these limits through reconstruction of the concept of rights is discursively possible, the reconstruction process inevitably comes up 'against the grain of historical formations' (Hall 1986, 54) – an 'accumulated historical weight which serves as a check on the potential "moveability"' of the liberal elements in rights discourse (Bennet 1990, 263).

Historically the liberal conception of rights developed in conjunction with the end of feudalism and the rise of liberal capitalism in the eighteenth century (Marx 1967; Pashukanis 1978; Weitzer 1980; Picciotto 1982). Where feudalism was defined by a rigid hierarchical social structure – in England, estates, lords, surfs, guilds – enforced by sovereign power, liberal capitalism separated civil society, and in particular economic relations, from the direct imperatives of sovereign power. In contrast to the rigid ranks of economic status in feudalism, under liberal capitalism all persons were equally free to own property and enter agreements for its exchange, a structure institutionalized in the laws of property and contract. This equality was, however, purely formal. The end of feudalism did not abolish economic inequality, it simply depoliticized it; inequalities officially enforced under feudalism were now reproduced within the very structure of society. Most people owned little more than the productive capacity of their bodies (their labour power), while a very few owned the bulk of society's wealth and productive property. The newly universalized rights of property and contract were thus imposed on, and served to enforce and maintain, a substantively unequal economic order. All individuals were treated as equals by the law, while they lived their lives in relations of radical inequality.

The elements of liberal rights discourse – atomism, anti-statism, formal equality – build on the presumption of liberal capitalism that political ('public') power can, and must, be separated from social and economic ('private') power. Their congruence with the dominant social system is as strong today as it was in the eighteenth century. Liberal rights discourse is sustained by, and helps sustain, the various elements of liberal and capitalist hegemony: an economic and social sphere that operates free of the immediate political imperatives of the state and is based on private ownership of property; agency and citizenship defined in terms of people's individual rights and freedoms to do, be, buy, and sell; and restrictions, both legal and conventional, on the degree to which public (state) power can legitimately be used to regulate social and economic life. The liberal message that social and economic relations are part of a private, atomistic, and depoliticized world is thus rooted in dominant patterns of social action, power, and structure, including those most central to people's lives, such as work (Bakan and Blomley 1992), gender relations (Ursel 1992) and child rearing (Kline 1992).

Liberal discourses are particularly strong within legal forums, where, in addition to the general relationships that exist between liberal discourse and social relations, law's unique ideological processes are in operation. Law is saturated with liberal ideology, and lawyers and judges are trained to believe that its elements are as natural as the air they breathe. The liberal ideologies of rights that dominate Charter litigation are thus built on solid historical and social foundations, both within and outside of law. Though Charter litigation appears a contest of language and symbols, ideological processes operate just below its surface to ensure, before the contest even begins, that liberal discourses of rights will prevail over others. The limits imposed by such discourses on the Charter's progressive potential, described and analysed in this and the next three chapters, are thus deeply rooted in history and social relations and cannot be avoided by reinterpretation alone.

IV

In conclusion, I have argued that litigation over equality rights is unlikely to advance social equality substantially, and I have tried to explain why this is so. Because of the anti-statist, negative, and dyadic form of dominant constructions of rights, litigation over equality rights is not a powerful tool for attacking the structures and institutions responsible for inequality in society. I do not deny that rights tactics may have a role in wider strategies for social transformation (see chapter 8) or that they are useful tools for attacking discrete instances of state discrimination and oppression. My aim, admittedly modest, is to mark the limits of equality rights in their social context. Litigation over Charter equality is likely to have some positive effects in particular and discrete contexts, as well as some negative ones. While it is not likely to have much effect at all on the structures and institutions of inequality, it undoubtedly will play some role, though relatively minor, in struggles to transform these. The arguments made about equality rights in this chapter hold for other Charter rights as well, and we thus revisit the general themes of this chapter in chapters 4–6.

4

Freedom of Expression and the Politics of Communication

Human life [unlike that of other animals] is sign-making – 'significant' – existence ... If squirrels, as far as we know, are not at this moment busy secretly constructing nuclear weapons, it is not particularly because they are a nicer crowd than we are but because they cannot deploy our kind of signs.
Terry Eagleton (1990, 25)

Communication is fundamental to human existence. Our thoughts, feelings, politics, identities, and power relations are all understood and expressed through language and other signs. That is why freedom of expression – the freedom to engage in communicative activity – is essential for human progress. Widespread consensus about the importance of free speech exists in Canada. Notorious examples of its repression, such as the massacre of demonstrating students in Tiananmen Square and Salman Rushdie's death sentence, excite outrage from people across the political spectrum and remind us of freedom of expression's historic role in struggles against state repression by non-dominant groups.

Focusing on official repression, however, can distort issues of free speech. People's capacities to speak are increasingly undermined by economic concentration, technological change, and privatization in the communications sphere. Yet the liberal discourses of freedom of expression that dominate public and legal debate tend to concentrate on discrete cases of governmental restriction of speech – censorship. In section I of this chapter I describe this liberal model, as it is manifest in the Supreme Court of Canada's jurisprudence. In section II I argue that social structures and processes profoundly constrain people's capacity to communicate effectively but lie outside the Charter's reach. Finally, section III looks at some of the distorting effects of mainstream freedom-of-expression discourse and offers alternative ways to think about the politics of communication that are more consistent with a progressive conception of social justice.

I

Disputes about free speech generally arise when a public institution, usually some part of the state, penalizes or prohibits a particular communicative act. The disputants each acknowledge the importance of freedom of expression, and also that it must sometimes be restricted to protect people from harmful consequences (such as those caused by shouting 'Fire' in a crowded theatre), but disagree on whether the particular speech at issue is sufficiently harmful to warrant its restriction. Four closely related elements define this paradigm and reflect the liberal tenets of anti-statism and atomism.

To begin with, only public (state or governmental) action is understood as a threat to freedom of expression (*Dolphin Delivery* 1986).[1]

Second, and closely related, people are presumed free to express themselves in the absence of external constraints, making unintelligible the idea that outside support might be necessary to enable them to speak. State intervention thus cannot facilitate freedom of expression; it is necessarily a coercive force. Though members of the Court have on occasion recognized the narrowness of this purely negative conception (per Justice L'Heureux-Dubé, in *Committee for the Commonwealth* 1991, 198, cited by the majority in *Haig v. Canada* 1992), the Court has refused to go beyond it (*Native Women's Association of Canada* 1994; Bakan et al. 1995; Trakman 1995a).

Third, formal equality among different speakers and messages is presumed. The content or meaning of speech is considered irrelevant for determing whether or not it falls within the scope of freedom of expression, as are questions about who is the speaker. '[A] necessary feature of our modern democracy,' according to the Supreme Court of Canada, is that 'everyone can manifest their [sic] thoughts, opinions, beliefs, indeed all expressions of the heart and mind, however unpopular, distasteful or contrary to the mainstream' (*Irwin* 1989, 968; see also *Keegstra* 1990, 729; *Zundel* 1992). The value of expression therefore lies in the fact that it is expression, not in how the judiciary or anyone else evaluates its particular contents. Corporate advertising, racial hatred, legislative debates, and lesbian/gay literature are thus united by their common form, and it is that form, rather than the particular contents of these different kinds of expression, that makes them presumptively worthy of equal protection from state suppression.[2] Though such 'content neutrality' is the norm governing interpretation of the right to freedom of expression, the Court does evaluate the substance of expression when determining whether a law found to limit that right should be upheld under section 1 of the Charter.[3] It tends to uphold laws that restrict expression that it considers harmful, such as some forms of hate literature, pornography, and advertising; or unrelated to the purpose of protecting freedom of expression;

or a threat to important competing social values, such as privacy and equality (*Irwin* 1989; *Keegstra* 1990; *Butler* 1992).[4]

Fourth, claims about freedom of expression are framed in dyadic terms, as challenges by an entity, group, or individual, to some discrete action (or inaction) of another entity. Rights to freedom of expression are triggered only by acts that restrict, or refuse to support, speech of a particular type, group, or individual; they do not contemplate the social, cultural, and economic determinants of people's communicative capacities.

There is an ongoing debate among academics and commentators about whether the Court has struck an appropriate balance between freedom of expression and competing social interests. Some of them object to almost any restriction on expression, while others are more tolerant of limits on modes of expression that have variously defined negative effects.[5] Each side trots out the well-worn arguments in support of its position when criticising or lauding the Court for its decisions. The debate, following the abstract and normative emphasis of internal legal analysis, focuses on questions about how courts should determine when legislative limits on freedom of expression are justifiable and ignores those about whether the Charter is likely to enhance people's actual capacities to communicate. I argue, in contrast, that a huge gap exists between the rhetoric – judicial and popular – concerning the importance of freedom of expression in a democracy and the actual communications capacities of most people and, further, that the liberal form of Charter rights means that Charter litigation can do little about this gap.[6]

The four characteristics of that form – anti-statism, a negative conception of rights, a formal conception of equality, and atomism – parallel the formal characteristics of equality rights. I argued in the previous chapter that while each of these characteristics imposes limits on the potential of equality rights to remedy social inequality, the most substantial limit is imposed by atomism. The same is true in the context of freedom of expression. The atomistic form of that right means that it is triggered only when one person's ability to engage in communicative activity is directly affected by a particular action of another person (or entity). People's capacity to communicate effectively, by contrast, is dependent on the interplay of multiple social and economic processes.

II

Of course I use the media! I can stand and speak for hours in [a shopping area], but if I'm not speaking beyond the immediate crowd, then I'm not effective.
Svend Robinson, MP (1994)

A combination of institutional and structural processes produces unequal power among people to communicate effectively – that is, 'beyond the immediate crowd.' Effective communication requires that people have access to audiences. Without an audience a person can only speak, not communicate, and her capacity to communicate effectively will depend on which, and how many, people hear her message. Mainstream notions of freedom of expression ignore this fact, implying that individuals are free to communicate so long as state restrictions are absent. 'Freedom of entry into opinion markets [is presumed] for any enterprise which thinks it has something individuals might like to hear, read or watch' (Keane 1991, 53).

This model may be appealing in the abstract, but it has little to do with the real world of communications. In sharp contrast to the presumption of equal freedom to enter the 'marketplace' of ideas, radical disparities exist among people in their capacity to gain access to the channels through which most communications reach most people. The communications domain is structured by 'asymmetrical relations of power ... differential access to resources and opportunities, and ... institutionalised mechanisms for the production, transmission and reception of symbolic forms' (J.B. Thompson 1990, 136). Over the last half-century cultural production has been almost completely incorporated into the vastly unequal domain of market relations (Inglis 1990, 114); today it occurs primarily in privately owned facilities, and the bulk of images, symbols, and representations that people see, read, and hear are produced for profit.

The consequences of private ownership of cultural production are the same as those of private ownership more generally: concentrations of social power and limited access for most people to major resources. Ownership and control of communications resources in Canada – television and radio broadcasting stations, newspapers, magazines, publishing houses, and movie studios – is concentrated and becoming more so (a tendency helped along by deregulation: Herman and Chomsky 1988; Inglis 1990; Curran and Seaton 1991), and Canadian media enterprises have substantial formal and informal ties to the international corporate community through cross-ownership and overlapping boards of directors. Most people do not own media facilities and cannot afford to buy media time and space from those who do. The average person's communications are unlikely to have much of an impact beyond her immediate geographic and social environment. She has easy access, however, to the cultural products of communications industries, which are often subsidized by advertisers and therefore free (television and radio) or inexpensive (magazines and newspapers). Much communicative activity is thus one way, characterized by consumption of cultural products, usually in a private setting. Though it involves, as John Thompson (1991) argues, 'mediated quasi-interaction,' where recipients form 'bonds of friendship, affection or loyalty' with communicators, this does not alter its predominantly one-way form. Nor is it likely that new communications media, such as the internet, will provide truly interactive communications.

Most people lack sufficient resources and skills – a computer, computer literacy, money to pay on-line fees – to log on to the internet.[7] More fundamentally, the internet cannot escape the pull of market forces towards the highly profitable, and decidedly non-interactive, pay-for-view form of 'information super-highway'; it is already taking the shape of 'a ten-lane highway coming into the home, with only a tiny path leading back out – just wide enough to take a credit card number or to answer multiple choice questions' (Besser 1995, 63; see also Postman 1992; J. Barlow 1995; Brook and Boal 1995; Kadi 1995; Saige 1995).

Public institutions and spaces have historically provided some openings, albeit limited ones, for people and knowledge closed out of market-driven communications spheres, but these are now subject to encroaching privatization (Schiller 1989, 88–91). The Canadian Broadcasting Corporation (CBC) is a good example of the problem. While it is hardly a bastion of non-dominant knowledge production, as a public broadcaster it at least has the potential (which it occasionally realizes) of providing programming that involves groups and viewpoints unlikely to be aired by commercial broadcasters. Its legislated mandate, for example, includes requirements that programming be predominantly and distinctively Canadian, reflect the multicultural and multiracial nature of Canada, be accessible to disabled persons, and include alternative programs (Broadcast Act 1991). Beginning in the mid-1980s, however, the CBC's capacity to achieve its legislated mandate was seriously eroded by funding cuts. Raboy (1990) describes the 1980s as a period during which there was an 'eclipse of public broadcasting'; 'the broadcasting environment was subjected to new scrutiny and federal policy began a process of transformation in which the public sector would be increasingly marginalised and reduced in function and importance' (267). It was, according to Raboy, a 'decade of steep decline' for public broadcasting (269), and the trend has only worsened in the 1990s.[8]

In addition to paring down public broadcasting, the federal government has cut or weakened a variety of programs that provide direct support for production and dissemination of alternative knowledge. As Phillips points out (1991, 196), 'a distinctive feature of the Canadian political system is that the federal government provides funding to public interest groups, many of which engage in vociferous criticism of their own benefactor.' Such programs were developed in the years following the Second World War and are a lifeline for production of alternative knowledge,[9] yet they are being reduced and eliminated in the name of deficit reduction.[10]

Arts funding has also been slashed, forcing visual and performing artists to look for corporate sponsors or produce commercially viable works. This process risks curtailing the ability of the arts to challenge conventional political, moral, social, and aesthetic conventions.[11]

Education, perhaps the most important and influential public arena of knowledge production, is also being pressed by privatization. Though governments still appear committed to publicly funded primary and secondary education for all children in Canada, insufficient funding has caused many schools to accept substantial corporate donations – usually with strings, if not ropes, attached (M. Barlow and Robertson 1994). Other institutions of public education, such as libraries and museums, are also facing serious erosions in public funding and are having to resort to corporate sponsorship.[12] University funding is increasingly dependent on private subsidies. The ability of universities to produce social criticism and alternative knowledge is threatened by this trend, which tends, as Newson and Buchbinder (1988) point out, 'to place the university in the service of the private sector, by tying its creative energies to the needs of production through various funding arrangements and contractual relationships' (72).[13] These developments do not bode well for the production of critical and alternative knowledge in universities (Readings 1996).[14]

Finally, public space is disappearing. Demonstrations, marches, and rallies, though quintessential images associated with freedom of expression, may soon be things of the past as social spaces, such as streets, plazas, and town squares, are increasingly privatized.[15] Privately owned malls have replaced streets and other public spaces as primary sites of social interaction in suburban and exurban population centres (Schiller 1989, 98–9), and mall owners have no obligation to allow expression on their property.[16] 'We simply don't want anything to interfere with the shopper's freedom to not be bothered and have fun' is how one mall owner justified consistently denying permission to groups wishing to pass out leaflets in a mall (Crawford 1992, 23).[17] In urban contexts, contemporary designs of downtown cores, which often rely on private, enclosed skyways, tunnel systems, and sidewalks in place of public streets, produce mall-like conditions. Even where these are publicly owned, and thus technically public space, they are often hostile to public expression.[18] They 'ensure a seamless continuum of middle-class work, consumption, and recreation, insulated from the city's "unsavory" streets' and have the effect of 'warning off the underclass Other' (Davis 1992, 159). In addition, many of the open spaces of downtown that appear public are in fact privately owned.[19] 'PUBLIC SPACE,' proclaims a plaque in the AT&T plaza in New York, 'Owned and Maintained by AT&T' (Schiller 1989, 102).[20]

Political, economic, and technological forces that directly exclude people from knowledge production are not the only limits on people's communicative capacities. Ideological processes work to the same end. In any society, dominant ideological discourses provide frames of reference that shape opinions and beliefs and ascribe credibility to some meanings while discrediting others.[21] Certain ideas are taken for granted as right and true, and others are thought to be wrong, dangerous, or deviant. In every area of social life (including law and rights: see chapters 2 and 3), images and representations exist that appear as 'simply descriptive statements about how things are (i.e., must be), or of what we can take for granted' (Hall 1990, 9). They 'accumulate the symbolic power to map or classify the world for others,' and they set 'the limit to what will appear as rational, reasonable, credible, indeed sayable or thinkable, within the given vocabularies of motive and action available to us' (Hall 1988b, 44). Dominant ideological discourses grant automatic value and credibility to messages that support existing social arrangements and conditions (J.B. Thompson 1990). These become part of society's 'common sense' and require no explanation or defence. The ideas of non-dominant groups, in contrast, are presumptively nonsensical because they contradict this common sense. The onus is on such groups to rebut this presumption and prove that their ideas are credible. The difficulties in meeting this task are compounded not only by the institutionalized inequalities of knowledge production discussed above, but also by the 'sound-bite' format of mainstream media, which makes it all but impossible to develop the kind of explanation and analysis necessary to challenge conventional wisdom (Hall 1980).

Dissident and oppositional ideas are thus denied effect by ideological processes that sustain the domination of mainstream knowledge. The overall result is similar to that of state censorship, but the processes are more subtle. To take an example, in 1992 New Star Books of Vancouver published a collection of essays, one of which, written by Gideon Rosenbluth, argues that the widespread concern about government deficits in Canada today is 'based on fallacies exposed in every respectable textbook on elementary economics published since the Second World War' (62). Rosenbluth's views are not shared by most Canadians, a point supported by survey data indicating widespread anxiety about government deficits and debt and a general view that they are dangerous and highly undesirable.[22] Most Canadians would reject Rosenbluth's argument automatically, and not because of disagreements over the finer points of macroeconomic theory. They would simply deny that Rosenbluth's views are credible in light of 'facts' about deficits and debt that are generally taken for granted and part of society's 'common sense.'

The mass audience, to which Rosenbluth arguably has at least some access as a published author, is thus predisposed against his views because of the divergence of those views from conventional wisdom. Within the current ideological environment, arguments, such as Rosenbluth's, not premised on the need to reduce deficits are presumptively invalid. Thus, while both Rosenbluth and the editorial writers at the *Globe and Mail* enjoy the right to freedom of expression, the latters' persistently anti-deficit message is more powerful, not only because the *Globe and Mail* reaches a wider audience than most New Star books but also because that message accords with dominant ideological discourses about public finances, while Rosenbluth's does not.

The question still remains of why some discourses, such as concern about deficits, become dominant in society – matters of 'common sense' – while others do not. The key lies in the relationship between discourses and other processes of social power (see chapter 3). We can break this relationship down into three analytically (if not actually) distinct parts. First, discourses that serve the interests of powerful groups in society – that are, in Stuart Hall's words, the 'cultural and ideological underpinning of ... particular structure[s] of power' (1986, 53–4) – have a substantial edge over others.[23] The short-term material interests of business, for example, are well served by anti-deficit discourses, as the latter help justify policies such as privatization, deregulation, cuts to social services, lay-offs, and roll-backs of wages and benefits and impose blame for economic hardships on governments rather than on the private sector. Not surprisingly, big business has used its substantial resources to create a culture of fear around government debt and deficits. Second, the institutional organization of knowledge production helps support the dominance of certain discourses (Zhao 1993, 30–1). For example, because most media enterprises make profits by selling space to advertisers, program content is designed to attract corporate customers. This probably contributes to the media's uncritical adoption of business's perspectives on public deficits and debt.[24] Third, the social context and constitution of the audience help determine which discourses become dominant (Lewis 1991). People are not likely to attribute much weight to ideas radically at odds with their knowledge, interests, and life conditions.[25] Popular readiness to accept an anti-deficit discourse does not indicate mass stupidity or false consciousness, but rather flows from a combination of the grain of truth on which such discourse is built (deficits do exist and are, in the abstract, not desirable) and people's need to understand, explain, and feel that there may be a solution to their worsening economic circumstances.

III

Thus the most substantial constraints on our freedom to participate in effective communicative activity are found in social institutions and structures, and these are beyond the range of even a very generous interpretation of the Charter's right of freedom of expression. The atomistic, anti-statist, and negative form of the right to freedom of expression excludes consideration of the most important limitations on people's power to communicate effectively: the economic and technological organization of knowledge production and the effects of ideological processes.[26] This does not mean that the Charter's protection of freedom of expression is useless. It is an effective tool for resisting discrete examples of legislative and administrative repression of ideas – censorship[27] – which certainly exists in Canada. The effects of explicit state censorship are relatively insignificant, however, when compared to the wide range of social constraints on people's capacity to communicate effectively.

Moreover, the latter kind of constraints are obscured by the emphasis on censorship in freedom-of-expression discourse. People are wrongly presumed to have freedom of expression in the absence of censorship, or at least that seems to be the implication of anti-censorship positions. Three distinct difficulties flow from this presumption.

First, this presumption exaggerates the potential importance and gains of traditionally framed struggles for freedom of expression. *Little Sisters v. Canada* (1996), a case widely understood to be at the forefront of the anti-censorship movement, illustrates the point. A complete victory for Little Sisters would have invalidated certain customs and tarrif regulations and thus denied Canadian customs officials the authority to seize lesbian and gay literature at the border. The actual decision in *Little Sisters* (1996) was a partial victory: though it declared that the regulations validly proscribe entrance into Canada of lesbian and gay material that is 'obscene' under the Criminal Code, it also recognized that customs officials often stray beyond their legislative authority in seizing lesbian and gay materials that are not obscene. Criticisms of the decision tend to focus on the relative merits of different potential outcomes, the relationship between the case and censorship law more generally, and the perils of state censorship. I want to make a different point: namely, whatever its eventual outcome in the appellate courts, this case can only very minimally enhance the communicative power of lesbians and gays. It focuses narrowly on a discrete set of governmental restrictions on expression and does not touch the institutionalized exclusion and repression of lesbian and gay knowledge, in broadcasting, newspapers, publishing, and school curricula. Nor, more generally, does it contemplate the power of homophobia to restrict, through discrimination and violence, the expression of lesbian and gay identity. Explicit state repression of lesbian and gay expression is, in short, only part of the wide range of social and ideological processes responsible for repressing lesbian and gay expression. While I fully support Little Sisters bookstore and others who struggle against such repression, my concern is that the intense focus of the anti-censorship movement on discrete state restrictions on freedom of expression effectively masks, or at least de-emphasizes, wider repressive processes.

Second, mainstream discourse on freedom of expression wrongly presumes that the state is necessarily antagonistic to freedom of expression. Its caricaturistic representation of the state as repressive censor – 'big brother' – effectively paints progressive people into a conceptual and political corner: once state power is identified as the primary threat to free speech, it makes little sense to ask the state for anything other than non-interference. Yet, as noted above, positive state initiatives – such as funding education, broadcasting, arts, and social advocacy; creating public spaces (such as parks and plazas); and building libraries and museums – can enhance the ability of non-dominant groups to speak. State power can, in other words, be harnessed to progressive ends in relation to knowledge production. The anti-statist basis of anti-censorship campaigns may implicitly deny this if it presents state power as the entire problem rather than as potentially part of the solution.

Censorship itself, in addition to positive forms of state support, may promote freedom of expression in some contexts. Inequalities of both communications resources and the relative credibility attached to different ideas by ideological processes create a social field in which 'unrestricted speech by some can actually inhibit the willingness to speak and the capacity to be heard of others' (Greenwalt 1995, 151). In the absence of legislative and administrative restrictions on expression, existing patterns of domination in communications spheres, such as those described in section II, may overwhelm and effectively silence ideas and voices with no social power behind them. Such domination can be met either by enabling of those who are dominated to speak louder or by requiring the dominant to speak more softly. If, in a roomful of people, some have access to a public address system, and the rest have just their unamplified voices, the latter will be drowned out. Their right to freedom of expression will be empty, its exercise entirely ineffective. A rule forbidding use of amplification devices would limit the power of microphone holders to get their points across, but it might enhance the capacity of the unamplified to express their views.

By analogy, legislative restrictions on the speech of dominant groups, ones that have access to communications resources and whose ideas are part of the mainstream, may enable non-dominant groups to express themselves and be heard. The purpose of the limits placed in the Broadcasting Act, 1991, on American content, for example, is to give Canadian voices a chance to be heard by turning down the volume of much louder American ones. Similarly, restrictions on the amount of money that people can spend on advertising during an election campaign are designed to enhance the expression of ordinary people's views by limiting the substantial capacity of rich people and corporations to express their views. In both cases governments place direct restrictions on some people's expression (the American culture industry, those who have money) in order to increase the expressive power of others.[28]

A similar approach can be developed in relation to racist, sexist, homophobic, and other ideological processes that mark some groups 'as Other, deviant in relation to the dominant norm' (I. Young 1990, 123). In theory, legislative power might be used to attenuate the repression of non-dominant identities, values, and beliefs caused by such processes. The silencing of lesbians and gays by widespread homophobia, for example, might be at least partly addressed by legislative silencing of homophobic speech. Criminal Code measures that increase penalties for hate-motivated assaults on lesbians and gays, or human rights legislation that proscribes homophobic hate speech – both of which have been characterized as violations of freedom of speech – may[29] help create a social environment in which lesbians and gays can express who they are in all aspects of their lives without fear of reprisal. The same kind of argument can be made in defence of anti-hate legislative protections for other groups, such as racial minorities (see, for example, *Ross* 1996, 31).

Legislation restricting expression – censorship – may thus serve the very values that underlie freedom of expression; it can silence the silencers.[30] This is a different, and I think better, way to think about restrictions on racist, sexist, and homophobic speech than the more common 'harm' approach. Many believe that restrictions are justified only when they are necessary to protect certain groups from harm.[31] All concerns about freedom of expression are thus placed on the side of individuals subject to legislative restrictions. The harm caused to groups that are targeted by the speech, though taken seriously, is defined as something other than repression of their expression – hurt, humiliation, degradation, offence, or incitement of violence against the group. Unintelligible within this framework is the idea that racist, sexist, and homophobic speech effectively undermines freedom of expression itself by creating an environment in which people feel threatened for expressing who they are and what they think. A further difficulty with this approach is that, because it presumes that freedom-of-expression interests are very weighty, the alleged harm caused by someone's speech must be severe to justify restricting it. Proponents generally think that extreme forms of racism, sexism, and homophobia meet this standard, on the ground that they are deviant, destructive, and intended to villify people and cause deep hurt and grave humiliation (Greenwalt 1995, 54, 63–4). But they consider day-to-day discrimination and harassment normal and merely offensive, though perhaps regrettable, and thus deserving of toleration as exercises of free speech.

Controversies about so-called political correctness illustrate the limitations of this model. Beginning in the mid-1980s some North American universities and colleges created policies designed to discourage and penalize verbal harassment or insults based on sexual, racial, or other characteristics and to open up the 'Western civilization' canon in the humanities to writers and ideas from non-dominant groups. Some condemn these measures as violations of free speech and academic freedom; they chastise proponents – usually members of historically oppressed and marginalized groups – for being 'thought police' who seek to enforce political conformity.[32] An argument often made against 'political correctness' is that it wrongly presumes that 'the rights of those offended by what someone says outweigh the rights of the person who says it' (M. Harvey 1993, 143). Language that insults, ignores, or excludes people may be offensive and even painful to its targets, the argument goes, but that is the price we must pay for living in a free society: 'no words or expressions should be illegal simply because they offend those who hear them' (Greenwalt 1995, 58) – though campus speech codes might be justifiable if 'directed primarily and carefully at the intentionally injurious use of speech' (in other words, *real* harm) (77). Opponents of political correctness often claim that, because effective speech will always offend somebody, little would be left of freedom of expression if speech could be restricted on that basis.

This argument, though superficially compelling, incorrectly assumes that protecting people from offence is the primary reason behind anti-discrimination and anti-harassment codes. The purpose of such measures is not to protect groups from mere offence, and it is not limited to protecting individuals from being intentionally injured by speech. Rather, it includes the promotion of values that lie at the core of freedom of expression itself. Ideological processes, I have argued, largely determine who can speak and what can be said. In universities, a predominantly white, middle-class, and male professoriate has established over the years what methods and subjects of inquiry are valid, what modes of behaviour in and out of the classroom are acceptable, and what levels of deference to its members by students and junior colleagues are appropriate. It has enforced these norms through the substantial power it has over students and junior members of faculty, in terms of grading, writing letters of reference, making admissions and appointments, and granting tenure and promotions. Though Canadian universities are more diverse places today than they were in the past, those who do not fit the dominant mould – women, racialized groups, and working-class and poor people – are often effectively silenced by an environment in which they may be invisible, denigrated, or harassed, and where criteria for truth, beauty, morality, and scholarship have been shaped in their absence. The purpose behind restrictions on certain forms of verbal behaviour, and requirements to diversify curricula, is to remove at least some of the factors repressing the expression of non-dominant groups. Though it is true that questions about whether particular restrictions have this effect must be considered on a case-by-case basis (Michelman 1992), opponents of political correctness reject such restrictions a priori. In their view, any direct restriction of expression is necessarily destructive of freedom of expression, while the coercive silencing effected by dominant norms and practices is of no concern. Only within such a distorted framework could the quite limited restrictions on expression found in most campus codes be perceived as substantial threats to freedom of expression. Ironically, this framework has itself become an orthodoxy – *the* correct view on issues concerning regulation of speech – leaving 'little free thought about free thought, little free inquiry about free inquiry, and little free speech about free speech' (Schauer 1992).

Returning to the 'harm approach,' my argument that its range is too narrow is not meant to deny its usefulness in some contexts. Communicative activity by some can cause various kinds of concrete harm to others beyond silencing their speech. Shouting 'Fire' in a crowded theatre is the paradigmatic example. There are many other examples. Speech that belittles or harasses employees or students on the basis of their race or sex can cause substantial hurt, loss of self-esteem, and even illness in those to whom it is targeted; it may also unduly persuade others not to employ or promote them or to evaluate their performance negatively. Protesting and picketing by anti-choice advocates in front of abortion clinics may cause direct physical and emotional harm to women seeking abortion services and interfere with their ability to avail themselves of those services (Bakan 1995; *Lewis* 1996). Advertising of tobacco products may cause harm by promoting smoking among young people (*RJR-MacDonald* 1995, per Justice LaForest). Some forms of hate literature and pornography may directly cause harm to racial groups and women or incite others to cause them harm (*Keegstra* 1990; *Butler* 1992; *Ross* 1996). The harm approach is useful for considering whether expression should be restricted in these kinds of scenarios. My argument against it is that its range does not extend beyond such examples to recognize as harm the silencing of some people by the speech of others.

A further difficulty with the approach has to do with how it operates within its range. Harm is neither a neutral nor an apolitical concept. Presumptions about the social world necessarily affect how it is construed by interpreters and therefore help determine the range of permissible speech. 'Harm' may be interpreted by decision makers to mean anything that does not comport with dominant conceptions of politics or morality.

The approach's proscription of modes of speech that are extreme and exceptional can thus serve to reinforce domination by legitimating state repression of non-dominant discourses. The point is illustrated by the Supreme Court of Canada's decision in *Butler* (1992). The Court upheld criminal prohibitions on certain forms of obscenity on the basis that they are necessary to protect society, particularly women and children, from harm. According to Justice Sopinka, writing for a majority, contemporary understandings of harm in relation to obscenity focus on sexual inequality and are no longer linked to conservative moral values. Many have hailed *Butler* as a victory for sexual equality – a 'virtually full endorsement of the feminist challenge to obscenity' (Greenwalt 1995, 120). Some passages in the judgment, however, equate harm with 'anti-social conduct' in general (485) – a definition that can easily be used to justify repression of lesbian and gay, feminist, leftist, and other 'dissident' material.

Post-*Butler* jurisprudence bears out this concern. In one case, *Glad Day Bookshop* (1992), a lower court applied *Butler* (1992) to hold that gay erotic materials are obscene, even though the materials contained no violence or domination of women. According to the court, the material is anti-social because it concerns gay sex. To similar effect, in *Little Sisters* (1996), the court interpreted *Butler* as being concerned primarily with harm to society caused by 'anti-social conduct' (126) and breaches of 'community standards' (129). Sexual equality, a central concern in

Butler, received only scant attention. These two cases illustrate how conservative values can be read into the definition of harm, thus turning the nominally liberal 'harm approach' into a vehicle for conservative moralism.

V

In conclusion, the liberal conception of freedom of expression that dominates the Court's jurisprudence on section 2(b) and popular debates about free speech cannot accommodate a progressive politics of communication. The reason is simple: it draws on a model of human communication that has little to do with reality. Our capacity to communicate effectively is shaped by social and economic processes of two basic kinds. First, much knowledge is produced by those who own or can afford the use of communications facilities. Most people do not have substantial access to such facilities and therefore are unable to reach a significant audience with their message. Their principal relationship to culture is as consumers, not as participants in its production. Second, this mode of cultural production, along with wider ideological processes, shapes the kind of culture that is produced and, in turn, popular conceptions of what is right, normal and true. Ideas, beliefs, and aesthetics that exist outside the terms of this societal 'common sense' often appear to lack credibility, and the people communicating them may be variously ignored, ridiculed, or vilified. It should be apparent that the two issues – the first relating to communications resources and the second to ideological context – are closely tied in practice. Those who own or have access to major communications resources may be able, through repetition and mass distribution, to give their messages the exposure and presence necessary for them to become dominant.

The traditional liberal model focuses only on discrete state restrictions on speech. As a result, it catches both too little and too much. It is too narrow to redress most restrictions on our capacity to communicate effectively, and broad enough to prohibit state measures aimed at freeing the speech of groups effectively silenced by the domination of others.

Thinking about freedom of speech requires consideration of how knowledge production is organized in society and the possibility that state measures directed at facilitating non-dominant communications, and restricting dominant communications, might enhance people's communicative capacities. The liberal model of freedom of speech tends not to contemplate these ideas. It should be replaced with a model that attaches significance to people's relative social and economic ability to communicate effectively. Debates about when and where to restrict and allow expression surely would not end under such a model, nor should we want them to. These debates would, however, be improved for having to grapple with the actual politics and practices of communications.

5

Freedom of Association and the Dissociation of Workers

Industry has long used spatial dispersion and the geographical isolation of employees as one of its prime mechanisms of labour control ... But recent transformations in industrial organisation, flexible locational choices and deregulation have ... been turned into a totally unsubtle form of coercive exploitation.
David Harvey (1993, 88)

Freedom of association, guaranteed by section 2(d) of the Charter, has long been a touchstone for workers' struggles against exploitation. The idea of association was at the heart of early French socialism, which envisioned a society controlled by associations of workers (Harrington 1989), and Marx (Marx and Engels 1988), saw 'permanent associations' of workers, and their 'ever expanding union,' as key to ending capitalist exploitation (228). Throughout this century, freedom of association has served to articulate the labour movement's aspirations and those of domestic and international organizations devoted to protecting workers' interests. Today, however, Canadian workers' freedom of association is severely restricted. Workers' capacities to form and join trade unions, bargain collectively and strike have been undermined by political-economic shifts – increased mobility of capital, new workplace technologies, and new modes of workplace organization – that lie far beyond the reach of the Charter's right of freedom of association. Because of its atomistic and anti-statist form, that right contemplates only direct state interference with workers' freedom of association.

Section I of this chapter reviews the Supreme Court of Canada's leading decisions on freedom of association and labour relations, as well as the academic debates that they generated. In section II I argue that political-economic developments over the last two decades have seriously undermined workers' collective power and overshadow whatever potential the Charter might hold in this area. The right of individuals to join and form trade unions is increasingly difficult to exer-

cise as new modes of workplace organization literally *dis*sociate workers; unions'
rights to strike and bargain collectively are substantially weakened by firms'
capacities to relocate to jurisdictions where labour is cheap and workers have little
collective power. The Charter right of freedom of association cannot address these
difficulties. Thus, I argue, even if unions had won their Charter challenges to legislative restrictions on strikes and collective bargaining (which, in fact, they lost),
workers' collective power would not have been substantially enhanced.

I

Collective action by workers in Canada has increasingly been repressed over the
past two decades. To the extent that there ever was a genuine commitment to
workers' rights in the post-war period, this has given way to new practices and ideologies. Governments began in the early 1980s to use legislation to control wages
and other benefits of public- (and, to a lesser degree, private-) sector employees and
to attenuate employees' rights to bargain collectively and to strike. 'Exceptional'
measures against workers are now the norm, with, for example, workers engaged in
legal strikes routinely being legislated back to work (Panitch and Swartz 1988;
1993).[1] Though New Democratic Party (NDP) governments in Ontario, British
Columbia, and Saskatchewan have countered this trend with enactment of labour
laws that strengthen workers' collective bargaining rights, such reforms tend not to
survive beyond the NDP's hold on power.[2] Moreover, NDP governments, just like
their Liberal, Social Credit, and Conservative counterparts, have been prone to
curtail the rights of public-sector workers in the name of fiscal management or protection of essential services (though with more hand-wringing and, arguably, less
vindictiveness).

With the Charter's entrenchment in 1982, many saw constitutional litigation as
a strategy to stop legislative roll-backs of labour rights. Since then, unions have
gone to the Supreme Court on seven occasions seeking constitutional protection of
picketing, strikes, and collective bargaining, and they have lost every time.[3] In a
1987 trilogy of cases, unions claimed that the Charter's guarantee of freedom of
association protected them from legislative restrictions on strikes (*Alberta Reference*
1987; *Public Service Alliance of Canada* 1987; *Saskatchewan Dairy Workers* 1987).
In rejecting this claim, the Court held that freedom of association protected the
freedom only of individuals to associate with one another, not of associations to
engage in their essential activities, such as strikes. A minority of judges disagreed,
holding that freedom of association protected trade unions qua associations, not
just individuals, and that legislative restrictions on strikes violated freedom of association because strikes are an essential activity of unions.[4] The majority's approach
was, however, confirmed in subsequent cases, where it was relied on to exclude col-

lective bargaining, in addition to strikes, from constitutional protection (*Professional Institute* 1990). The overall effect of the Court's decisions is that while the Charter does not protect strikes and collective bargaining,[5] it does protect the right of individuals to form and join trade unions. This latter right, according to Justice LeDain's plurality decision in the *Alberta Reference* (1987), is fundamental in a democracy, its repression a characteristic of totalitarian regimes (391).[6] By implication, repression of the rights to strike and to bargain collectively, which Justice Ledain and the other members of the majority held permissible under the Charter, is perfectly consistent with democratic principles.

No one (except perhaps those on the far right) would accuse the Court of having gone too far in protecting the right to form and join unions. The Court has, however, been substantially criticized for not going far enough. Critics argue that its majority decisions are incoherent, granting individuals a right to form and join unions, while denying unions the rights to strike and bargain collectively. This criticism can be found in two dissenting judgments: 'A union can only exist if it is allowed to bargain collectively. That is the raison d'être of a union ... To say that the union exists as long as the individuals can meet and discuss their grievances is, with respect, to cast a spell of unreality over the situation. The voiced grievances would have no more effect than casual complaints about the weather' (per Justice Cory, *Professional Institute* 1990, 382–3). 'If freedom of association only protects the joining together of persons for common purposes, but not the pursuit of the very activities for which the association was formed, then the freedom is indeed legalistic, ungenerous, indeed vapid' (per Chief Justice Dickson, *Alberta Reference* 1987, 362–3). Academic critics agree with the dissenting judges that the majority's reasons are conceptually and analytically flawed. Beatty and Kennet (1988), for example, argue (correctly in my view) that the ban on strikes meets Justice McIntyre's test in the *Alberta Reference* (1987) for determining whether legislation restricts freedom of association but that faulty logic precludes him from seeing this.

More generally, critics argue that the Court's decisions are wrong in principle. They lionize Chief Justice Dickson for holding in dissent that the Charter should protect unions' collective rights and for articulating a progressive conception of freedom of association. According to Chief Justice Dickson: 'Throughout history, workers have associated to overcome their vulnerability as individuals to the strength of their employers. The capacity to bargain collectively has been recognized as one of the integral and primary functions of associations of working people ... Collective bargaining remains vital to the capacity of individual employees to participate in ensuring fair wages, health and safety protections and equitable and humane working conditions' (*Alberta Reference* 1987, 368).[7]

Building on his judgment, critics argue that the majority decisions are seriously flawed – 'inimical to the very values of democracy and social equality which the

Charter exists to protect' (Harmer 1989, 422), a 'national embarrassment' (Macklem 1992, 14), an affront to workers' dignity and autonomy (Harmer 1989, 427), and a result of judicial reluctance, based on 'conservativism and fear' (Macklem 1992, 14; see also Wedderburn 1989), 'to protect unions from the state' (Christian and Ewing 1988, 75). According to Christian and Ewing (1988):

The majority rejected the idea that freedom of association was the fundamental value which both anchored and energised labour legislation – a scheme of particular laws which themselves articulated the compromise between the interests of the community in the provision of services and the interests of employees in the terms and conditions of their employment. There is no constitutional home for the reality that workers, throughout history, have taken collective action to secure goals that are now accepted on the street as basic rights. Constitutional recognition of the engine of collective action would have established a principled starting point for measuring legislation which limited the freedom to engage in collective action where the interests of society were seen to be paramount to those of workers in a particular occupation or in special circumstances. Without this constitutional footing there is no first principle against which labour legislation can be judged. Instead there remains a morass of political rationales to be invoked by legislators. (89)

Beatty (1991) agrees that the majority's position in the *Alberta Reference* (1987) flies in the face of the principles underlying labour law and notes that confirmation of that position in subsequent cases unfortunately proves correct 'the instincts and original predictions of those who were sceptical and critical of modifying our system of government by the addition of a process of constitutional review' (860).[8]

Critics of the Court's decisions, particularly Beatty, have themselves been criticized for being somewhat naïve for ever expecting that courts would protect workers' rights under the Charter (Bakan 1990; 1991; Mandel 1994, 275–8, 282–3; above, chap. 2). Here I want to make a different point: namely, that these critics were (and are) also wrong to believe that union victories in this set of cases would have significantly advanced workers' rights. Strongly implied by their passionate advocacy of constitutional labour rights is the view that such rights would substantially enhance workers' freedom to act collectively; that protecting workers from direct state interference with their rights to collective action would actually ensure that they have freedom of association. This position manifests the limits of atomism and anti-statism. It emphasizes the power dyad of state versus workers/unions in isolation from its social determinants, thus ignoring the effects of political-economic processes on workers' actual capacities to unionize, bargain collectively, and strike, and even making them invisible.

Yet it is principally these latter processes that are rapidly decreasing the power of workers to protect their common interests through collective action. From the end of the Second World War to the late 1960s, economic growth consistently created high profits, which were passed on to workers in the form of high wages. Mass production and consumption were based on stable capital investments and continued expansion and strength of consumer markets. Workers gained legislative rights to bargain collectively and strike (Hyman 1989, 87). Expansion began to slow in the early 1970s, with markets becoming saturated (in part because of more competition in production). In Canada, the crisis was particularly acute because of reliance on export-led growth and the collapse of world markets for many resources (Drache and Glasbeek 1989, 3–5). Producers have maintained levels of profit during this period of stagnation by lowering production costs, the primary component of which is labour (Jacobi 1986b, 34–6). They tend to use two strategies towards this end. First, they may reduce the size of the workforce and introduce 'flexible' production methods (such as part-time and temporary work, subcontracting, smaller workplaces, and home work), while maintaining or increasing levels of production. Second, they may move production to jurisdictions where labour is cheap, such as those of the developing world or the southern United States. These strategies are the real threats to workers' freedom of association today. They combine to create conditions in which legal rights to unionize, bargain, and strike have lost much of their power to protect workers' interests. Because the scope of the Charter's freedom of association is limited to protecting these rights, Charter victories by unions, though certainly better than defeats, cannot significantly enhance workers' collective power.

II

Changes to the law ... have helped curb the unions since 1979 ... [but even] if the law had been left unchanged, other factors would have reduced union clout. Unemployment soared, making workers less willing to put their jobs at risk. It rose furthest in manufacturing, which outside the public sector had a far greater union presence than other parts of the economy ... Job growth since 1979 has largely been in parts of the labour market, where unions have been weakest; in the service sector, in smaller firms.
Economist 1996

Let me begin this section by analysing workers' rights to form and join trade unions – rights that all members of the Supreme Court agree the Charter protects (*Alberta Reference* 1987; *Professional Institute* 1990). Until quite recently, capitalist production typically took place in large workplaces with relatively consistent shift systems. Substantial numbers of workers would regularly inhabit the same spaces at the same times, an important condition for their developing a sense of common interest and struggle. 'With the development of industry,' according to Marx

(Marx and Engels 1988), 'the proletariat not only increases in number, it becomes concentrated in great masses, its strength grows, and it feels that strength more' (228). Over the last two decades, new production methods and deindustrialization have had the opposite effect, fragmenting the worksite in time and space and thus creating real obstacles to workers' development of solidaristic ties.[9] The steady rise of part-time and temporary work arrangements[10] means that the worksite is no longer a temporally cohesive unit. Workers come and go and are unlikely to have contact with the same co-workers for any substantial period of time.[11] Moreover, as they rush from one part-time job to another – all the while, especially if they are women, juggling other obligations, such as care of children and elderly relatives, tasks themselves becoming more time consuming because of cuts in social services (J.G. Robinson and McIlwee 1989, 128–9) – workers have less contact among themselves. Sharing among workers of concerns, complaints, and aspirations – a necessary basis for creating a sense of common interest (and thus successful union organizing) – is difficult in the absence of regular and consistent contact.

Spatial (in addition to temporal) fragmentation of work worsens this situation. Increasingly, firms are 'downsizing' and relying on subcontractors to meet production needs previously met within the firm. Large plants may become medium-sized ones and then subcontract with small, specialized firms and even single home-workers.[12] Workers are thus spread out in space and isolated from each other, geographically dissociated, and thus less able to develop solidaristic ties. Moreover, small firms are prohibitively costly for unions to organize and thus allow for greater resistance by employers to certification.[13] The likelihood that a firm's employees will be represented by a union thus decreases with the size of the firm – a further obstacle to unionization (and thus workers' association) in light of the trend towards smaller firms.

Spatial and temporal dissociation of workers also results from new forms of work organization within firms. There is, for example, a movement in manufacturing and other sectors away from assembly line–type production towards smaller units, often called 'quality circles,' where groups of multi-skilled employees work in production teams. Industry bills 'quality circles' as representing a 'new humanism' and reducing conflict in labour relations.[14] Because they break a firm's workforce into easily managed and monitered units, however, they also serve as 'an extremely attractive form of worker control and union busting' (Grenier 1988, 17). They tend to focus workers' sense of community on the small group, rather than on the plant's workforce as a whole, and they also allow management to monitor closely workers' behaviour and attitudes concerning the union and promote peer pressure against pro-union employees (4, 17–19).

In addition, 'quality circles' and other forms of team production help cultivate an ideology of individualism – an 'enterprise culture' – that encourages workers to view themselves and each other as entrepreneurs, in partnership with management and in competition among themselves (Foster and Woolfson 1989, 52; Hyman 1989, 190; Fairbrother and Waddington 1991, 34–5). As one commentator states: 'The potential value to the company of [quality circles and other such programs] lies not just in the economic returns of shop floor suggestions, but also in [their] integrative potential. To the degree that workers believe it is their responsibility to share with management the burden of plant efficiency and profitability, an enterprise consciousness may supplant broader solidarities between workers in general or between workers in a particular union' (Rhinehart 1984, 83). Other 'human resource strategies' – such as company-sponsored grievance procedures, 'neighbourhood checks' and 'snitch lines' (employees reporting to management on poor performance by their co-workers), various channels of direct communication between management and workers, and tying remuneration to levels of productivity – have similar effects (Rhinehart 1984; Jacobi 1986b, 44; Fiorito, Lowman, and Nelson 1987; Kane and Marsden 1988, 120; Fairbrother and Waddington 1991, 34–5).

Where workers are materially and ideologically dissociated from each other by new production methods, their Charter-protected right to form and join a trade union has little value. The possibility of union representation is increasingly remote for many Canadian workers, despite their legal rights to organize, as flexible schedules and small work units become the norm. Evidence of the effects of such changes can be found in the steady decline of union density in the United States and United Kingdom. Union jobs disappear, because of plant downsizing and closures, and the new jobs that replace them are part-time, temporary, and in small workplaces – in a word, union-resistant.

Though overall union density levels have not dropped substantially in Canada (a point relied on by some to argue that economic restructuring may not be the primary cause of union demise: Rose and Chaison 1990), this is only because serious declines in the private sector's union density have been compensated for by increases in the public sector.[15] Because downsizing and contracting out are now destroying union jobs in the public sector, as well as in the private sector, overall union density is likely soon to drop.[16] The relationship between political-economic developments and declining union density demonstrates the basic contradiction underlying the Charter's protection of freedom of association (and, indeed, constitutional rights more generally): the right to form and join a trade union is protected by the Court as a fundamental constitutional right, a hallmark of freedom and democracy, while at the same time being persistently and systematically undermined by the routine operation of social and economic structures and institutions.

What about the rights to strike and to bargain collectively? I have argued that the constitutionally protected right to form and join a trade union does not substantially enhance workers' actual power to do what the right purportedly enables them to do. The same would be true of constitutional rights to strike and bargain collectively, if the Court had decided freedom-of-association cases differently and created such rights. An example illustrates the point (reported in *Globe and Mail* 5 and 6 April 1993). On 28 March, 1993, 220 employees of a Nestle plant in Chesterville, Ontario, were locked out. Through their union – Retail, Wholesale and Department Store Workers – they had refused the company's request for certain concessions (including elimination of overtime pay for weekend work within the first forty hours of the work week). Nestle responded to the union's intransigence with a veiled threat to close the plant. 'I'm just trying to save jobs,' a plant manager stated. 'The clock is ticking. We either come to terms [with competition] or we'll suffocate a slow death.' In other words: concede, or we will move to the United States – a possibility opened up by the Canada–United States Free Trade Agreement (FTA), which allows companies unfettered access to Canadian markets from the United States.[17] The 'choice' for the workers was to give up hard-fought-for benefits or lose their jobs – a daunting prospect in light of high unemployment in the region (itself partly a result of the FTA). The legal rights to bargain collectively and strike were close to useless for the workers because political-economic conditions denied them the power to exercise those rights. Nestle effectively had a gun to their head – the threat to close down the plant. As one union local president from a different jurisdiction (where Nestle workers had made the required concessions) stated: 'Sometimes it's a good time to go on strike, and sometimes it isn't. This wasn't one of the good times.'

Nor are there likely to be many 'good times' in the future. High unemployment, liberalized trade laws, cheaper transportation, and new communication technologies enable big business to shop around the planet to find the place or places where it is cheapest to produce a product or service. Production does not have to take place in the country or region where a company has its headquarters and markets (Price 1985, 134–5; Warrian 1987, 22; Drache and Glasbeek 1989, 519). This is true for services as well as manufacturing: keypunch, clerical, and bookkeeping services can be shipped to cheap labour zones as easily as the assembly of motors (Drache and Glasbeek 1989, 534). A firm's threat to relocate is a significant trump for overriding union concerns in the bargaining process, for extracting concessions (G. Clark 1989, 53; Drache and Glasbeek 1989, 523; Hyman 1989, 170), for dampening the will of employees to strike (Jacobi 1986b, 44; Hyman 1989, 171), and for getting the union to agree to introduction of 'human resource management' policies (Hyman 1989, 170).

High unemployment is the background condition that gives these threats their power. Hundreds of thousands of jobs in Canada have disappeared over the past two decades in manufacturing, resource, and service industries, a result of firms moving to jurisdictions where labour is cheaper, contracting out, and new technologies[18] and production methods. The problem is exacerbated by fiscal and monetary policies aimed at lowering inflation, too great a reliance on export-led growth, and intensification of the pain of unemployment for workers through roll-backs in unemployment insurance and social welfare (Cohen 1993). Workers and their unions have little bargaining power in this context; employers can ignore their demands without consequence.

In short, while workers have legal rights to bargain collectively and strike, increasingly they cannot use them effectively. Victories for unions in the constitutional labour cases would have protected these rights only from direct state interference. They would have done nothing to curb rapid erosion of workers' collective power.

IV

To conclude, the Charter's right of freedom of association suffers from some of the same limitations as the rights to equality and freedom of expression. Because of its dyadic, negative, and anti-statist form, freedom of association can contemplate only restrictions on workers' collective action directly imposed by the state. Though such restrictions are not insignificant, they are only part of labour's problem. Economic forces are primarily responsible for eroding labour's power. Despite the impression that may be left from reading the arguments on freedom of association of progressive scholars (such as Beatty) and judges (such as Chief Justice Dickson), much more than a generous interpretation of the Charter right of freedom of association is necessary to ensure that workers have genuine freedom of association. Ways must be found to resist and overcome the increasing isolation of workers from each other and the weakening of unions' bargaining power in the new political economy. The solution lies not in the Charter, but in curbing business's power and capacity to dissociate workers from each other and ignore their collective voice. The state has a major role to play here – a fact obscured by the anti-statist form of Charter arguments. Legislation extending collective agreements achieved in one or several businesses in a particular sector to all businesses in that sector, for example, would counter some of the difficulties faced by unions in organizing small workplaces. Strengthening laws on employment standards and extending their coverage to part-time and temporary workers would help ensure adequate protection for employees in difficult-to-organize sectors, despite the absence of unions (Fudge 1991). Requiring companies to provide regular meeting times for employees (scheduled to maximize the number who will be able to attend), and better access for union organizers to company property (Macklem 1990), would ameliorate some of the effects of workers' temporal and spatial dissociation. Penalizing companies for moving their plants (or threatening to do so) to avoid unions or their demands would improve unions' bargaining power. More generally, policies aimed at reducing unemployment, promoting job security, providing better social programs (including child care), and creating disincentives to businesses' leaving Canada (abolishing or radically altering existing trade deals, for example) would greatly improve workers' collective power in Canada.

These things must be done if Canadian workers are to have real freedom of association. Yet none of them is within the Charter's reach.

6

Power to the Powerful

If Charter idolatry were to persuade the vast majority of Canadians that the Charter really does embody their most fundamental rights and freedoms and that the key to social progress is restricting government activity, then indeed the Charter would have contributed mightily to a shift of the entire political spectrum to the right.
Peter Russell (1994, 41)

Social injustice is not only difficult to address under the Charter but may also be worsened through the Charter's implementation. Right-wing and corporate attacks on government regulation, taxation, and spending have become increasingly stri-dent through the 1990s and have succeeded (with the media's help) in cultivating popular suspicion of just about everything that governments do. This suspicion is manifest in highly publicized attacks on mandatory bicycle-helmet laws, photo-radar speeding tickets, gun registration, and all forms of taxation and in business's persistent (and effective) lobbying for less governmental spending and regulation. There exists an unfortunate symbiosis between the anti-government ideology of the right and the deregulatory form of Charter rights. Both build on the same lib-eral presumptions: governmental regulation is presumptively undesirable because it encroaches on individual liberty (anti-statism), and all persons must be equally protected from it (formal equality). Consequently, individuals, groups, and corpo-rations can use the Charter to avoid legislative restrictions designed to prevent them from harming and exploiting others.[1]

Historically, at least in Canada and the United States, when judges have had the authority to review and nullify legislation under a constitution, they have often used it to strike down progressive legislation. Before the Charter was entrenched in the constitution, corporations and individuals used judicial review under sections 91 and 92 of the British North America Act, 1867 (renamed the Constitution Act, 1867), to deregulate their activities (Weiler 1974). In 1937, for example, the

Supreme Court of Canada, in decisions confirmed by the Judicial Committee of the Privy Council, held that Parliament could not enact a series of social welfare bills – a Canadian new deal – to address the social insecurity created by the Depression.[2] To similar effect, the U.S. Supreme Court cited that nation's Bill of Rights in prohibiting certain forms of progressive economic regulation[3] (though it effectively reversed these decisions in the wake of President F.D. Roosevelt's threat to pack the Court with five new judges).[4]

The history of judicial review in Canada and the United States was very much on the minds of early left-wing opponents of the Charter, who feared that it might be used to undermine progressive legislation.[5] Their concerns turned out to be well founded. Business corporations have relied on the Charter to deregulate their activities, and individuals accused of sexual assault and hate crimes have used it to weaken criminal constraints. In section I of this chapter I examine decisions of the Supreme Court of Canada in response to claims of business corporations that their Charter rights have been violated. I conclude that, despite the Court's explicit stance against protecting economic rights under the Charter, the jurisprudence that it has developed does just that. In section II I review cases relating to hate literature and sexual assault that illustrate the Charter's potential to be used against legislative measures designed to protect racial minorities and women. In section III I argue that the Court's explicit embrace of social-democratic and pro-regulatory principles is, at best, only a thin defence against potential use of the Charter for regressive ends.

I

Business corporations have not been given everything that they have asked for under the Charter, but the Supreme Court of Canada has consistently met them part-way. Despite holding, for example, that corporations are not directly protected by Charter rights to life, liberty, security of the person (section 7), and freedom of religion (section 2a) – because only humans can have these rights – the Court has relied on these rights to acquit business corporations accused of criminal and regulatory offences. Moreover, it has held that Charter rights other than those stated in sections 7 and 2(a), including freedom of expression and some criminal-procedure rights, do provide direct protection to corporations. In addition, though the Court has explicitly held that the Charter does not protect 'purely economic' interests, it (along with lower courts) has construed many economic interests as not purely economic, thus clearing the way for constitutional protection. Finally, in some cases corporate interests receive protection under the Charter even though corporate actors are not directly involved in litigation, a point illustrated by the Charter activism of the National Citizen's Coalition. There are then a number of openings for corporations to advance their interests under the Charter, each of which I examine in the following paragraphs.

The Court's jurisprudence on corporations and the Charter distinguishes two kinds of rights: the first protects only human interests; the second, corporate interests as well as human ones. The logic of the boundary between the two is that corporations, though often considered 'persons' (but not individuals) for legal purposes (*CIP* 1992, 852–5), do not reasonably fit into the concepts of some Charter rights. They do not, for example, practise religion, and they cannot be killed, incarcerated, or physically or emotionally injured. Therefore courts have held that they are outside the scope of the rights to life, liberty, and security of the person (*Irwin Toy* 1989), freedom of religion (*Big M* 1985), and several other Charter rights. There are, however, two openings for corporations within this framework, and thus two ways for them to get standing to bring a Charter challenge.

First, a corporation charged under a criminal or regulatory law can argue that the law must be struck down (thus leading to an acquittal) because that law infringes the Charter rights of human persons. Thus a corporate claim that a law violates a Charter right may succeed even if the right in question has been held not to afford direct protection to corporations. While a corporation does not have interests protected by freedom of religion or the rights to life, liberty, and security of the person, if the legislation under which it is charged potentially limits human beings' exercise of these rights, the corporation will be able to claim that the legislation is unconstitutional. In *Big M* (1985), for example, a corporation charged under the Lord's Day Act for opening on a Sunday successfully argued that the act violated the freedom of religion of individuals who belonged to religions that observed the sabbath on a day other than Sunday. Though the Court recognized the obvious point that corporations cannot practise religion, it held the Lord's Day Act unconstitutional because it violated the religious freedoms of human persons such as Jews and Muslims. It therefore acquitted Big M Ltd., which could not be convicted under an unconstitutional statute.[6]

This back door into Charter protection has been used successfully by corporations since *Big M*, particularly to challenge enforcement mechanisms in regulatory legislation. Such laws (which regulate corporate activities in areas such as the environment, worker safety, and product liability), unlike criminal laws, do not generally require proof that an accused had a 'wrongful intention' (*mens rea*) in order for a conviction to be secured. Establishing such proof within the traditional contours of criminal law is difficult when the accused is a corporation. There is often no clear 'directing mind' of the corporation that can be proved, beyond reasonable doubt, to have intended to commit a proscribed act.[7] Regulatory legislation therefore usually states that an offence is either one of 'absolute liability' (liability following simply from proof that the accused committed the proscribed act) or 'strict liability' (liability following from proof that the accused committed the proscribed act, unless the accused can prove on a balance of probabilities that it exercised due diligence in trying to avoid the act's commission[8]).

The Court has held that certain legislative provisions creating each form of liability limit Charter rights if they might include human beings, such as corporate officers, within their scope. In such circumstances, according to the Court, absolute-liability offences automatically breach section 7 (if imprisonment is a possible sanction: *Motor Vehicle Reference* 1985), and strict-liability offences limit the Charter right of being presumed innocent (if, as is usually the case, the onus of proving due diligence rests with the accused). In *Wholesale Travel* (1991),[9] the leading decision in this area, the Court states that it will be quick to strike down absolute-liability offences, but somewhat more tolerant (under section 1) of strict-liability offences.[10] The general tenor of the decision, however, is, according to Tollefson (1992), 'strongly suggestive of the extent to which sympathy and support for the regulatory mission of the state ... has waned in favour of a more sceptical rights-driven classical liberalism' (370). As a consequence of *Wholesale Travel* (1991), along with the *Motor Vehicle Act Reference* (1985), most absolute- and strict-liability provisions must meet section 1 criteria or they will be struck down by a court.[11] Consequently, the state's capacity to enforce legislative standards in relation to the environment, workers' safety, and consumer protection, among other areas, is now subject to judicial determination and may thus be substantially weakened.[12]

Second, where a Charter right is interpreted by a court to protect interests that a corporation *can* have, that right will be available to corporations. Freedom of expression is one such right. Though corporations cannot have or practise religion, they can, at least in the Court's view, express beliefs, opinions, and ideas – just like humans.[13] All governmental regulation of advertising is put at risk by this approach: restrictions on what can be advertised (such as those relating to children's toys, dental services, and tobacco, to cite a few examples that have come before the Court) and how things can be advertised (such as standards concerning false and misleading advertising or sexist and racist content) now constitute prima facie breaches of section 2(b) and thus depend for their validity on judges' willingness to uphold them under section 1. The same is true for regulation of other kinds of corporate communication, a point acknowledged, for example, in Justice L'Heureux-Dubé's statement that 'the government's regulation of [all broadcasting] resources ... constitute [*prima facie*] violations of s. 2(b)' (*Committee for the Commonwealth* 1991). Legislation designed to level power imbalances in communications, such as the Canadian content and election-spending regimes discussed in chapter 4 and later in this chapter, must also be justified under section 1.

Other Charter rights have been held by the Court to include corporations within their scope. The right to be secure against unreasonable search and seizure (section 8) is one of these. In *Hunter* (1984), the Court stated that the purpose of this right is to protect individuals from unjustified state interference in their private lives. Corporations also appear to require such protection, however, as is implied by the Court's holding that Southam Inc. was deprived of its section 8 rights by the Combines Investigation Act.[14] The Court has also held that the right to be tried within a reasonable time – section 11(b) – protects corporations. In *CIP* (1992) a corporation, charged under occupational health and safety legislation with causing the death of an employee, invoked section 11(b) in its defence. Shortage of court space had led to several adjournments of the trial, and, almost two years after the charge had been laid, a provincial court judge stayed the proceedings, holding that the delay constituted a violation of the corporation's section 11(b) right. The case was appealed up to the Supreme Court of Canada, which held that section 11(b) includes corporations within its scope. The purpose of that section, according to Justice Stevenson, is to ensure that the accused, whether a human or corporate being, has a fair trial.

Taken together, these decisions establish that if a Charter right can reasonably be interpreted to protect corporate (non-human) persons, then corporations may be protected by it.[15] This approach begs a large question: namely, whether the Charter – a human rights document – should be concerned with the interests of non-human beings. Nothing more than conceptual believability is offered by the Court to justify treating corporations and individuals in the same way under the Charter (Tollefson 1993, 318). There is no principled basis in its stated reasons for holding that the 'privacy,' 'expression,' or speedy-trial interests of corporations are on a par with those of humans. Indeed, the Court itself casts doubt on such equivalence by suggesting that Charter rights protect inherently human interests – it links privacy to human dignity and self-worth (*Hunter* 1984), freedom of expression to human fulfilment and self-actualization (*Ford* 1988; *Irwin Toy* 1989), and the right to a speedy trial to emotional and physical harm that may result from delay (*Mills* 1986, 919–20; Tollefson 1992, 347). It ignores such links, however, when holding that corporations can have Charter rights. Despite its rhetoric to the contrary, the Court ultimately presumes that human and corporate persons are the same (at least for those rights where such a presumption is conceptually feasible) and thus provides further evidence of its formal and abstract orientation.

Assuming that a corporation has standing to bring a Charter challenge (through one of the two routes just described), how will the courts deal with its claim? The cases indicate that corporations (or, for that matter, individuals) succeed under the Charter only when their claims are construed as something more than or different from purely economic. In *Irwin Toy* (1989), for example, the Court held that 'the intentional exclusion of property from s. 7, and the substitution therefore of "security of the person" ... leads to a general inference that economic rights as generally encompassed by the term "property" are not within the perimeters of the s. 7 guarantee' (1003) and that 'corporate-commercial economic rights' are therefore not protected (1004). Though this holding relates specifically to section 7, the Court has stated more generally that protection of purely economic rights is not one of the Charter's purposes (see, for example, *Alberta Reference* 1987, per Justices McIntyre and LeDain). Lower courts too have rejected the idea of protecting purely economic rights, refusing to shield businesses from legislation relating to, for example, rent collection (*A&L Investments* 1993), running a business (*Miles of Music* 1990), liquor licensing (*R.V.P. Enterprises Ltd.* 1988), collective bargaining (*Arlington Crane* 1988; *Metro Stores* 1988), patent rights (*Imperial Chemical Industries* 1990), and contracts (*Skalbania* 1989). The line between 'purely economic' and 'something-more-than economic' is, however, ambiguous, and a good argument can usually be made in a particular case that more than purely economic interests are at stake.[16] The 'economic plus' argument appears implicitly in cases such as *Hunter* (1984) and *CIP* (1992), where corporate interests are represented as more than economic (that is, as privacy or fairness).

Similarly, the Court has justified Charter protection of commercial advertising on the basis that such advertising, though motivated by profit, is not purely economic because it 'serve[s] an important public interest by enhancing the ability of [consumers] to make informed choices' (*Rocket* 1990, 247).[17] Some kinds of cigarette advertising, for example, help consumers learn 'about product availability to suit their preferences' and to protect their health by allowing them to 'compare brand content with an aim to reducing the risk to their health' (*RJR-MacDonald* 1995, 95).[18] The commercial advertising cases, taken together with the others discussed, demonstrate that the Court mutes its unwillingness to protect purely economic interests by characterizing economic interests as not purely economic.

The cases looked at to this point involve a corporation's invoking the Charter to protect its immediate interests. There is a further avenue through which the Charter may serve corporate interests. Numerous non-profit organizations exist to serve the needs of for-profit corporations, and one of these, the National Citizens' Coalition (NCC) (a right-wing, corporate-supported, non-profit group), has used the Charter to advance the general interests of corporate Canada. The NCC's cases demonstrate how the Charter can bolster corporate power, even where no corporation is directly involved in litigation.

In *National Citizens' Coalition* (1984), for example, the NCC challenged, as violating freedom of expression, sections of the Canada Elections Act that prohibited political advertising during an election campaign by 'third parties' (individuals or groups other than nominated candidates, registered political parties, and agents thereof).[19] The sections were struck down by an Alberta court.[20] Consequently, in the 1988 federal election the sections were not enforced.[21] The central issue in that election was the Canada–United States Free Trade Agreement, and, because of the *NCC* decision, third-party groups were able to spend tens of millions of dollars in favour of the deal, which was supported by only one of the three major parties.[22] The Canadian Alliance for Trade and Job Opportunities spent $2.5 million to promote free trade prior to the election campaign and another $2 million during the campaign, and it also supported other free-trade advocacy groups such as the Artists and Writers for Free Trade (Gray 1989, 17; Whitaker 1989, 11). The NCC itself spent $842,000 to promote free trade and portray the NDP as 'very, very scary.' According to Michael Adams, president of Environics (a polling firm), such advertising 'played a significant role' in voting patterns and explains the 'remarkable' recovery of the Conservatives after the leadership debates (*Globe and Mail* 1990). It is possible that, had the third-party restrictions been in place, the Conservatives would not have been returned to power in 1988, and the free-trade deal would not now exist – a possibility that makes the judgment in *NCC* (1984) potentially one of the most important in Canadian history.

In the wake of the 1988 election, a royal commission looked into reforming electoral laws. A bill[23] was introduced in Parliament which followed many of the royal commission's recommendations, including new restrictions on third-party electoral spending. The report's reasons for including these restrictions are instructive: 'Restrictions on the election expenditures of individuals or groups other than candidates or parties were central to the attempt to ensure that the financial capacities of some did not unduly distort the election process by unfairly disadvantaging others ... [The *NCC* decision and its implementation by Elections Canada] destroyed the overall effectiveness of the legislative framework for promoting fairness in the exercise of freedom of expression and of democratic rights during Canadian elections. The experience of the 1988 election demonstrates this. The gaping hole in our existing framework in relation to independent expenditures is patently unfair ... Without fairness we may continue to have a "free" society, but we would certainly diminish the "democratic" character of our society' (Royal Commission 1991, as cited in Mandel 1994, 291). In April 1993, approximately one month before the bill was assented to, David Somerville, president of the NCC, launched a Charter challenge against the bill in an Alberta court. Once again, the restrictions on third-party contributions were struck down (*Somerville* 1993; 1996; Jenson 1994).[24] The NCC is now supporting a court challenge to BC legislation that restricts third-party election spending (Pemberton 1995).[25]

Lavigne (1991) is another case involving the NCC. While Mr Lavigne, a college instructor, did not officially represent the NCC, it supported his long and expensive litigation under the Charter. Lavigne was part of a staff unit at his college for which the Ontario Public Sector Employees Union was collective bargaining agent. He was not a union member. Under the collective agreement, however, an amount equivalent to the monthly union membership fee was automatically deducted from his pay cheque. Lavigne challenged this arrangement,[26] arguing that it violated his freedom of association because it compelled him to associate with the organizations and causes supported by the union. The Court rejected his claim. A majority of judges (four of seven) held, however, that freedom of association could be violated by legislation that compels people to associate: three judges held on this basis that the compelled payment of dues breached Lavigne's freedom of association but should be upheld under section 1;[27] a fourth found no limitation on Lavigne's freedom of association, since he was not forced to associate with the union or its causes but only to give it money.[28] The NCC's pro-business agenda was not directly advanced by the outcome because the agency-shop arrangement was upheld. *Lavigne* (1991) can, however, be used on behalf of business interests to attack other kinds of union security arrangements, such as the union shop (which requires newly hired employees to become members of the certified union for that shop, rather than just paying dues to it) and the closed shop (which requires a person to join the certified union before being employed). These can be distinguished from the agency-shop arrangement upheld in *Lavigne* (1991), on the ground that they more severely constrain individuals' freedom not to associate, and future courts may therefore refuse to uphold them under section 1.[29] (The European Court of Human Rights has held, for example, that closed-shop provisions violate freedom of association: *Sigurjonsson* 1993.[30]) The Court's creation in *Lavigne* (1991) of a right not to associate thus provides business interests, and groups such as the NCC, with another weapon in their anti-union arsenals.

II

Individuals accused of sexual assault and hate crimes can take advantage of the deregulatory form of Charter rights to challenge legislation constraining their activities, again demonstrating the Charter's regressive potential. These individuals may not be powerful actors themselves, in the way that large business corporations are, but their uses of the Charter similarly illustrate its potential to undermine legislative attempts to promote social equality and other public interests. With respect to hate crimes, the Court has held that anti-semitic hate speech is prima facie protected by the right to freedom of expression (*Keegstra* 1990). Keegstra, a school teacher in Alberta, was exercising his freedom of expression, according to the Court, when he taught students that Jewish people are evil, sadistic, money-loving child killers who have caused the world's ills, sought to destroy Christianity, and fabricated the Holocaust. The 'invidious and obnoxious' (730) character of Keegstra's speech, and the fact that it was 'virulently unsupportive of freedom of expression values' (765–6), were not reasons, in the Court's view, for denying it protection under section 2(b); content neutrality had to be maintained to guard against 'a slippery slope on which encroachments on expression central to section 2(b) values are permitted' (765–6; see also above, chapter 4). The Court thus found that the Criminal Code's restrictions on hate speech, under which Keegstra had been charged, limited his freedom of expression. It upheld the restrictions under section 1, however, on the grounds that they are necessary to protect minority groups from harm and that they advance constitutional values such as equality and multiculturalism (see *Ross* 1996 for a similar result).

In the subsequent case of *Zundel* (1992), the Court was more sympathetic to the hatemonger's claim. Ernst Zundel is one of the leading producers of Holocaust-denial literature in Canada, and indeed the world (Lipstadt 1993). He was charged under section 181 of the Criminal Code for publishing a 32-page booklet entitled 'Did Six Million Really Die?,' the central theses of which are that the Nazis did not kill six million Jewish people and that dissemination of the 'fact' that they did is part of a worldwide Jewish conspiracy. Section 181 created an indictable offence punishable by a maximum prison term of two years for a person 'wilfully publish[ing] a statement, tale or news that he knows is false and that causes or is likely to cause injury or mischief to a public interest.'[31] Consistent with *Keegstra* (1990), the Court found that the section limited freedom of expression. False news, such as hate literature, might be undesirable or even harmful in some cases, according to the majority judgment of Justice McLachlin, but that is not sufficient reason to deny it prima facie protection as a form of expression (*Zundel* 1992, 759). The majority refused, however, to uphold the restriction under section 1.

According to Justice McLachlin's majority opinion, this case, unlike *Keegstra*, was 'not about the dissemination of hate' (743), but about 'false news.' In her view, permitting the state to restrict speech – even that involving denial of the Holocaust – on the basis that it is false would risk suppression of the truth: 'The question of falsity of a statement is often a matter of debate, particularly where historical facts are at issue. Historians have written extensively on the difficulty of ascertaining what actually occurred in the past, given the difficulty of verification and the selective and sometimes revisionist versions different witnesses and historians may attribute to the same events' (747–8); 'where complex social and historical facts are involved, [determining truth and falsity] may prove exceedingly difficult' (756). In the context of this case, these statements imply that Zundel's views on the Holocaust might be valid. Moreover, according to Justice McLachlin, even if his views are false they still have some value. Holocaust denial conveys the message, for example, that 'the public should not be quick to adopt "accepted" versions of history, truth, etc., or that one should rigorously analyze common characterizations of past events' (757, see also 754–5). In other words, the viciously anti-semitic practice of denying the Holocaust performs a public service by keeping us on our toes. This idea is, in my view, disgusting, as is the implication that denial of the Holocaust might be valid. More to the point of this chapter, however, *Zundel* (1992) vividly illustrates how the Charter can serve to protect a professional racist such as Zundel.

Racists are not the only people who find refuge in the Charter; those accused of sexual assault have found a place there too. Two years after the Charter's equality rights had come into operation, Fudge (1987) noted what she considered the 'ultimate paradox of the Charter' – while feminists were developing theories of equality aimed at addressing women's social and historical subordination, 'innumerable other litigants, including defendants charged with sexual assault offences ... [were] simultaneously invoking the Charter to claim a formal equality which may well erode victories which feminists believed they had already won' (529; see also Petter 1989).[32]

The 'victories' to which Fudge is referring were legislative changes to the rules governing sexual assault to bring them more in line with the interests and concerns of victims (who are overwhelmingly women).[33] Throughout the 1970s and early 1980s, feminist organizations had lobbied for such changes, and by 1983 their efforts had had an impact. Amendments to federal legislation lightened evidentiary burdens for sexual assault convictions, restricted admission of evidence about previous sexual conduct, and prohibited publication of victims' names in the press. These changes provided valuable safeguards for women against sexual bias in the justice system, removed disincentives to their coming forward with complaints, and increased conviction rates for sexual offenders (Fudge 1989; Michael Smith 1993). They demonstrated the effectiveness of feminist lobbying in persuading Parliament to consider some of the realities of the justice system's response to sexual assault when balancing the rights of victim and accused.

Under the Charter, the Court has shifted that legislative balance towards greater protection of defendants and, correspondingly, less for victims. Taken together, its decisions under the Charter represent a substantial setback for women's equality in the context of sexual assault. In *Hess* (1990) the accused had been charged under section 146(1) of the Criminal Code, which made it an indictable offence (with liability for life imprisonment), for a male to have sexual intercourse with a female under the age of fourteen years 'whether or not he believes the female is fourteen years of age or more.'[34] The latter phrase created absolute liability for the offence, meaning that the provision constituted a *prima facie* breach of section 7 of the Charter. A majority, led by Justice Wilson, held that the provision could not be justified under section 1 and declared that it must operate with the usual presumption in criminal law of full *mens rea*. Justice McLachlin disagreed. Absolute liability was necessary, according to her, to prevent defendants from escaping conviction by claiming that they honestly believed a girl to be fourteen or older. A *mens rea* requirement, or even a lower standard of strict liability, would facilitate such a defence, in her view, and thus undermine legislative protection of children from sexual abuse and assault. Justice Wilson's majority ruling, however, confirmed that Parliament's earlier replacement of absolute liability with strict liability (in response to the lower court decision in this case) was required by the Charter.[35] The introduction of strict liability to the offence makes it more difficult for prosecutors to secure convictions when a victim might reasonably be thought to be fourteen or older. In such cases, which are not infrequent, the defence can easily persuade a jury that the accused was honestly mistaken about the victim's age, which establishes innocence under the strict liability standard.

Seaboyer (1991) is another case, like *Hess* (1990), where the Court holds against a legislative provision designed to protect victims of sexual assault. The provision prohibited introduction of evidence in a sexual assault trial that 'concern[ed] the sexual activity of the complainant with any person other than the accused.'[36] It had been enacted in response to strong lobbying by women's organizations, which criticized common law rules permitting evidence of past sexual history on the grounds that such evidence has little probative value, leads to biased and stereotypical inferences about 'unchaste' women (for example, that they are more likely to consent to sexual activity and to lie), and discourages women from reporting sexual assault because of the ordeal of being cross-examined on their past sexual histories. None the less the Court (with Justice McLachlin now writing for the majority) struck down section 276(1) on the ground that it violated the accused's right, protected by section 7, to present a full answer and defence to a charge. There are situations, according to Justice McLachlin, when the accused must call evidence of past sexual conduct to establish his innocence, and operation of section 276(1) could therefore lead to conviction of the innocent (613–17). Justice L'Heureux-Dubé refuted Justice McLachlin's arguments in a strong dissent, but to no avail. The end result of *Seaboyer* (1991), like that of *Hess* (1990), is a diluted[37] version of provisions originally designed to protect victims of sexual assault.[38]

Finally, in *Daviault* (1994) the complainant was a sixty-five-year-old woman, partially paralysed and confined to a wheelchair. The accused sexually assaulted her. He claimed, however, that he was so intoxicated that he was not aware of his actions and had no memory of them. The applicable common law rule states that drunkenness never negates *mens rea* in sexual assault and therefore is not a defence. The accused successfully challenged this rule before the Supreme Court of Canada as violating sections 7 and 11(d) of the Charter. A majority of the

Court (including its two female members) held that in very rare cases, such as this one, an individual could be so drunk as to make it impossible to say that he intentionally or recklessly commited sexual assault. Because the common law rule allowing conviction of such an individual would contravene the Charter, according to the Court, it had to be modified. The new rule would be this: if an accused can establish on balance of probabilities that he suffered extreme intoxication at the time of the offence, akin to automatism or insanity, then he will be acquitted. The fact that he voluntarily chose to get so drunk is not enough, in the Court's view, to hold him liable for the consequences of his actions while drunk. Despite the Court's speculation that the extreme-drunkenness defence would only rarely succeed, its new rule has been frequently used by lower courts to acquit or order new trials for men accused of assault, sexual assault, and other crimes (see, for example, *Blair* 1994; *H.S.* 1995; *Misquadis* 1995; *O'Flaherty* 1995; *Johnston* 1995; *Levy* 1996; *McShane* 1996).

III

The analysis to this point indicates that, because of its deregulatory form, Charter litigation is a powerful tool for attacking legislation designed to ameliorate various forms of social injustice. Concern about the Charter's politically regressive potential is not the domain only of advocates of social justice. Members of the Court themselves seem anxious about their power under the Charter to advance a regressive program. They regularly warn themselves against using the Charter in this way, and the Court has held in numerous cases that legislation protecting 'vulnerable groups,' if found to limit a Charter right, should be deferred to by judges under section 1 (see, for example, *Edwards Books* 1986; *Irwin Toy* 1989; *Slaight Communications* 1989; *Ross* 1996).

Such ideas are at odds with the classical liberal tone of so much of the Court's work, though consistent with ideological themes in Canadian political culture more generally (Macklem 1988; Bakan et al. 1995). This oft-cited passage from *McKinney* (1990, per Justice Wilson) articulates a social-democratic theme that can be found throughout the Court's jurisprudence on section 1: 'Canadians recognize that government has traditionally had and continues to have an important role to play in the creation and preservation of a just Canadian society ... It is ... untenable to suggest that freedom is co-extensive with the absence of government. Experience shows the contrary, that freedom has often required the intervention and protection of government against private action' (356). In this spirit, the Court has upheld restrictions of hate speech (*Keegstra* 1990; *Ross* 1996), obscenity (*Butler* 1992), advertising aimed at children (*Irwin Toy* 1989), and potentially oppressive employment practices (*Edwards Books* 1986; *Slaight Communications* 1989; *Potash*

1994) on the ground that they are necessary to promote social justice and protect 'vulnerable groups.' Should these decisions assuage fears about the Charter's potential to facilitate regressive deregulation? Certainly not.

I am sceptical about the Court's 'vulnerable groups' approach for several reasons. First, it has not stopped the Court from striking down legislation at the behest of corporations and individuals accused of sexual assault and hate crimes, as illustrated by the cases analysed above. Second, the concept of 'vulnerable group' is too ambiguous to serve as a sufficient hedge against regressive results. One can usually argue reasonably that legislation designed to protect a vulnerable group does not in fact do so. Justice McLachlin argued in *Rocket* (1990), for example, that restrictions on advertising by dentists, designed to protect consumers of dental services, a vulnerable group in her view, actually served to undermine that group's interests; in *Keegstra* (1990), in dissent, she argued that criminal prohibitions of hate literature did not stop racism and therefore could not be justified as necessary to protect vulnerable groups.[39] Ambiguity also surrounds the issue of who is a vulnerable group, and judges are likely to make this determination from their own, generally conservative perspective (see, for further discussion, Bakan et al. 1995, 110–19).[40]

Third, even taking the Court's concerns at face value and assuming that it is genuinely committed today to the social-democratic principles that it espouses under section 1, what about the future? The words of section 1 invite judges to define 'free and democratic society' and use that as a standard for judging whether to uphold or strike down legislation. The tendency of judges to embrace social-democratic values over the last decade and a half is probably a reflection of the dominance of those values in Canada's post–Second World War political culture. Social-democratic values, however, have recently come under serious attack, and the vision underlying the Court's doctrine of vulnerable groups is out of step with ascending ideals of economic neo-liberalism and social neo-conservatism. Given judges' propensity to stay within the boundaries of dominant ideological thought (a point explored more fully in the next chapter), the doctrine is itself vulnerable. As I, with several others, recently stated: 'If the last few years have seen dominant views shifting toward the right of the political spectrum in Canada and elsewhere – as the state gives in more and more to the ideological pressures of capitalism and individualism, and as the legitimacy of the welfare state diminishes – one might expect that future decisions of the Court will reflect that trend' (Bakan et al. 1995, 126).[41]

My prediction – and I hope I am wrong – is that the broad and liberal approach to Charter rights that extends prima facie rights protection to corporations and others who might harm 'vulnerable groups' will increasingly result in regressive judicial deregulation as, in response to the rise of neo-liberal and neo-conservative ideology, section 1 hurdles are set higher and higher for governments trying to defend progressive regulation.[42]

Finally, the Charter will serve as a substantial brake on activist progressive governments of the future, even if the Court maintains its current levels of deference to legislation designed to protect vulnerable groups. The broad and liberal approach to Charter rights means that survival of many areas of regulation depends on judicial views of whether they are 'reasonable' (as is apparent from the above analyses). Many of the interventionist programs of a decidedly leftist government would probably fall outside judicially established boundaries of current (let alone future) doctrine under section 1. The difficulties posed by the Charter for mainstream governments, as illustrated in the examples discussed above, are even greater for governments wanting to take more substantial and pro-active measures against social inequality. Even the NDP government in British Columbia, hardly a radically leftist one, has been dogged with the threat and reality of Charter litigation in its attempts to crack down on hate speech, create buffer zones around abortion clinics, promote accuracy in reports of political polling, and limit third-party spending in electoral campaigns. In short, transferring authority over many areas of social policy to the judiciary inevitably constrains governmental activity, including that aimed at promoting social justice and equality in society.

PART III

7

Judges and Dominant Ideology

The best solution [to interpretive questions under the Charter] lies in seeking the dominant views being expressed in society at large on the question in issue.
Justice McLachlin (1991)

The education, socialization, and selection of judges ensure that they are likely to value and support existing social arrangements and to stay within the bounds of society's 'dominant views' when deciding cases. This does not mean that judges are 'biased' – only that they, in contrast to the advocates who make progessive Charter arguments before them, are unlikely to think social change necessary or desirable. Judicial conservatism, in addition to the liberal form of rights, helps define the Charter's relationship to social justice and equality. This is illustrated by the Supreme Court of Canada's Charter cases on labour picketing and strikes, corporate advertising, and spousal benefits for lesbians and gays, in which the majority judges rely on anti-union, pro-business, and morally conservative presumptions in coming to their decisions. In contrast, the minority judges in these cases occasionally draw on more progressive elements of society's dominant views, demonstrating that neither judges, nor society's dominant views, are necessarily homogeneous. In section I of this chapter I discuss judges' tendency to embrace dominant ideological discourses (and usually more conservative ones). Sections II and III analyse the above-noted cases to demonstrate the influence of such discourses on Charter law.

I

Judicial bias is generally thought of as exceptional. Though few dispute that judges, being human, are not perfect, and that on occasion they may 'favour one side unfairly' (*Metropolitan Properties* 1968, 309–10), as a general rule judges are presumed to be free of 'personal interest in biased interpretation one way or the other'

(Lederman 1976, 11). Contemporary debates about judging do sometimes challenge this presumption, raising questions about how judges might view whole groups, such as women or people of colour, in stereotypical and derogatory terms.[1] Even group-oriented conceptions of bias, however, tend to imply that discriminatory attitudes on the part of judges are exceptional and that bias involves judges in consciously favouring one side of a dispute or deliberately trying to advance their own views. This view is both too hard on the majority of judges and too easy on judicial decision making as a whole. Assuming (correctly, I think) that most judges sincerely try to apply laws fairly, and do not intend to favour one person, group, or view over another, their unconscious premises and beliefs about what is right, just, normal, and natural still influence their decisions. Judicial decision making is, for this reason, best understood as an ideological process, one shaped by, as Kline (1994) states, 'the power and pervasiveness of ... dominant ideology in the wider society [rather] than individual ... prejudice on the part of judges' (452–4).

Because of their social backgrounds and professional training, most judges are unlikely to question prevailing social arrangements and the dominant ideological discourses that legitimate them (Griffiths 1981; Petter 1986; 1987).[2] To begin with, most judges are white, male, and relatively wealthy, and they are always lawyers. The judiciary is not representative of the Canadian population in terms of class, race, ethnicity, gender, culture, or education. Most appointments to the bench are from elite strata of private practice, where women, members of visible minorities, and lawyers who practise poverty law, union-side labour law, and other forms of progressive or activist law are under-represented. As a result, women constitute a small percentage of federally appointed judges in all jurisdictions,[3] and members of racial minorities an even smaller percentage.[4] In addition to these social and demographic influences, political patronage continues to be a factor in many judicial appointments.[5]

Professional training also plays a filtering role in determining who becomes a judge and how judges view the world. To be a judge, one must be a lawyer, and to be a lawyer one must go to law school. Most law students are white and from middle-class or wealthy backgrounds,[6] and until quite recently men substantially outnumbered women.[7] Certain structural features of legal education create barriers for students from working-class and poor families. Such students are unlikely to have had the same pre-law educational opportunities and financial support as their wealthier counterparts, and they therefore suffer a relative disadvantage in the intense competition for admission to law school.[8] Moreover, because of heavy workloads and full-time attendance requirements,[9] it is difficult, if not impossible, for students to attend law school if they cannot afford to be unemployed for three years, or if they have substantial family or community commitments.

The content of legal education also helps shape the viewpoints of those who eventually become judges. All judges, and the lawyers who appear before them, have received roughly similar legal educations, and, despite the efforts of many law professors, law schools remain conservative institutions. Research and curricula are geared primarily to the needs and perspectives of elite law firms. The knowledge and skills necessary for alternative practice, government work, and even non-elite general practice are at best sporadically presented. Critical approaches to law, or those connecting law to wider social processes, are often altogether absent (Arthurs 1983; Glasbeek and Hasson 1987).[10] None of this denies the development in North American law faculties, especially over the last two decades, of courses and research that focus on legal services for oppressed and exploited groups and that are critical, theoretical, and interdisciplinary. However, a look at what is predominantly taught and researched in Canadian law schools quickly reveals continued domination of conservative values, traditional legal methods, and elite lawyers' perspectives.[11]

Given the nature of judicial appointments, the legal profession, and legal education, it is not surprising that judges tend to rely on and reproduce dominant ideological discourses in their opinions. It does not follow, however, that all judges always view things the same way. Dominant ideological discourses are not uniform on all issues – they may even contradict one another and compete for dominant status.[12] Both conservative ('family values') and liberal (freedom of choice) notions of sexuality, for example, can be found among dominant discourses (Cooper and Herman 1991), and, as we see below in the discussion of *Egan* (1995), members of the Court disagree along this ideological divide. In other areas, dominant views may be more homogeneous, though some variation will usually exist. Trade unions, for example, are most often portrayed negatively in dominant discourses, though occasionally they will be deemed tolerable or necessary; business (as a whole) is generally represented in uncritical terms, though rogue corporations are sporadically identified. Thus judges need not be radicals to disagree among themselves on these and other issues: there is a range of acceptable opinion on which they can draw. Personal differences among judges, of background and experience, are probably responsible for the particular positions they take within that range. At a minimum, patronage seems to be divided among Liberals and Conservatives,[13] women are increasingly being appointed to the bench, and occasionally judges with progressive views, such as Bertha Wilson and Claire L'Heureux-Dubé, are appointed despite the filters discussed above. The ideological divisions that exist among current Supreme Court judges on some issues are thus attributable to variation among judges, as well as that within dominant ideological discourses. None the less judges' perspectives still tend to lean towards the more conservative side of the dominant ideological spectrum.[14]

The Court's Charter decisions on trade unions, business corporations, and gays and lesbians illustrate this ideological 'tilt' (Holt 1984b). In these cases, judges rely on, reproduce, and reinforce dominant ideological representations to justify denying constitutional protection to unions, while providing it to corporations and rejecting the claim to equality rights of lesbians and gays. In section II below, I examine a series of decisions in which the Court depicts labour picketing and strikes as coercive, irrational, violent, and harmful to the public interest, while celebrating corporate advertising as facilitating rational and free choice and serving the public interest. The next section analyses the Court's decision in *Egan* (1995). I demonstrate how judges draw on 'family values' rhetoric to justify refusing to extend spousal benefits to lesbian and gay partners and also how they invoke dominant ideological ideas about lesbian and gay identity to explain why sexual orientation should be included as a ground of discrimination in section 15. Taken together, these cases provide some illustrations of how judges rely on and reproduce elements of dominant ideological discourses – and usually those at the conservative end of the dominant ideological spectrum – in the cases they decide.

II

Working-class political action is, and has always been, represented in dominant discourses as violent, irrational, and harmful to the 'public interest' (Parenti 1986; Puette 1992; Silva 1995; Salutin 1996). Such negative imagery is often invoked by employers and state agencies to legitimate initiatives against workers' collective actions, and it is pervasive in media and popular culture. Media accounts of labour strife tend to be one-sided. They often present union intransigence as the sole cause of conflict; ignore workers' concerns (making union positions seem irrational, stubborn, and greedy), while frequently discussing company offers (making companies look reasonable and conciliatory); and emphasize public inconvenience and economic damage allegedly caused by strikes. The negative consequences to workers of not going on strike, or of giving in to company demands, receive little, if any, attention, and coverage of picket lines focuses on incidents of violence and confrontation, implying that these are the norm.[15] The general impression created by media, and other dominant accounts, is that unions are coercive, destructive, selfish, and greedy – 'adept at advancing their own interests at the public's expense' (Freedman and Medoff 1984, 4).[16]

Dominant accounts of business corporations are the exact opposite. They present the interests of business as symbiotic with those of the public. They either glorify consumerism or take it for granted; they evaluate economic performance from the perspective of business (obsession with deficit reduction is one example; another is the presumption that economic performance is an entirely separate issue from that of social welfare – and that the latter must be sacrificed to the former).

The media report stock market activities as frequently as the weather and devote entire sections and programs to business issues, profiles, and analyses.[17] In contrast, the power of business to coerce and exploit employees, manipulate consumers, destroy communities by relocating, and ruin the environment, is seldom, and certainly not systematically, an issue. Nor are the media likely to emphasize (except perhaps in the business press) that business's primary concern is to make profit. Instead, the general message is that business exists to serve the public good by creating jobs, supporting community and cultural activities, and providing people with an array of goods and services.

These dominant ideological discourses of labour and business emerged in a series of Charter cases where restrictions on unions (picketing and strikes) and business (advertising) were challenged as violations of freedom of expression and association.[18] Two dichotomies – coercion versus freedom and self-interest versus public interest – structure the Court's reasons in these cases in ways that reproduce some of the discursive elements discussed above. The first dichotomy can be illustrated by comparing the Court's decisions on picketing with those on advertising.[19] 'A picket line,' according to a majority of the Court, 'has great power of influence as a form of coercion'; '[a] picket line both in intention and effect, is a barrier'; it 'set[s] up a barricade' (*BCGEU* 1988, 231–2) and is designed to cause injury and induce unlawful behaviour (breaches of contract) (*Dolphin Delivery* 1986, 587–8).[20] The person who refuses to cross a picket line is automatonic, unthinking, and irrational: 'picketing sends a strong and automatic signal,' generating, at least for union workers, an 'automatic, almost Pavlovian' response (*BCGEU* 1988, 231–2, quoting Paul Weiler). The decision not to cross a picket line is motivated not by rational choice but by a kind of religious zeal: it is a matter of 'faith and morals,' a 'commandment ... obeyed ... by all true believers' (231, quoting *Heather Hill*).[21]

Advertising, according to the Court, in marked contrast to picketing, plays a significant role in enabling individuals to make 'informed economic choices' and is 'an important aspect of individual fulfilment and personal autonomy' for the consumer (*Ford* 1988, 767; *Rocket* 1990; *RJR-MacDonald* 1995). Though there are exceptions to advertising's positive qualities – such as misleading and fraudulent advertising and advertising aimed at children (*Irwin Toy* 1989) – these only prove the rule that it generally facilitates informed choice and promotes autonomy. Even some cigarette advertising has this effect, according to the Court, in enabling consumers to choose between more and less healthy brands (*RJR-MacDonald* 1995, 95).

A second dichotomy, self-interest versus public interest, is also apparent in the cases on unions and advertising. Unions are depicted by the Court as 'overwhelmingly, though not exclusively, concerned with the economic interests of their members' (*Dolphin Delivery* 1986) rather than the public interest; and, related to this, the rights they seek are matters of economic policy (*Alberta Reference*, per Justice McIntyre), rather than 'fundamental' rights (*Alberta Reference* 1987, 413–14, per Justice McIntyre, 391, per Justice LeDain). Moreover, the judges persistently suggest, with no supporting evidence (and sometimes in the face of contradictory evidence: *BCGEU* 1988), that strikes and picketing are harmful to the public interest and 'the social cost [of these activities] ... great' (*Dolphin Delivery* 1986, 591).[22]

Again, the contrast with judicial representations of advertising could not be sharper. Advertising, according to the Court, 'involves more than economics' and serves 'an important public interest by enhancing the ability of [consumers] to make informed choices' (*Rocket* 1990, 241, 247; see also *RJR-MacDonald* 1995), thus promoting the values of self-fulfilment and discovery of truth underlying freedom of expression.[23] Furthermore, in contrast to the Court's presumption that picketing and strikes are inherently harmful, in the case of advertising a substantial burden of proof must be met by those alleging that particular kinds of advertising cause harm.[24]

Though the Court's representations of picketing, unions, and advertising may contain, as ideological discourses often do, a 'grain of truth' that makes them believable, they also distort their subject matters through exaggerations, partial truths, and outright falsehoods (Eagleton 1991, 19). Contrary to the Court's implications about unions and their activities, for example, violence on picket lines is rare and is in most cases a response to provocation and attempts by management, often with police assistance, to bring in replacement workers (Geary 1985, 91, 114–16, 142–7; Forbath 1989).[25] Moreover, in contrast to the Court's characterizations, picketing provides consumers with important information, enabling them to make informed moral and political decisions, about whether or not to support a strike, and therefore serves an essential aspect of freedom of expression – promoting political speech and debate (Glasbeek 1990a). Related to this, workers who respect picket lines are not irrational or blinded by class loyalty, as the Court would have it, but acting on previously held beliefs and commitments, in much the same way people do when joining political parties or voting in elections (Getman 1984).[26] Finally, the Court's depiction of unions as self-interested, and as acting against the public interest, implies that organizations and actions designed to give workers some control over the conditions in which they work do not benefit, and in fact harm, the public. This presumes that members of the public have interests only as consumers who are denied goods and services during a strike, not as workers who stand to gain directly or indirectly through labour solidarity and power.[27]

The realities of advertising are also distorted by the Court's characterization of it as generally facilitating informed and rational choice. While some advertisements may include useful information about products, most eschew such mundanities and instead create fanciful images and irrational associations.[28] According to one industry executive, 'advertising is the art of arresting the human intelligence just long enough to get money from it' (cited in Bagdikian 1987); according to another, it is designed to imbue products that have little use value with 'pre-logical' and 'non-rational psychological overtones.'[29] Far from promoting informed decision making, most advertising is, by both design and effect, anti-rational.[30] It aims to imbue commodities with magical powers and to create an 'enchanted kingdom of magic and fetishism where goods are autonomous, where they enter into relations with each other and where they appear in "fantastic forms" in their relations with humans' (Jhally 1989, 224). It often presents products as having powers to transform people's lives, satisfy their needs and wants, make them happy and popular, give them a community and social relationships, and even harness for them the forces of nature.[31] You will have friends if you drive a Honda; get promoted in your job if you Ban under-arm odour; have more sex if you drink beer; and be clean – really clean – if you use this or that soap. To suggest that any of this is rational or informative is strained, to say the least.

III

Dominant ideologies of family and sexuality play an important role in many areas of adjudication, as has been revealed within the feminist and lesbian and gay legal studies literatures (Boyd 1991; 1993; Cooper and Herman 1991; Gavigan 1993; Kline 1993; Herman and Stychin 1995). Here I want to look at the effects of such ideologies in *Egan and Nesbit v. Canada* (1995), currently the leading case on discrimination against lesbians and gays.[32] In that case, the Court rejected (in a 5–4 decision, with strong dissenting judgments) Egan and Nesbit's claim that section 15 requires spousal benefits be available to same-sex partners. At the same time, all members of the Court agreed that sexual orientation is a ground of discrimination under section 15, despite its not being stated in the text. I want to analyse this latter aspect of the case first.

The nine members of the Court differed among themselves on the reasons why lesbians and gays should be protected by section 15. We can identify two competing ideological discourses about sexual identity in their decisions. The first constructs sexual orientation as an immutable characteristic, such as race and disability, rather than something that is chosen by an individual. Therefore, the argument goes, discrimination against lesbians and gays is wrong: people should not be blamed for what they cannot help. Justice LaForest (with whom Chief Justice Lamer and Justices Gonthier and Major concurred) articulates this view in his decision: 'Whether or not sexual orientation is based on biological or physiological factors, which may be a matter of some controversy, it is a deeply personal characteristic that is either unchangeable or changeable only at unacceptable personal costs ... [It is] an innate and unchangeable characteristic' (528). Justice L'Heureux-Dubé, in separate reasons, partly agrees with Justice LaForest, noting that sexual orientation is 'quite possibly biologically based,' but she also suggests that it is 'at the very least a fundamental *choice*' (567; emphasis added). The latter idea – that sexual orientation is chosen by individuals – lies at the heart of Justices Cory and Iacobucci's judgment (with which Justice McLachlin concurred). For these judges, it is because sexual orientation is a matter of choice – 'choice of a life partner' (601) – that it must be protected: people's 'tastes [on everything from prosaic to fundamental matters] will vary infinitely' because of the 'uniqueness of individuals,' and though the majority of people in society will find characteristics of some groups 'extremely peculiar and vastly perplexing,' those groups must be 'tolerated' and protected by the Charter (595). Thus, 'so long as [sexual preferences] do not infringe on any laws, they should be tolerated' (595).[33]

Though both approaches to sexual orientation draw on liberal concerns that minority groups such as lesbians and gays should be protected from imposition of majority preferences, their explanations of lesbian and gay identities are contradictory: one is based on immutability, the other on choice. Neither approach, however, strays beyond the boundaries of dominant ideological discourses. Gays and lesbians either choose to reject the norm of heterosexuality or they have no choice but to do so; the norm of heterosexuality itself, however, is not questioned. Consequently, both approaches may 'restrict rather than broaden social understandings of sexuality' (Herman 1994, 44) in at least two ways.[34] First, 'lesbians and gay men are granted legitimacy, not on the basis that there might be something problematic with gender roles and sexual hierarchies, but on the basis that they constitute a fixed group of "others" who need and deserve protection' (Herman 1994, 44). This may serve to reinforce the dominance of heterosexuality by depicting it as 'natural' and to 'contain [the] challenge to dominant social relations' represented by lesbians and gays (44; see also Ryder 1991, 295). Second, both the immutability and choice constructs elide important differences between lesbians and gays and among members of each group (Herman 1994). The obvious gender differences between the two groups, and differences of race, class, and politics within them, are effectively overridden by the unified construction of 'homosexuality' in both the choice and the immutability approaches. Because of these kinds of effects, Herman

(1994) argues that articulating lesbian and gay political claims in liberal rights discourse may serve to narrow and distort such claims (see also Herman and Stychin
1995).

I now want to develop a second ideological analysis of *Egan* (1995). Having
established that lesbians and gays fall within section 15's scope, the Court then had
to determine whether denial of spousal benefits to same-sex partners constituted
discrimination. Dominant familial ideology played an important role in Justice
LaForest's decision that it did not. 'Family values' has, over the last decade or so,
become the code-word on the right for a constellation of morally conservative ideas
about gender relations, work, sex, and sexuality. It lies at the more conservative end
of the dominant ideological spectrum, representing 'family' as exclusively and nat-
urally a heterosexual married couple raising children with a male wage earner and a
stay-at-home mother, thus pathologizing (always implicitly and sometimes explicitly) gay and lesbian partnerships.

Yet 'family values' rhetoric is central to Justice LaForest's reasons. Marriage,
according to him, is 'the fundamental social unit' (539) and 'is by nature heterosexual' because of the 'biological and social realities' (536) that only 'heterosexual couples have the unique ability to procreate' and to raise children; it is fundamental to
the 'stability and well-being of the family' and 'fundamentally anchors other social
relationships and other aspects of society' (536). This is demonstrated, according
to Justice LaForest, by the fact that 'children brought up by single parents more
often end up in poverty and perhaps impose greater burdens on society' (537). His
expression of 'family values' rhetoric, though drawing upon a 'grain of truth'
(Gavigan 1993), distorts reality in what it emphasizes and omits. Its idealization of
'the family' masks both gendered relations of power and dependence that characterize familial relations and the violence and abuse against women and children
these often cause. Moreover, it articulates a privatized vision of social reproduction
that has served historically to reinforce women's financial dependence on men and
politically to limit the role of governments in funding child care and other social
services.

A kind of blame-the-victim thinking follows from its logic, as is evident in
Justice LaForest's linking of child poverty to single parenthood: children would not
be poor, he implies, if mothers married and stayed married.[35] This obscures the
political-economic causes of child poverty and the lack of an alternative to single
motherhood for many women forced to leave relationships with men because of
violence and abuse against them and their children. Finally, the 'family values' rhetoric is blatantly homophobic. Ryder (1991) has observed that 'the most common
argument used to rationalize the oppression of lesbians and gays is the fact that
their sexuality is not procreative' (294), and that is exactly the argument deployed

here. Related to this, the justice's statement that child rearing among lesbians and gays is 'exceptional and in no way affects the general picture' (538) conveniently ignores the fact that its infrequency may be a result of homophobic laws, practices, and social pressures relating to adoption, custody, and reproductive technologies, that make it difficult, and often impossible, for lesbian and gay couples to be in a position to raise children.

The minority judges disagree with Justice LaForest's characterization of spousal benefits and 'family values,' again illustrating variation among both dominant ideological discourses and judicial viewpoints. For these judges, spousal pension benefits have as their purpose 'the alleviation of poverty among cohabiting elderly "spouses"' (*Egan* 1995, 608, per Justice Iacobucci), and should not be interpreted to exclude lesbian or gay couples who, but for their sexuality, are like spouses and require similar protection from poverty (608, also 598–604, per Justice Cory, 567, per Justice L'Heureux-Dubé). The minority judges also challenge the elements of Justice LaForest's 'family values' rhetoric. Justice Iacobucci, for example, notes (adopting a passage from Justice L'Heureux-Dubé's decision in *Mossop* 1993): 'It is possible to be pro-family without rejecting less traditional family forms. It is not anti-family to support protection for non-traditional families. The traditional family is not the only family form, and non-traditional family forms may equally advance true family values' (616).

At the same time, however, the minority judges seem anxious not to be misunderstood as going too far in challenging traditional conceptions of the family. Justice Cory reassures us, for example, that Egan and Nesbit's claim does not 'challenge ... either the traditional common law or statutory concepts of marriage' (583), and, in a similar vein, Justice Iacobucci notes that the case does not require exploration of 'whether same-sex couples ought to be constitutionally entitled to adopt children or get married' (617). In other words, the elements of dominant familial ideology need not be seriously disturbed by extensions of spousal pension benefits to lesbian and gay couples: heterosexual privilege would still rule in the legal definitions of who can get married and have and raise children.

IV

I have argued that the process through which judges give meaning to the Charter's ambiguous concepts is an ideological one. Because of who they are, where they come from, and how they are socialized and trained, judges are likely to draw, uncritically and unquestioningly, on dominant ideological discourses when interpreting and applying the Charter. The actual operation of this process, however, is complicated. Despite a generally homogeneous judiciary, differences exist among judges, in terms, for example, of social backgrounds, gender, and previous political affiliations, and these factors may affect their view of the issues that come before them. Moreover, dominant ideological discourses themselves are not uniform but may articulate competing, even contradictory, positions. Such variation, among both judges and the discourses they draw on, helps explain ideological divisions among members of the Court and, in particular, the occasional progressive decision. At the same time, however, the majority of judges are conservative individuals, socially and professionally members of the elite, involved in a fundamentally conservative enterprise. They, and the legal profession in general, are about the last group we should expect to act as agents of progressive social change.

PART IV

8

Rights as Political Discourse: The Charter Meets the Charlottetown Accord

The question of the liberatory or egalitarian force of rights is always historically and cultur-
ally circumscribed.
Wendy Brown (1995, 97)

This chapter examines the politics of rights outside the immediate context of Charter litigation. More specifically, it looks at how the media represented arguments
about rights made by two organizations, the Native Women's Association of Canada
(NWAC) and the National Action Committee on the Status of Women (NAC), in
the period leading up to the national referendum on the Charlottetown Accord.[1]
Both NWAC and NAC made issues concerning rights major parts of their strategies
to defeat the accord. They argued that the document, if entrenched in the constitution, would override the Charter's equality rights, and they succeeded (at least
outside Quebec) in generating opposition to the accord on this basis.

In their support of Charter rights, neither NWAC nor NAC adopted the classical liberal discourses of dominant rights ideology (as described above, in chapter
3). Each organization's claims of rights contained elements that differed from, and
often opposed, those of classical liberalism. Yet those claims were almost invariably
represented by the media as supporting a 'consensus' against the accord based on
elements of classical liberalism: individualism, suspicion of governmental and collective power, and formal equality. I describe this process in section II (after a general discussion of the 'rights debate' in section I) in an effort to illustrate how
progressive claims to rights can be transformed into dominant ideological terms,
even when made outside the confines of courts and litigation. In section III I discuss potential implications of this process for the internal politics of social movements; section IV analyses some of the ideological processes that sustain the
dominance of liberal rights discourse and thus contain the effectiveness of progressive rights strategies.

I

Many contemporary analysts of rights are concerned less with the capacity of litigation to advance specific political goals than with the influence of rights discourse on the terrain, tactics, and balance of forces in the political field itself.[2] In short, the equation of rights strategies with litigation tactics has given way to a more complex understanding: rights are not just inert tools that can be used by social movements to advance their causes through litigation; rather, they actively structure the very nature of political struggle (E.M. Schneider 1986; J. Williams 1987). Moreover, rights discourse is an important and unique political language because of its universal form and presumptive validity in liberal-democratic societies. It is 'hegemonic' in two senses: first, it elevates particular claims to the 'plane of the universal' (Laclau and Mouffe 1985; Hunt 1990, 320), and, second, it is a dominant form, perhaps *the* dominant form, of political discourse in Western capitalist states such as Canada (see Nedelsky and Scott 1992). Rights discourse is also 'indeterminate'; its elements are unstable and thus open to reinterpretation. The combination of hegemony and indeterminacy, rights advocates claim, gives rights discourse a unique capacity to mobilize social movements, affirm marginalized identities, and attract support for progressive goals in the wider community.

I agree that expressing a social movement's positions in rights language may have these kinds of effects. However, I think it is important to question the nature of these processes. What is actually symbolized, mobilized, or affirmed when movements employ rights strategies in specific contexts? This is the general question that I address in my analysis of the politics surrounding the Charlottetown Accord. In any time and place, ideological processes lend credence to certain conceptions of the concept of a right, thus creating a 'common sense' in society about what rights are – a dominant ideology of rights.[3] Central to such ideology in Canada today (and other Western capitalist societies), as we saw in chapters 3–6, are the liberal discourses of anti-collectivism (or anti-statism), formal equality, and atomism. The concept of a right surely can be interpreted to reject these elements of dominant rights ideology, a point that lies at the heart of proposals for use of rights strategies by progressive social movements; it can indeed accommodate collective rights (E.M. Schneider 1986), communal rights (Lynd 1984), rights as sites of dialogue (Nedelsky and Scott 1992), and social rights (Brodsky 1992a), as well as rights claims relevant to historically subordinated identities and groups (P. Williams 1991). Such claims to rights, however, despite their conceptual feasibility, may be absorbed into and limited by dominant rights ideology in wider public debates.

This last point is illustrated by Herman's (1994) analysis of the public debate in Ontario around Bill 7, an amendment to human rights legislation concerning sexual orientation. Herman shows how the articulation of gay and lesbian identities in the form of rights discourse during this debate yielded constructions of sexual identity that served to reinforce a view of lesbians and gays as abnormal members of an immutable sexual minority. In similar terms, Crenshaw (1988) has shown how use of rights strategies by African Americans, while working to their benefit in attacking formal inequality, has also served to 'absorb, redefine and limit [their] language of protest' (1370). More particularly, it has helped legitimate material subordination of African Americans by creating 'an ideological framework that makes the present conditions facing underclass blacks appear fair and reasonable' (1382–3).

Both Herman and Crenshaw concur with those who suggest that rights strategies mobilize social actors and affirm marginalized identities. Yet they remain ambivalent about rights, largely because their work also reveals how the effects of these processes – what is actually mobilized and affirmed – can sometimes be politically regressive. In their analyses the reinterpretation process appears as a two-way street. Alongside the potential gains to social movements of progressive rights strategies exist the channelling effects of ideological processes which may engender regressive and narrow interpretations of social movements' politics and positions. Herman and Crenshaw's work shows us that the effects of rights always depend on the social and political conditions shaping their use; 'rights have no inherent political semiotic, no innate capacity either to advance or impede radical ideals' (Brown 1995, 97). The fate of rights claims made by NWAC and NAC during the period leading up to the referendum on the Charlottetown Accord illustrates this point.

II

The reasons for the defeat of the accord in a national referendum on 26 October 1992 are complex. That event was, however, hailed in the dominant media as a watershed for Canadian democracy – a historical moment in which the vast majority of 'ordinary Canadians' abandoned their habitual political quiescence to deliver a resounding 'No' to Canada's 'elites,' despite the apocalyptic forecasts of the consequences of rejecting the accord. The people had prevailed over their governments, and a new era of politics had begun. Politicians now had to earn, rather than take for granted, the trust of the electorate. A central part of this story involves provisions in the accord relevant to the Charter's application to Quebec and First Nations governments. Throughout the campaign leading up to the referendum, one of the most frequent arguments made by those on the 'No' side was that the accord threatened to undermine Charter rights and freedoms. This concern came to shape the very terms of debate about the accord, and the accord's final defeat was hailed in popular forums as a victory for people's rights.

I postulate that discourses about rights had profound effects on political struggles over the accord. I would make two points, however, before making this argument. First, rights discourse, though the focus of this study, was not the exclusive dynamic in the politics of the accord. Wider issues of race, gender, culture, language, class, and so on were central, as were more traditional debates about the relative merits of centralized or decentralized federalism. A further factor was the federal government's profound unpopularity at the time. The following analyses of rights discourse thus explain only one aspect – albeit an important one – of the political anatomy of the Charlottetown Accord.[4] Second, throughout the following discussion I rely on an account of 'common sense' ideas about certain features of the accord. I base that account on my experience of events as they unfolded, as well as on subsequent analysis of the print media. Any attempt to identify a coherent 'common sense' involves selection and interpretation and hence is bound to eliminate some of the complexity of multifaceted political phenomena. Nevertheless, I believe that I have captured a sense of how the public debate about the accord was shaped by elements of rights ideology.

The Charlottetown Accord was designed in part to address some of the contradictions of Canadian nationhood. The idea of a Canadian nation, founded as it is on histories of conquest and colonialism, has long been vulnerable to competing claims of nationhood from First Nations and Quebec. Historically, Quebec nationalism was minimally accommodated through creation in 1867 of a federal system that provided Quebec, along with the other provinces, some measure of political autonomy; First Nations nationalism, in contrast, was constitutionally denied and brutally repressed. Today, Quebec nationalism and First Nations nationalism are substantial factors in Canadian politics. The Charlottetown Accord attempted to accommodate them in the constitution by modifying Canada's federal political system, which currently recognizes two basic socio-political units: federal and provincial.[5] The accord would have gone some way towards adding a third unit, First Nations, and it thus would have used the federal structure to constitutionalize First Nations self-government. It might also have affected the current distribution of political authority among existing units by recognizing Quebec as a 'distinct society,' and thus breaching the constitution's underlying principle of formal equality among the provinces. Overall the accord would have required Canadian federalism to recognize, albeit in limited terms, First Nations and Quebec as collective entities, defined in terms of their respective histories, languages, and cultures.

An analysis of the Charter of Rights and Freedoms, particularly in relation to its imposition of obligations on all legislatures and governments (including the national assembly and government of Quebec) to respect individual rights and freedoms, is important for explaining the defeat of the Charlottetown Accord. Quebec opposed the Charter from the start as a general limitation on the collective power of the Quebec 'nation,' and more specifically as an attempt by the federal government to deepen protection of anglophone language rights in Quebec (sections 16–23). The sovereigntist government of Quebec refused to assent to the Charter's entrenchment in the Canadian constitution.[6] The Liberal federal government of Pierre Trudeau overrode Quebec's objections and proceeded with entrenchment – a source of continuing resentment among Quebec nationalists.

The difficulties raised by the Charter for Quebec nationalists apply with equal, if not greater, force in relation to First Nations. Both Quebec nationalists and First Nations nationalists resent the Charter's imposition of Canadian national standards that potentially constrain the political autonomy of their respective 'nations.' For First Nations this problem is exacerbated by the cultural specificity of the Charter's liberal concepts, ones firmly rooted in European political traditions often incompatible with those of First Nations (Turpel 1991). Many people within the movement for First Nations self-government argue on these bases that the Charter should not apply to First Nations' governments.

The Charlottetown Accord responded to Quebec's and First Nations' concerns about the Charter by proposing provisions that would have exempted Quebec's or First Nations' governments from Charter scrutiny in relation to policies designed to preserve and promote languages, cultures, and traditions.

During the referendum campaign, the perceived clash between the Charter's individual rights and the (arguably quite minimal) collective powers gained by Quebec and First Nations in the accord became a central point of contention. Most interesting for our purposes is the way in which the concerns of the 'No' side were regularly expressed through the discursive elements of dominant rights ideology, which soon became firmly entrenched in popular discourse. They served not only to foreclose alternative accounts of rights within the debate but also to articulate the claims and identities of various oppositional movements in liberal terms. Most notable was the way the relationship among individual rights (women's equality rights being the most-discussed example), nationalism (that of First Nations and that of Quebec), and state power was constructed within the traditional liberal frameworks of dominant rights ideology – atomism, anti-statism, formal equality – in 'common sense' accounts of the accord. The dominant message conveyed by the media (and I focus on the print media) was simple and unequivocal – namely, there is a fundamental contradiction between collective power (especially when harnessed to nationalist politics) and women's equality, and the only way to ensure the latter, in light of the threat posed to it by the former, is through the Charter.

The media and pundits were persistent, and largely unquestioning, in reporting the 'fact' that the accord threatened individual rights and formal equality by granting collective powers to Quebec and First Nations. 'When collective rights take precedence over individual liberties,' noted Pierre Trudeau in a strategically timed and reverentially reported intervention, 'We see what can happen to people who pretend to live freely in these societies. When the citizen is not equal to all other citizens in the state, we're in the presence of a dictatorship which sets the citizens in a hierarchy based on their beliefs.' Trudeau continued by arguing that the accord would create 'an unacceptable hierarchy of classes of citizens ... threatening the survival of official language minorities and depriving women and racial, ethnic and religious minorities of true equality before the law' (Van de Wille 1992). The point was picked up by other liberals, such as Sharon Carstairs (formerly leader of Manitoba's Liberal party), who decried the 'group-based shopping list we find in the new Canada Clause [which] risks turning the Charter into a hierarchy of claims for rival interests' (Carstairs 1992); and William Johnston, columnist for the *Montreal Gazette*, who was concerned that the accord 'create[d] a hierarchy of rights as a basis of discrimination' (Johnston 1992).

Such statements usefully illustrate how the various elements of dominant rights ideology were effective in criticizing the accord. Taken on their own, these comments are of little interest – they are predictable, given the well-known liberal proclivities of their authors. Their positions, however, largely reflected a developing 'common sense' about the accord, at least outside Quebec and First Nations. Media accounts in particular tended to emphasize classical liberal themes when describing and analysing the positions of various groups on the accord. Reports of right-wing attacks on the accord focused on how the self-government proposals and the distinct society clause would undermine individual rights and the threat posed to formal equality by the so-called special status granted to First Nations and Quebec in the accord.[7] Not dissimilarly, feminist concerns about the effect of 'government rights' (of First Nations and other governments) on the individual equality rights of women, especially First Nations women, were a primary focus of media attention. To this extent, groups with fundamentally contradictory political positions were forged – at least within media constructions – into a de facto coalition (the 'NO side') that opposed the accord because (among other reasons) its conferral of collective powers, whether on First Nations or Quebec, threatened the Charter's rights and freedoms. This construction served to override concerns about the historically unequal power relations among First Nations, Quebec, and the rest of Canada, rooted in histories of conquest and colonization. It also created a substantial obstacle to promotion of constitutional recognition of collective powers as a way to redress social injustice.

NWAC and NAC's arguments about rights and the Charter tended to be swept into and (re)presented as part of this liberal 'common sense,' despite its contradictions with NWAC and NAC's actual positions.

Among media and academic pundits, and in political and legal circles more generally, the issue of equality rights for First Nations women quickly became a focal point for opposition to the accord. The accord extended already-existing limits on the Charter's application (section 25) to include protection of First Nations' language, cultures, and traditions from the Charter. It also granted First Nations' governments the power that provincial legislatures and the federal Parliament already have to enact laws 'notwithstanding' certain provisions of the Charter (section 33). NWAC had taken a position against these proposals on the ground that they subordinated the Charter's equality rights to the collectively defined powers of First Nations. It received strong support (and assistance) from non–First Nations pundits, media, and lawyers for doing so.

Conspicuously absent from statements of this support, however, was any discussion of one of NWAC's basic presumptions – that the causes of sexual inequality in First Nations lie in the colonial policies of the Canadian state. The need for Charter protection of First Nations women originated, according to NWAC, in the fact that 'the *Indian Act* ... imposed upon [First Nations] a patriarchal system and patriarchal laws which favour men' (NWAC 1992, 4): 'By 1971, this patriarchal system was so ingrained without [sic] our communities, that "patriarchy" was seen as a "traditional trait." In other words, even the memory of our matriarchal forms of government, and our matrilineal forms of descent were forgotten or unacknowledged' (5). From this perspective, First Nations communities are inherently non-patriarchal but have been restructured in patriarchal terms through a history of colonialism; because of that history, First Nations' women now require the protection of the Charter's rights to equality. Consistent with this analysis, NWAC supported constitutional recognition of an inherent right to self-government, so long as the Charter applied to First Nations' governments (7–8).

Mainstream media tended to reduce NWAC's position, with its understanding of patriarchy as a product of colonialism and its support of First Nations self-government, to the much simpler elements of classical liberal ideology – a clash between the collective powers of First Nations polities, construed as intrinsically patriarchal, and the individual's right to gender equality – with the only tenable solution lying in application of the Charter to limit the scope of First Nations self-government. Within this framework, the accord's limitations on the Charter's application to First Nations' governments appeared as dangerous steps towards authoritarianism. Their effect, according to columnist Michele Landsberg (1992), was to '[cast] native women out into the cold,' and the accord was consequently the 'greatest crisis in civil liberties in Canada since the internment of the Japanese' (Landsberg 1992, quoting Weinrib et al. 1992). In similar spirit, Johnston (1992) noted that, should the accord pass, 'the aboriginal citizens [among them women] will be left relatively powerless before the swollen power of the aboriginal state, sanctioned by the Constitution of Canada.' Such comments indicate profound distrust of First Nations' governments – a sense that, free of Charter constraints, they would wield their collective power against women with impunity. NWAC's actual position on the accord undoubtedly included elements of such distrust. However, the mainstream media's obsession with the issue, along with its failure to discuss NWAC's analysis of patriarchy and its support of self-government, indicated what Greschner (1992) has referred to as 'the bias of aboriginal patriarchy': a '[false, per-nicious, and racist, but none the less pervasive] belief in an inherent or irremedia-ble chauvinism of aboriginal men worse than the chauvinism of non-aboriginal men' (339).

Equally disturbing is the related implication, found throughout media portray-als of NWAC's challenge, that gender equality and self-government are irreconcil-able without the protection of liberal rights. A group of Canadian law professors, in a widely circulated and reported memorandum, expressed the concern that, in the absence of the Charter, clashes between First Nations traditions and women's equality would necessarily be resolved in favour of the former (Weinrib et al. 1992). The implication is that the two are inherently contradictory, a notion belied by NWAC's recognition that the tension between them is a symptom of colon-ialism, not of something inherent in First Nations culture (NWAC 1992). The representation of women's equality and First Nations traditions as inherently con-tradictory, along with the 'bias of aboriginal patriarchy,' not only distorts history but also draws on and reinforces racist stereotypes of First Nations as lacking a req-uisite degree of 'civilization' to restore and develop their own conceptions and practices of sexual equality.

Compounding these tendencies was the view expressed by some that rejection of rights and the Charter by First Nations organizations was itself a sign of backward-ness. Again, according to Weinrib et al. (1992): 'The Charter reflects ideas of indi-vidual dignity now accepted by a large variety of countries, many of which are neither western or white.' The implication that First Nations are outside the steady march of progress in the international community is unfortunate, but not surpris-ing. Rights, and liberal notions of law more generally, have often been construed by Western observers as indicators of civilization, with their absence in a society confirming its status as uncivilized 'other' (Fitzpatrick 1992; Kline 1993).

Behind such criticisms of the accord's limitations on the Charter's application to First Nations' governments was the further, questionable presumption that Charter equality rights are necessary, and even sufficient, for protecting and advancing women's equality. The media presented limitations on the Charter's application as restrictions on women's equality itself, implying that the Charter unproblemati-cally translates into actual equality for women. As one columnist noted in discuss-ing NWAC's position: 'Canadians' equality is protected by the Charter. Anyone who believes they are being discriminated against can go to court, claiming a violation of their Charter rights' (Graham 1992). This statement, however naïve and unquestioning of liberal ideology, succinctly expresses the common assumption in the media that the Charter's application to First Nations' governments would have ensured gender equality for First Nations women (and this despite the absence of such equality where the Charter does apply). The causes and effects of inequality are largely beyond the Charter's judicially determined reach, a point developed above (chapter 3). There is some irony, indeed hypocrisy, in a patriarchal society such as Canada's imposing its values (the Charter) on other societies in the name of sexual equality – especially when its colonial policies are implicated in creating and perpetuating the inequalities that exist in those societies (NWAC 1992, 4; Musqueam Indian Band 1992).

Moving from First Nations to other issues concerning Charter equality rights, we find further examples of the media's emphasizing traditional liberal themes. The National Action Committee on the Status of Women (NAC) condemned the accord's 'Canada Clause' – an interpretive provision that stated 'fundamental characteristics' of Canada and was designed to guide application of the accord, of the Charter, and of other parts of the constitution. Included as 'fundamental characteristics' in the Canada Clause were First Nations self-government, Quebec's distinctiveness as a society, democratic government, official-language minorities, equality (for provinces, men and women, and racial and ethnic groups), and respect for individual and collective rights. NAC argued forcefully that the clause would unduly circumscribe judicial interpretations of Charter rights and thus undermine its guarantees of equality. Day (1992), vice-president of NAC, stated that it would '[claw] back rights that were won in 1982,' ones that were still 'new and fragile' (22). The clause articulated mainly 'government rights' (those relating to First Nations' and Quebec's governments and the parliamentary system), according to NAC, and failed to affirm as fundamental the individual and group equality rights of the Charter. Moreover, its statements of gender and racial equality were weaker than those in the Charter and excluded altogether grounds of discrimination such as religion, age, disability, sexual orientation, and poverty. The clause therefore created, according to NAC, a 'hierarchy of rights,' placing 'government rights' at the top and individual and group rights at the bottom: it wrongly conferred rights on governments and obligations on individuals, when the real need was endorsement of 'the commitment of governments to the rights and freedoms in the Charter and to a high standard of protection and promotion of rights' (21).

NAC's position appears consistent with the liberal suspicion of governmental power found in dominant rights ideology, and this is exactly how it most often appeared in the media. NAC, however, is not an adherent of classical liberal ideology. To the contrary, it supports an activist state and the collective empowerment of Quebec and First Nations. Consistent with this, NAC's support of the Charter is based on a distinctively non-classical liberal conception of constitutional rights, in which equality rights require governments to take positive action against poverty and other social disparities (Day 1992; Brodsky 1992a). Viewed in this light, NAC's concern about the Canada Clause overriding Charter rights, far from expressing liberal anxiety about the overbearing state, was clearly motivated by fear that the Clause would in fact reduce governmental obligations to support social equality.

Not surprisingly, most media accounts ignored these subtleties in NAC's understanding of equality rights. They construed NAC's position in terms indistinguishable from, and supportive of, the developing liberal 'consensus' that the accord unduly bolstered the power of government to trample individual rights. Simpson (1992), for example, an influential columnist with the *Globe and Mail*, suggested that Day's position on the Canada Clause was the same as Pierre Trudeau's, thus placing her among 'les enfants de Trudeau.' More generally, media reports tended to treat NAC's concerns about women's equality as wrapped up primarily in Charter issues, separate from its wider concerns about social equality and programs (Canadian Press 1992).

NAC is, however, partly responsible for how its positions were portrayed in the media. Its strategists must have known that NAC, by condemning expansion of collective powers as an illegitimate conferral of 'government rights' and using the phrase 'hierarchy of rights,' risked being misunderstood as advocating traditional liberal positions. NAC, however, may have considered that risk worth taking, given the power of anti-government themes to attract publicity and media attention.

III

The analysis above of NWAC and NAC's rights strategies vis-à-vis the accord illustrates how progressive political positions of social movements may be absorbed into dominant discourses of rights and reframed in liberal terms inconsistent with the movement's wider political aspirations and positions. Recognition that rights strategies can give a social movement's 'public face' a liberal complexion raises questions about the effect that such strategies might have on ongoing political struggles within the movement – particularly those between liberals, whose positions will be consistent with and affirmed by the discourses of dominant rights ideology, and those, such as socialists and nationalists, for whom collectivist values are central.[8]

Miliband (1991) usefully notes that most social movements are internally divided among liberals, radicals, and socialists. Liberals seek reform in particular areas but eschew analyses and strategies that locate the roots of oppression in the nature of the social order itself; radicals 'are moved by a search for entirely new ways of life' and include nationalist movements; socialists believe that oppression is rooted in class relations (Miliband 1991). I agree with Miliband, and others who have made this point, that these (and other) different and conflicting positions can be found within most contemporary social movements – the women's movement (Weir 1993), lesbians and gay men (Duggan 1992; Herman 1992), environmental and peace movements (Miliband 1991), and anti-racism (Tushnet 1987). Their presence militates against any easy inference that social movements are politically homogeneous or that, as 'new social movement' theorists (Laclau and Mouffe 1985; McClure 1992) would have it, they represent a decisive break with older political identities and cleavages.

The political diversity of social movements is a matter that must be considered in analysing rights strategies. If a group within a social movement has a political orientation consistent with the tenets of dominant rights ideology (a liberal one), then rights strategies may serve to advance the political goals of that group at the expense of groups representing conflicting positions within the movement, such as socialists and nationalists. Herman (1992) argues that this kind of dynamic was one of the 'unintended implications, and under-considered effects' of the use of rights strategies by the Coalition for Gay Rights in Ontario (CGRO) when lobbying the Ontario government for reforms of human rights law in the early 1990s: 'CGRO's choice to be a voice of lesbian and gay liberalism, implicitly meant that the organisation was not speaking for feminists, socialist and other progressive lesbians and gay men. Thus, whilst some apolitical people may have been gathered into the process, others, such as myself at the time, became increasingly marginalised from the "public face" of the lesbian and gay movement' (120–1).

The history and politics of other social movements reveal similar dynamics. Liberal rights strategies of the U.S. National Association for the Advancement of Colored People (NAACP), for example, which came to represent the public face of African Americans' struggle for equality, did not speak for socialists (such as William DuBois and his followers) or nationalists (such as Malcolm X and his followers) within that movement (Tushnet 1987). Once it is acknowledged that social movements are internally divided among political tendencies, it becomes difficult to speak, in the abstract, of rights strategies being appropriate or useful for a social movement.

The public debate about the Charlottetown Accord once again illustrates the point. During that debate, opposition to women's oppression came to be synonymous, at least within the media, with support of the Charter (which itself was reduced to support of liberal ideology, as noted above). This construction was built on the pro-Charter positions of NWAC and NAC. It implied that women who did not support the Charter, and rights more generally, were not part of the struggle to end women's oppression. The effect of this implication was to simplify the issue of women's oppression and to discredit and exclude from the 'women's movement' those whose struggle against unequal gender relations involved politics and strategies that did not conform with the liberal contours of the debate. In this section I examine this dynamic in relation to nationalist women and socialist feminists in First Nations and Quebec.

Many First Nations women in the self-government movement, including those in NWAC, consider colonialism to be at the root of gender inequality in First Nations communities. According to them, equality for First Nations women requires a break with colonialism, and the First Nations 'women's movement' is therefore inseparable from the struggle for self-government. It follows for some – and this is where women in the Assembly of First Nations (AFN) disagreed fundamentally with NWAC's position on the accord – that the Charter, as an instrument of the colonial (Canadian) state, is part of the gender-inequality problem for First Nations, not its solution. Moreover, the Charter's Eurocentric homage to individual rights and freedoms is viewed as alien, and potentially harmful, to First Nations cultures and traditions. 'Divisions between First Nations people based upon the non-native fascination with extreme individualism,' according to a statement by the Musqueam Indian Band in British Columbia, 'simply support the assimilation of our people into non-native culture' (Musqueam Indian Band 1992). The AFN's opposition to the Charter was part of its wider project of breaking with colonialist power and ideology; because it considered colonialism a root cause of patriarchy in First Nations communities, it viewed such opposition as necessary for achieving sexual equality. On this basis many women within the self-government movement supported the accord's limitations on application of the Charter.

The idea that opposition to the Charter might be part of a strategy to promote women's equality, at least for First Nations women, was too easily dismissed – when considered at all – in debates concerning the accord. Not surprisingly, it made little sense in a dominant framework that equated women's equality issues with liberal rights and the Charter. Weinrib et al. (1992), for example, condemned the accord's limitations on the Charter's application to First Nations on the basis that the concept of rights is universally valid. They agreed with the Federal Court of Appeal that 'the norms of *Canadian society* dictate that the Charter should apply to aboriginal governments' (emphasis added), thus demonstrating startling disregard for the fact that an important aim of First Nations self-government is precisely to avoid imposition of Canadian norms and institutions. Moreover, as already noted, Weinrib et al. (1992) argued that Charter ideals reflect ideas that are 'now accepted by a large variety of countries, many of which are neither western nor white,' thus ignoring the fact that liberal rights regimes were often forcibly imposed on these countries and were central components of colonial strategy in

Canada and elsewhere. This denial of history is disingenuous: it perpetuates the notion that rights are one of the 'gifts *we* gave *them*' (Fitzpatrick 1987, 130) and implies a dangerous colonialist ambition (Parekh 1993, 167–8). More to the point, however, liberal rights are neither the only, nor the best, mode of governance and political action. To argue that they are is Eurocentric and analytically suspect and ignores the intimate connection between (neo)liberal doctrine and *current*, as well as past, modalities of Western imperialism (Lazarus 1990, 157). The position of First Nations nationalist women demonstrates that the struggle against women's oppression within colonialism may involve collective resistance to rights rather than embrace of them.

This kind of connection between gender and nationalism in the First Nations context has a parallel in the other major nationalist struggle in Canada, that of Quebec. For many of Quebec's feminists, issues of gender equality are indissolubly bound up with Quebec's pursuit of greater political autonomy (either within Canadian federalism or as a sovereign state) – a sentiment captured by the slogan 'no women's liberation without Quebec liberation; no Quebec liberation without women's liberation' (Vickers 1993, 267). Because it is a pan-Canadian document, many Québécois see the Charter as an unwarranted extension of Canadian federal power over the Quebec 'nation' – a point underlined by Quebec's refusal to assent to the Charter in the first place. Moreover, some Quebec feminists question the necessity of the Charter on the grounds that, first, there is already a Quebec Charter of Rights, and, second, women's equality receives greater protection under Quebec's social and human rights policies than it does in other provinces or at the federal level. Like First Nations women in the self-government movement, nationalist feminists in Quebec do not necessarily accept the 'Charter must be paramount' view so strong elsewhere in Canada (Hiebert 1993).[9]

Quebec nationalism has posed some difficulties for NAC, a national organization that is insistently pan-Canadian, supports the Charter, and advocates a strong federal presence in social programs (Hiebert 1993; Vickers 1993). In the debates surrounding the Meech Lake accord (a predecessor of the Charlottetown accord defeated in June 1990), for example, NAC was critical of the 'distinct society' clause, fearing that it could be used to undermine the Charter equality rights of women in Quebec. Nationalist feminists in Quebec, in contrast, saw in the distinct society clause minimal, though welcome, recognition of Quebec's unique status in Canadian federalism (Duclos 1990). Tension developed between NAC (and other women's groups) and nationalist feminists in Quebec, which was exacerbated by the media's portrayal of NAC as anti-Quebec.

In the Charlottetown debate, NAC endorsed the distinct society clause and, perhaps more important, the central argument of nationalist feminists in Quebec.

According to Judy Rebick, 'We understand in the women's movement ... that equality doesn't mean treating everyone the same way. Equality often means special measures – that terrible word – to correct historical inequalities ... We also need special powers ... for Quebec ... to recognize the fact that they have a disadvantage in being the only French-speaking nation or province in the whole of North America. They need those powers and they want those powers to protect their language, their culture and their institutions' (as cited in Hiebert 1993, 127).

Presumably it was on the basis of similar reasoning that NAC supported the idea of First Nations self-government. Given this parallel, it is curious that NAC refused to accept any restrictions on the Charter in the First Nations context while endorsing the distinct society clause for Quebec. The message of Quebec's nationalist feminists appears to have had more of an impact on NAC in this regard than that of women in the AFN.

Quebec and First Nations nationalist women are not the only groups opposing women's oppression whose politics were effectively overridden by the liberal 'public face' given to women's struggles during the Charlottetown accord debates. Vickers (1993) has noted that women's movements throughout Canada have tended to be sceptical of equality rights strategies because they risk abstracting issues out of their socio-political and economic context. This is especially true of socialist feminism, where women's equality is considered politically and analytically inseparable from class structure. Socialist feminists have argued that the anti-statist form of dominant rights ideology, and the Charter more specifically, obscure the structural gender/class inequalities of 'private' social relations, such as those of work and family, and restrict the state from playing a positive role in transforming the loci of women's subordination (see Fudge 1987; Currie and Kline 1991). This does not deny recognition among socialist feminists that in some contexts rights strategies can have tactical utility (Herman 1992). However, socialist feminism, like nationalist feminism, relies on analyses and strategies that emphasize the need for collective mobilization to change social structures. Its central tenets are often contradicted by the classical liberal elements of dominant rights ideology. Thus the classical liberal spin put on feminist politics during debate on the Charlottetown Accord did not represent the views of socialist groups within the women's movement.

IV

Perhaps the analysis so far demonstrates only that oppositional rights strategies share with all other political strategies the risk of cooptation. The fact that NWAC and NAC's rights strategies were (re)presented as part of the liberal hegemony around the accord may illustrate only that these organizations used the wrong kinds or amounts of reinterpretive work in their particular strategies (Hunt 1990; Hunt and Bartholemew 1990) or that they made strategic choices to risk such (re)presentation so as to secure the accord's defeat. The analysis would not then contradict the central claim of advocates of rights strategies that progressive and counterhegemonic reinterpretation of rights discourse can be an effective tactic for advancing social movements' claims (Laclau and Mouffe 1985; Hunt 1990; Nedelsky 1993). The latter argument, however, often plays down the fact that rights discourse is produced within material and ideological constraints that, at least in Western capitalist states, tend to favour traditional liberal articulations over radical ones (see above, chapter 3).

The playing down of such constraints is apparent throughout the rights advocacy literature but is most pronounced in the work of 'left pluralists' Laclau and Mouffe (1985) (McClure 1992). For them, politics is primarily a struggle over symbols – language, discourse, and other modes of cultural representation – and less (if at all) over other dimensions of existing social and political institutions and economic relations: 'discursive practice ... does not have a plane of constitution prior to, or outside, the dispersion of the articulated elements' (109). Cooper's (1993) observations about Mouffe's discussion of discourses of citizenship are equally applicable to Laclau and Mouffe's (1985) account of discourses of rights: 'Mouffe's focus is on the process of rearticulation ... But where and how do we rearticulate? What kinds of struggles are appropriate for what kinds of terrains? How do we deal with discursive and material limitations and constraints? And how do we decide which articulations are the right ones? Mouffe's work is perhaps not intended to deal with such "practical" considerations. However, if radical democracy is to be empowering beyond the level of theoretical struggle, texts with greater specificity are required' (Cooper 1993, 164).

In similar spirit, Hall (1986) has said of left-pluralist work that it views society as a 'totally open discursive field' where 'there is no reason why anything isn't potentially articulable with anything' (56). Left-pluralists attach too little weight to the wider social context in which rights discourse is produced, a context that creates differential power relations, narrows the scope of conflict, and favours some positions over others. There is no clear sense of 'how [rights] discourses are constituted and reproduced, nor how some [rights] discourses come to be more powerful and privileged than others' (Boyd 1991, 97).

The rights positions of NWAC and NAC, despite their counter-liberal elements, were ultimately appropriated to support an undifferentiated liberal hegemony that developed around the Charlottetown Accord, largely because the deep social and historical roots of rights discourse 'served as a check on the potential "moveability"' (Bennet 1990, 263) of its liberal elements. In chapter 3 I discussed the nature of these roots in relation to Charter litigation. NWAC and NAC made their rights claims outside the immediate context of litigation, directing them at a wide public audience, where ideological processes additional to those discussed in chapter 3 (and similar to those discussed in chapter 5 as sustaining anti-debt and -deficit discourses) were probably in operation. For example, production of rights discourse for public consumption takes place largely within an ideological infrastructure – media, schools, political institutions, and so on. These institutions help construct and disseminate dominant ideological discourses, including those of rights (Kellner 1990; J.B. Thompson 1990, 136; Zhao 1993). Moreover, the way people understand and react to discourses of rights will depend, at least in part, on their life conditions (Lewis 1991). Laclau and Mouffe (1985), Hunt (1990), and other rights advocates presume that counterhegemonic discourses on rights will have certain effects, in relation to social-movement activists, potential members, and the public in general, yet they tend not to consider how the varying social conditions of people's lives might shape their responses to such discourses. To take one example, economic fear and insecurity, such as that fomented by capital's current 'restructuring,' may dampen receptivity to egalitarian ideals, as the contemporary rise of egoism and xenophobia within liberal democracies might suggest (Smarden 1992, 134).

There are thus major constraints, material and ideological, affecting the articulation process of rights discourse. At a general level, rights are more than a discursive problem. The power of dominant rights ideology and its role in absorbing and distorting the rights claims of NAC and NWAC was probably the result of a combination of the factors discussed here and in chapters 3 and 5. Knowledge about the precise dimensions of this process would require an analysis much broader and deeper than I have attempted. This does not prevent me from concluding, however, that social movements that use rights strategies risk having their positions and internal politics distorted by rights ideology – a prospect not necessarily avoided through careful construction of arguments and interpretations within rights discourse. Rights are rooted in material and ideological conditions. These conditions, in addition to interpretive questions about rights discourse, must be at the core of analyses and strategies involving rights. Failure to consider them may engender not only wasted efforts and resources but also the real possibility that rights strategies will backfire.

V

Let me now draw together the various strands of my discussion. I have argued that dominant rights ideology may construct the values and identities of social movements' actors in ways that distort their positions and implicitly delegitimate and suppress non- or anti-liberal political tendencies within a movement. Section II demonstrated how the mainstream media presented the rights-defined positions of NWAC and NAC in the Charlottetown Accord debates so as to reflect classical liberal anxiety about collective power and a corresponding celebration of individual rights, thus attributing political commitments to these organizations that contradicted their actual positions. This was the result at least in part, I claimed, of the channelling effects of dominant rights ideology. In section III I argued that the media's liberal construction of the 'women's movement' tended to marginalize, and implicitly delegitimate, the alternative view that women's struggle is inseparable from nationalist or class struggle. However, the discursive effects highlighted in sections II and III provide little more than a basis for speculation regarding the impact of dominant rights ideology on the post-Charlottetown Accord political dynamics of women's movements in First Nations, Quebec, and the rest of Canada. Finally, in section IV, I argued that the potentially distorting and narrowing effects of dominant ideological discourse on rights cannot be avoided by reinterpretation alone, because the elements of such discourse are anchored in wider material and ideological structures.

My central point throughout this chapter has been that strategies involving rights discourse are necessarily shaped by dominant rights ideology. The effect of this is not only to limit the utility of such strategies in advancing progressive goals but also to create the risk of negative political consequences. I do not want to suggest that rights strategies are unique in being problematic: any political strategy may fail or backfire. It is not possible to say in the abstract that rights strategies are necessarily worse than other strategies. I do believe, however, that it is possible to identify some of the particular difficulties raised by use of rights strategies, and that is what I have tried to do. Such analysis does not lead to the conclusion that rights strategies should be abandoned. It only underlines the point that they, like all other political strategies, have a constitutive effect on the politics of social movements that is not always positive. This is, in my view, a significant finding, not least because it tends to be discounted, even ignored, in some of the more sanguine academic writing on rights as vehicles for progressive social change. The analysis of such change must assess not only the possible advantages of rights strategies but also the full range of potential drawbacks and constraints.

9

What's Wrong with Social Rights?

The welfare capitalist society defines the citizen primarily as a client consumer ... Corporate advertising, popular culture media, and government policy collude to encourage people to think of themselves primarily as consumers ... to evaluate their government's performance according to how well it provides them with goods and services ... Such a client-consumer orientation toward citizenship privatizes the citizen.
Iris Marion Young (1990, 72–3)

Social rights have been proposed by some as a solution to the Charter's limitations. During the constitutional debates leading to drafting of the Charlottetown Accord, progressive governments and organizations advocated entrenching another charter in the constitution, which would explicitly protect social (or positive) rights and thus compensate for the courts' failure to interpret the existing Charter as including such protections.[1] I argue here that it is unlikely that a social charter would have done what those who supported the idea wanted it to do. The limitations of social rights[2] resemble those of existing Charter rights. First, because of their abstract formulation, there is no guarantee that social rights would be interpreted progressively by judges or other authoritative interpreters, and there is a risk that they would be given regressive meanings. Second, because the form of social rights is atomistic, such rights would address only discrete symptoms, not the complicated causes, of social inequality. Third, as a consequence of these features, the symbolic message of social rights implies a client-consumer model of citizenship. Section II of this chapter canvasses these arguments after section I develops a brief history of the social charter idea in Canada.

I

In the fall of 1990 the New Democratic Party (NDP) was elected in Ontario. Soon after, in the spring of 1991, the idea of entrenching a charter of social rights in the Canadian constitution was raised in the Ontario legislature, followed by release of a series of discussion papers in the fall of 1991.[3] That fall also saw electoral victories for the NDP in Saskatchewan and British Columbia, ensuring the party a powerful presence in ongoing constitutional negotiations. A 'social union' provision modelled on Ontario's original proposal, which had been largely adopted by the Beaudoin-Dobbie Report (Canada 1992c), was eventually included in the Charlottetown Accord. Advocates of a social charter shed few tears, however, when it was defeated, along with the rest of the accord, in the 1992 referendum. For them, the accord's proposals were too weak, providing insufficient protection of people living in poverty and no real safeguards against cuts to social programs. Proposals for a social charter are likely to surface again, and they are of continuing relevance in international and European politics. Many progressive people see broad rights to health, education, and social welfare as essential components of full citizenship (Turner 1986; see also Scott and Macklem 1992, 35–6; but see for a critical view Waters 1989).

Two concepts of citizenship underlie social charter advocacy in Canada: citizenship as participation and citizenship as national standards. The first presents the social charter as a means of empowering, and including as citizens, poor and disempowered people in Canada. Porter (1991), for example, argues that citizenship means 'participation of persons and groups within the economic, political and legal community' and is effectively denied for 'growing numbers of people ... in Canada by poverty, homelessness, malnutrition, sexual violence and environmental degradation' (2). Accordingly, 'citizenship must include the right to an adequate standard of living, including adequate food, clothing, housing, health care, education, social security, just and favourable conditions of work and reasonable employment opportunities' (27). The second – national standards – underlies the proposal by Ontario's NDP government for a social charter. It assumes that the social welfare state which has developed since 1945 is a central feature of Canadian citizenship and should be in the constitution: 'Over time, the idea of Canadian citizenship has evolved and broadened ... Taken together, [major social] programs represent and symbolize Canadians' sense of themselves as members of a community where solidarity and mutual responsibility are fundamental social norms' (Ontario 1991, 2). Similarly, the Beaudoin-Dobbie (1992) Report states: 'Our intention in recommending a social covenant is to reinforce the [commitments to social programs currently expressed in the constitution] and express other governmental commitments to social programs which Canadians see as part of their national identity' (87); 'many people are deeply attached ... to national standards, seeing this as an essential part of Canadian citizenship' (64).

The idea of a social charter meets some of the concerns of those who are critical of rights, especially in its articulation of rights that cohere with ideals of citizenship in the modern social welfare state. In all social charter proposals and instruments, for example, the stated rights and commitments impose positive obligations on the state, thus avoiding the libertarian form of civil and political rights (as discussed in chapter 3). A social charter would thus undoubtedly increase the resources available to defend rights and provide another arena of struggle for social change. At the same time, however, social rights share many of the limitations of more traditional equality rights, such as those of the Charter. I analyse these limitations in section II.

II

All proposals for a social charter or covenant, official or unofficial, have this in common: the rights included, whatever their content, are couched in broad and general language, providing few constraints on those responsible for their interpretation (see above, chapter 2). This means, among other things, that the progressive aspirations of supporters of a social charter may not find their way into authoritative interpretations of social rights.[4] Whether or not they do will depend on who is doing the interpreting. Concepts such as 'adequate social services and social benefits,' 'high-quality education,' 'just and favourable working conditions,' and 'the highest attainable standard of physical and mental health'[5] are broad enough to accommodate interpretations from different groups with conflicting interests that are at once contradictory and plausible. Conservative governments and business groups, for example, would probably advance narrow interpretations of social rights, which imposed limited duties on governments and private actors, and starkly oppose the broad interpretations of progressives.[6] There is no reason to believe that progressive activists would be more likely (they may actually be less so) to win these arguments about social policy under a social charter than in other political forums.

'So what?' one might respond. 'A social charter may not get everything progressives want, but surely it is better than nothing.' Maybe it is, but it may be worse than nothing. The vagueness of social rights will allow conservative groups and governments to use a social charter offensively to articulate regressive aims and policies (as already happens under the Charter: see chapter 6). For example, a government could defend ungenerous and regressive social policies by arguing that they meet social charter standards. The discourse of rights, including social rights, is well suited for such arguments because of its 'on/off' quality – either a right is breached, or it is not. Thus a government might seek to justify its decision to lower or not raise social assistance rates, or minimum wages, by claiming that the current or new rate is equal to or higher than the minimum rate required by the social charter (as determined by an enforcement agency, or the government's own legal advisers).

Ironically, a social charter might actually prompt governments to cut spending and lower regulatory standards if the minimum levels determined acceptable under a social right are lower than existing ones. A government could also use social rights against public-sector employees. It might, for example, defend back-to-work legislation for striking teachers or nurses on the ground that individuals are denied rights to education or health by strike-related school or hospital closures, or it could justify rejection of wage demands by the same groups of employees by arguing that meeting such demands would require cutting education and health services in ways that would violate social rights.[7]

Some business groups would also want to take advantage of a social charter, as they have of the Charter (see above, chapter 6). Where rights do not explicitly identify government as solely responsible for providing a service, businesses may claim that certain kinds of economic and social regulation deny that service to consumers and thus violate a social right. Landlords could argue, for example, that rent controls or standards of habitability violate the right to 'adequate housing' because they induce capital flight from the market and thereby reduce rental housing stock; or doctors and pharmaceutical firms could say that a right to the 'highest attainable standard of health' is violated by legislative restrictions on the services and goods they can provide and, possibly, in the case of doctors, by the whole structure of 'socialized medicine.' Some businesses might argue (as they have successfully in Europe and in the southern United States) that a 'right to work,' or even one to 'access to employment opportunities' (National Anti-Poverty Organization 1992), precludes union security provisions in legislation and collective agreements.

Supporters of a social charter recognize that social rights will not necessarily be interpreted progressively. That is why they are concerned about who would have authority to interpret and implement such a charter. Some argue that social rights should not be justiciable because judicial conservatism and unfamiliarity with 'positive' rights would result in narrow and possibly regressive interpretations (Ontario 1991, 16). Others predict that, if social rights are not justiciable, they will be ineffective and not taken seriously (Jackman 1992). Both positions may be partially correct, though neither deals adequately with the legitimate concerns of the other. The anti-justiciability thesis wrongly implies that difficulties raised by the vagueness of social rights are avoided by adopting non-judicial enforcement. While the judiciary may be more likely than other institutions to interpret social rights narrowly and regressively, other bodies may do the same. Whatever enforcement mechanism is chosen, narrow, even regressive interpretations of social rights will remain a possibility. Moreover, large businesses and governments will always be better equipped than social activists, in terms of access to media, lawyers, lobbyists, experts, and so on, to advance their interpretations.

Social charter activists have used two techniques to limit the risk of regressive and ungenerous interpretations. First, they have specified in draft proposals that social rights protect only 'vulnerable groups' (Nedelsky and Scott 1992), thus nominally barring powerful groups from using a social charter. But what is a 'vulnerable group'? As Brodsky (1992a) points out, this term will not necessarily keep out the wrong plaintiffs and allow in the right ones; groups with regressive ambitions will always be able to find members of 'vulnerable groups' to serve as plaintiffs, as they have under the Charter (20–2; see also chapter 6 above and Bakan et al. 1995). Furthermore, even if complainants could be restricted to these groups, powerful and conservative governments and groups will still be able to make their narrow and regressive claims about social rights as respondents before the enforcement agency and, more generally, in the media and public debate.

Second, activists may include in their draft proposals language that requires decision makers to consider the plight of poor and disadvantaged people. The Alternative Social Charter (ASC), for example, requires that policies be justified in terms of people's 'security and dignity' and stipulates that 'alleviating and eliminating social and economic disadvantage' are its main goals (Nedelsky and Scott 1992). I am sceptical about the effectiveness of this strategy in avoiding regressive uses of a social charter. The articulated aspirations of the ASC are neither denied by, nor inconsistent with, the rhetoric of the mainstream right. Indeed, security, dignity, and elimination of poverty are often presented by people on the right as the purpose behind their favourite ideas – free markets, competition, deregulation, privatization, and individual responsibility.

A further difficulty with social rights (at least those requiring government spending) is that, assuming governments do not raise taxes, revenue for implementation will come out of existing budgets.[8] By necessity, a social charter, if it is effective, will 'prioritize' some social goals over others, and its priorities, not to mention the tradeoffs they will require, may be undesirable from the perspective of many on the left and in social movements. Not all would agree, for example, that spending on health or education, each explicitly protected by a social right, is more important than that on shelters for battered women, First Nations media and advocacy groups, foreign aid, and public broadcasting, for example. While social spending always requires tradeoffs, a social charter would freeze a particular set of tradeoffs into constitutional law and placed them outside the scope of political debate and change. Though it may be appealing to place certain things beyond the contingencies of politics, whether it is progressive or not will depend on what priorities are frozen into place, and from whose perspective the question is being asked.

A solution to some of these difficulties would be for governments to raise taxes to pay for implementation of social rights, thus avoiding the need for cuts in other areas. However, it is unlikely that any agency will have power to compel a government to raise taxes in the name of social rights; it is also improbable that governments will do so on their own (especially in the current political climate). In any event, increased taxation to pay for social rights is not necessarily desirable – governments may use regressive taxes such as Canada's Goods and Services Tax and thus effectively force low-income and poor people to pay for implementation of their rights.

Perhaps most important, social rights, because of their atomistic form, will not touch the real causes of poverty and other social ills. Social rights that oblige government to provide services,[9] even if they are effective in protecting and improving those services – a big 'if' – are unlikely to affect the social and economic relations that produce the need for those services in the first place. Despite all the rhetoric about Canada being a caring and compassionate society, its social welfare system has done little to address economic maldistribution, even at the worst end of the scale. Universally provided services, such as health and education, do not redistribute income or wealth; nor does the income security system as a whole.[10] Social assistance is the only program that is genuinely progressive, but it provides little more than means for survival, allowing people to live in poverty rather than die from it. Universal access to state services may provide a 'safety net,' but it has not transformed (nor will it) socially and legally enforced structures of economic inequality and the unequal distribution of suffering and want that they engender (see chapter 3). Nor should we expect constitutionalizing of universal access to such services through a social charter or covenant to change very much.

Health care provides a good example of the problem. All the proposals for a social right to health place on the state an obligation to ensure that all Canadians have access to health care. They say nothing, however, about the social determinants of ill health, particularly the unequal social relations that have much to do with why and to whom illness happens. The emphasis is on access to treatment of illness, which implies that 'the determinants of health and illness are predominantly biological, so that patterns of morbidity and mortality have little to do with the social and economic environment in which they occur' (Doyle 1979, 12). Yet measures of morbidity and mortality consistently demonstrate that low-income earners, poor people, and those who are unemployed or threatened with unemployment are sicker, die earlier, and have higher infant mortality rates than those with higher incomes (Doyle 1979; Thursten 1988; Rachlis and Kushner 1989, 178–86; Baumeister, Kupstas, and Klindworth 1991; Delamothe 1991. See also:

Mattiasson et al. 1990; National Council of Welfare 1990, 6; Jin, Shah, and Svoboda 1995).

This conclusion is not surprising, given the obvious links between poverty/economic insecurity and inadequate nutrition and shelter, unsafe and unhealthy jobs, neighbourhoods with higher rates of violent crime, accidents, industrial pollution, and other health hazards. As one medical commentator states, 'If the health of the nation – the whole nation – is to improve then the distribution of the disposable income of its population needs to be made more equal. Establishing a classless society would not necessarily produce this outcome, although it would vastly increase the likelihood of doing so' (Delamothe 1991, 1050). Accessible and universal medical services are necessary but will never be sufficient for distributing good health equally. According to one study, 'the presence or absence of medical care accounts for only 10 per cent of the differences in mortality between different populations' (Haggerty 1985). The most that can be hoped for from a social right to health services is promotion of equal access to medical treatment, not equal access to health.

Many supporters of a social charter concede some of the points raised in this chapter. They are not sanguine about concrete effects but argue that the potential symbolic effects of a social charter make it worthwhile. For them, a social charter would be a symbol of citizenship for economically disadvantaged and disempowered people; and its absence would symbolize denial of that citizenship (Scott and Macklem 1992). In addition, they point out, the symbolism of social rights would inspire and mobilize people to demand that governments fulfil their social obligations.

I find little comfort in these arguments and am concerned that the symbolism of social rights might have the opposite effect. One of the symbolic effects of a social charter, for example, might be to obscure, and go some way towards legitimating, a reality of social wrongs. How many times does one hear that Canada is now a free and equal society because of the Charter of Rights and Freedoms, without any analysis of the actual impact of its provisions? A similar disparity is possible with social rights. The ideals they articulate may be misinterpreted as descriptions of reality, and the effect may be to create an illusion of progressive social change when nothing has actually happened. Smart has noted that 'the acquisition of rights in a given area may create the impression that a power difference has been resolved' (Smart 1989). My concern is that social rights may be understood as themselves remedies for social inequality and thus obfuscate the continuing need for social change.[11] 'Rather than providing a springboard to the future [a social charter might thus] trap the country in the past' (Myles 1992, 62).

More specifically, I am worried about what particular social rights, especially those to social services, might symbolize. I agree with supporters of a social charter that such rights symbolize something about citizenship, but what exactly is that 'something'? I am afraid that it may be a radically incomplete vision of citizenship, especially for poor and low-income people – 'You are a citizen because the state will treat your poverty with income assistance, and your illness with medical services.' Citizenship, in other words, is about the state treating suffering; the citizen is a client-consumer, seeking goods and services to deal with her afflictions (I. Young 1990, 72–3). Unnoticed within this vision of citizenship is the fact that the state supports and enforces social relations largely responsible for causing that suffering, for making people poor and making them sick. The political and economic causes of poverty and illness become invisible and irrelevant, implicitly relegated to the so-called private and depoliticized world of biology, individual choice and ability, family and the market. Many supporters of a social charter have criticized civil and political rights as symbolizing an impoverished ideal of citizenship. My point is that social rights may have the same effect. Their focus on how the state treats its subjects through particular programs and actions (albeit positive rather than negative) manifests the same atomistic form that characterizes civil and political rights and thus represents a conception of citizenship that is unrelated to, and unaffected by, the exploitation and suffering of the so-called private world of social relations.

This is not a message that progressive people should want to support. I believe social services such as universal health care and income security to be absolutely necessary in Canada today but that does not mean that rights to such services symbolize a progressive conception of citizenship. It strikes me as almost offensive to say, for example, that poor and working people are full citizens because they have access to universal, portable, and publicly administered health care, while ignoring the facts that they live and work in conditions that will make them sicker and kill them sooner than will the conditions of wealthier people.

The struggle for citizenship has to be about more than what the state should or should not do in terms of social services. It must challenge directly the exploitative relations of social life. As Thurshen (1988) has postulated in relation to health: the 'first line of defense against ill health in a capitalist society is income-producing employment in a workplace that has a strong union to protect workers' health on the job and to negotiate benefits for them and their families ... The second line of defense, when the first has failed, is a welfare state to supply life's essentials – the food, clothing, shelter and medical care that [people] no longer have the income to purchase' (212). The third, and most desperate, line of defence, in my view, is a social charter – especially one that glorifies the already 'second best' social welfare state as representing the achievement of full citizenship.

10

Conclusion

Let me begin by briefly summarizing the book's central points. First, Charter adjudication is political in the sense that it requires judges to decide, on the basis of vague and abstract legal norms, how power should be exercised. Neither the elaborate arguments of constitutional jurisprudence and theory, nor the subjective feeling of some judges and lawyers that their conclusions result from the law's indelible logic, alter this fact (chapter 2).

Second, the politics of Charter law are driven by ideological processes that narrow the range of meanings that lawyers and judges are likely to attribute to the Charter's otherwise open-ended words. Historical and social forces have engendered, and continue to sustain and anchor, the dominance of a liberal conception of rights. Within its terms, social injustice is construed as resulting from discrete actions by one entity (usually the state) against another; the processes that produce unequal patterns of power among people in the first place are beyond its grasp, as is the possibility of state action promoting equality and freedom. Consequently, constitutional rights have only a limited capacity to advance social justice – in relation, for example, to economic security (chapter 3), communications (chapter 4), work (chapter 5), and health (chapter 9).

Charter litigation can get results, however, where social injustice is congruent with the liberal form of rights (where it involves discrete state acts of repression or discrimination). Rights and courts have played important, though limited, roles in such areas as lesbians' and gays' struggles against discrimination and women's fight for reproductive choice (chapter 3). At the same time, rights strategies can be used against progressive initiatives (the point of chapter 6's examination of Charter challenges to regulatory, anti-hate, and sexual assault legislation), and even apparently progressive uses of rights can have unanticipated regressive effects (such as the cuts to unemployment insurance benefits that followed *Schacter* [1992]: chapter 3) or lead to narrow and distorted constructions of social movement politics (chapter 8) and citizenship (chapter 9).

Third, and finally, in addition to the limits imposed by rights' liberal form, judges tend to rely on conservative conceptions of society when interpreting the Charter, thus creating a further barrier to the Charter's having progressive effects (chapter 7).

For these reasons, I argued, the Charter has done little to advance social justice in Canada, despite its just words.

I

The conclusions that I draw from these arguments are rather modest: for progressive people and causes, constitutional rights strategies share with all other forms of political action some positive potential and various negative risks, yet their overall effect is unlikely to be substantial in light of the multitude of factors that produce social injustice. Analysing constitutional rights as social and ideological phenomena, rather than as purely conceptual and discursive ones, can provide insight into their limits and potential effects in different contexts. Such analysis can thus be a useful part of progressive rights strategies, and I hope that my work will be of some help in that respect. I hesitate to draw any stronger conclusions than these. Though scholarly critique is an excellent medium for generating knowledge and understanding about the world, academic expertise does not qualify people such as me to tell actors in social movements what they should or should not be doing. Academics undoubtedly have roles to play in social activism, as participating citizens, analysts, and critics, but working with ideas about the world is not the same as working in the world – a central point of this book – and the conflation of these two realms in academic work can lead, in my view, to arrogant, elitist, and undemocratic prescriptions, a kind of 'vanguardism with a vengeance' (Meikins Wood 1995). I am content to suggest that people who work with rights should add some social theory and analysis to their strategic thinking, if they have not already done so. They are better positioned than I, however, to determine where this will lead them.

I do not agree with those who draw the stronger conclusion that the overall effect of the Charter is profoundly negative and that it should therefore always be avoided, even where its immediate results might be desirable from a progressive perspective. Hutchinson (1995) argues, for example, that constitutional litigation and adjudication are 'constitutive of extant social conditions' in ways that 'subordinate people' (176). He continues: 'Ultimately, any gain through litigation will serve to lend popular credence to the legal system as a legitimate arena for successful transformative activism. To engender respect for any rights gained and to ensure their effective enforcement, it will be necessary to instill a general reverence for the courts as a whole. While such a strategy might allow small advances to be made, it will actually defer and inhibit the kind of profound changes necessary for truly progressive transformations' (177).

Similarly, Mandel (1994) argues that the Charter represents a 'fundamental [and conservative] change in the structure of Canadian politics' (82) and 'has undermined popular movements' because it has 'legalized our politics' (4); thus, in his view, resort to the Charter has the effect 'in the long run ... of legitimating this general form of politics and sinking us deeper into the quicksand' (456–7).

Holding the Charter responsible for serious erosions of democracy and social justice in Canada is perhaps a useful corrective to the exaggeration of the Charter's positive potential found in much constitutional scholarship and popular accounts, but it shares with that work a presumption that constitutional law is central in people's lives, a presumption that I have challenged above. Though the Charter undoubtedly has some negative effects on Canadian politics and social relations, the erosion of democracy and social justice in Canada today is radically overdetermined, driven by a wide array of economic, social, and political forces, of which the Charter is only one.

I believe (though this can never be proven) that the day-to-day lives of people in Canada would not be that much different – not that much better, nor that much worse – if the Charter had never been entrenched in the constitution. Constitutional law, including the Charter, imposes constraints on the exercise of political power. The social constitution – historically rooted patterns of power relations among groups and individuals that profoundly affect and determine the nature and quality of people's existence – is largely beyond its grasp. That is why the overall effect of the Charter on Canadian society, whether positive or negative, is probably not nearly as substantial as either its supporters or its detractors believe.

I therefore cannot agree with the implication in Hutchinson and Mandel's work that every use of the Charter has a sufficiently negative effect on Canadian politics and society to warrant avoiding Charter litigation even in those limited areas where it might do some good.[1] Charter litigation is not unique among political strategies in requiring engagement 'within existing social relations' (Hutchinson 1994, 176), and while there is some truth in the statement that 'if you legitimate the Charter by using it, you cannot claim foul when it is used against you' (Mandel 1994, 457), the same holds true for all political institutions. Though there are unique difficulties with Charter litigation (the subject of the chapters above), the Charter is not uniquely subject to the influences of regressive social pressures and the risk of strategies being ineffective or backfiring.

II

I stated at the beginning of this book that the purpose of criticism is not to prove that nothing is possible, but to understand what is. In arguing that the Charter's potential to advance social justice is limited, I have necessarily implied that the possibility of progressive social change depends on work that goes beyond the confines of Charter politics. The liberal form of constitutional rights discourse presumes that our analytical concerns and activist energies should be focused on discrete actions of governments and that government action is always part of the problem and never part of the solution for promoting social justice. I have argued in contrast that analysis of social and economic structures – including the class structure of capitalism – is essential for understanding and working to ameliorate social injustice and that progressive social change can be facilitated by an activist state. I am well aware that such arguments are currently out of vogue and likely to attract criticism. That does not, however, mean that they are wrong. As I explain below, class analysis and state activism continue to have major roles to play in the quest for social justice, despite the persistent refrain from pundits, the media, and even academics that they are irrelevant and old-fashioned notions.

Class, as defined in chapter 1, contemplates relationships and processes of capitalist economic production, particularly property and ownership, that establish dependence and unequal power among people. Two things are true of class relations within capitalism. First, subject to rapidly deteriorating social programs and regulation, and a shrinking public sector, most people's health and welfare depend on decisions of private economic actors to give them jobs with decent wages and benefits, invest in and provide goods and services to their communities, not ruin their environment, and make available affordable shelter. Second, profitability, not people's needs, is what drives the decisions of private economic actors.

The focus of much of this book is on how these dynamics can operate to undermine interests and values that Charter rights and freedoms are designed to protect. Social inequality results from decisions and actions of private economic actors that lead to economic insecurity, poverty, and discrimination (chapters 3 and 9); free speech is undermined by inequalities in access to communications resources and by the dominance of ideological discourses that are reinforced and sustained by class power (chapter 4); freedom of association is undermined by the capacity of business enterprises to move or reorganize production in ways that dissociate workers and thus impose barriers to their organizing unions, bargaining collectively, and striking (chapter 5); business can enhance its power by using the Charter to deregulate its activities (chapter 6); and anti-union and pro-business attitudes among judges are related in part to the wider dominance of these attitudes in society (chapter 7). Each of these arguments is concerned with class to the extent that it relates to issues raised by the exercise of powers and capacities that are derived from relations of property and ownership – in other words, class relations.

While recognizing the significance of class, however, I reject several positions that are often (and wrongly) associated with class analysis. First, I am not arguing, and do not want to imply, that the quest for social equality and justice is futile within capitalism; I do not foresee the development of a classless society any time soon, and there is much that can be done within capitalism to ameliorate that system's harsher effects. Related to this, I am not arguing that all private property should be abolished, nor that equality would be the result if it were. Private property relations are not necessarily exploitative or oppressive; it depends on how and in what context they are asserted. My aim in focusing on property relations is to identify a crucial source of social power and inequality in capitalism and to suggest that efforts at promoting equality must be concerned with curbing, and protecting people from, exploitative and oppressive uses of such power. I agree with Wright (1994) that 'capitalism [does not have] to be destroyed before inequalities can be significantly reduced; but ... the power of capitalists and other privileged elites cannot go unchecked if there are to be significant inroads on [inequality]' (50).

Second, I am not suggesting that wealthy people and business elites are morally wanting. I am concerned with the structure and logic of capitalist social relations, not making moral judgments about those involved in the system. In any event, at least in my experience, individual human qualities do not correlate with class position; personal kindness, integrity, and compassion seem to be roughly evenly distributed across the class spectrum, as are their opposites.

Another point must be made in relation to the connection between class and human experience: the analyses of this book relate to objective social relations of class, not to people's subjective experience of class identity. Without wanting to deny the importance and complexity of the issue of class consciousness (see, for example, Meikins Wood 1995), I am concerned more with the objective power derived from property rights within capitalism than with how those over whom such power is exercised understand their class identity. The fact that most people would define themselves as 'middle class' and may enjoy a reasonable level of material comfort does not immunize them from the dynamics and vulnerabilities of class relations. Their dependence on private economic enterprises for jobs, goods, and services is no less acute because of their subjective class consciousness – a fact painfully evident in the increasing economic insecurity of many people who identify themselves as middle class.

Third, in focusing on class I am not suggesting that social injustice and inequality are unique to capitalism. Injustice and inequality have been present throughout history and in all social systems, including putatively socialist ones. I certainly draw no inspiration from recent and contemporary examples of 'socialist' societies, such as the Soviet Union, the People's Republic of China, and North Korea; at best they provide some insight into how horribly sour movements for social justice can turn. As I indicate throughout this book, I am committed to the ideals of equality, democracy, and freedom, albeit fuller conceptions of these ideals than are realized within liberalism. The Marxist-Leninist and Maoist regimes of the twentieth century are about as far from these ideals as one can get. Totalitarianism is reprehensible, whatever form it takes, and the collapse of these regimes is a welcome development.

At the same time, however, the popular notion in the West that this collapse represents the triumph of capitalism, the end of history and ideology, and the termination of people's quest for social systems that are just and humane represents an incredible arrogance of the present. Those in power have always claimed (and worked to cultivate the belief that) history has ended with their power. Yet history, and the conflict and struggles over power that it entails, will go on. I cannot believe that human beings are so unimaginative, complacent, unvaried, and unchanging as to support the same social system for, say, the next thousand years (though they may for the next twenty, fifty, or one hundred years). Though the world is rife with social injustice today, and history reveals few examples of societies where ideals of social justice are genuinely reflected in everyday life, this does not mean that the struggle for social justice has ended in failure, only that it is not yet complete (or close to it).

Fourth, and finally, there is the issue of class reductionism. Traditional Marxian thought is often criticized for its exclusively economic focus and, correspondingly, its failure to deal with wider social relations, such as those of gender and race. I agree with this criticism. Class relations inevitably intersect with other social relations (see chapter 3's discussion of relationships among class, race, and gender); and social injustices, such as violence against women and racism (chapter 6), discrimination against lesbians and gay men (chapter 7), and colonialism (chapter 8), cannot and should not be reduced to class issues. The critique of such reductionism is welcome, but in some instances it has been taken too far. Laclau and Mouffe (1985), for example, argue that, because new social movements represent a fundamental break from the politics of the past, progressive social struggle today does 'not have a necessary class character' (58). In contrast, I see class as always relevant and necessary for those seeking to understand and work against social injustice, though it is never the only, and often not the primary, characteristic of social injustice in a particular area. So long as the production and distribution of economic power in society are based on relations of property and ownership – class relations – class analysis will be necessary (albeit not sufficient) for understanding social power, exploitation, discrimination, and oppression. Without reducing social movements to an exclusively class character, it is possible, and indeed necessary, to recognize the role of class relations in, for example, the anti-racism (Gabriel 1994; Small 1994), environmental (Frankel 1994), lesbian and gay (Duggan 1992; Herman 1994), and women's (Brodie 1995) movements.

Today, at the end of the twentieth century, with the 'triumph' of capitalism over the welfare state and socialism (much like at the end of the nineteenth century, with its triumph over feudalism), class power is increasingly consolidated and unrestrained, and analysis of it is crucial for understanding inequality and social injustice. Ironically, those most concerned about class today are business elites and their allies in the mainstream media. While many on the left have all but abandoned the idea of working-class struggle, class consciousness and solidarity among the business community (the capitalist class) are as strong as ever. Like the working class of another era, it is the capitalist class that today seeks radical and even revolutionary change on an international scale, in the dismantling of the social welfare state and the withering away of national sovereignty. Contrary to conventional wisdom, this is an era of intense class consciousness and class struggle (though it is business interests, not the working class, that are the new class warriors). Now is not the time to abandon class as an analytical and political concept.

Nor, for similar reasons, is this a good time for progressive people to abandon the notion of an activist state. Again, conventional wisdom holds that the role of the state in social and (especially) economic life must be reduced through privatization, deregulation, lower taxes, and less government spending. This has hardened into an anti-statist orthodoxy that obscures some of the disturbing consequences and contradictions of the policies proposed in its name. First, deregulation and privatization necessarily narrow the scope of democratic authority. Legislative regulation and state ownership are tools for promoting a measure of democratic control over social and economic life and some insurance against property rights being used in ways that cause harm to people and the environment. Lifting legislative restrictions on the activities of private actors is tantamount to immunizing their actions from the exercise of popular sovereignty; similarly, privatization transfers control of an enterprise from the democratic state to private actors who are accountable only to shareholders. The evisceration of democratic authority inherent in deregulation and privatization programs is seldom acknowledged or considered by those advocating radical withdrawal of legislatures and governments from economic life. At a minimum, political organizations and parties, such as the National Citizen's Coalition and the Reform party, that advocate both greater democratization and less authority for democratic institutions (through deregulation and privatization) should explain this apparent contradiction. Like other forms of governmental policy, regulation and state ownership are not perfect, have substantial limitations, and are more appropriate in some contexts than others, but their categorical dismissal is extreme and unwarranted.

Second, while deregulation and privatization restrict the authority of democratic state institutions, the suggestion by their advocates that such measures free the market from state intervention is disingenuous. It is simply nonsensical to reject regulation and state ownership on the ground that they involve state 'intervention' when their alleged opposite, the 'free market,' is itself made possible only through operation of an elaborate state apparatus. Deregulation of a particular area of social or economic activity means not that the state has pulled out of that area but only that legislative restrictions on the exercise of state enforced property and contract rights are lifted. After deregulation, laws, courts, police, and the penal system continue to create, enforce, and protect contract and property rights. The state is not absent, it simply abdicates its role of monitoring and restricting the exercise of property and contract rights in aid of variously defined public goods (such as health, safety, environmental protection, human rights, and employment standards). In a similar vein, privatization entails only a shift in property entitlements from public to private entities; enforcement of those entitlements remains with the state.

Calls for deregulation and privatization are about how, and in whose interests, state power should be exercised, not whether it should be exercised. Their aim is to free the market of democratic constraints, but they do not question any other aspect of the massive state apparatus needed to maintain and operate a market system. It is incumbent on the business elites who advocate such programs to explain why the state should support only their interests and not seek to promote, through regulation and public ownership, the often-conflicting interests of other groups and the general public.

Next, the dogma that governments can no longer afford to spend money on social programs, and that reduction of deficit and debt through cuts in spending must therefore be their primary concern, obscures the true complexity of public finances, as well as the potential costs, in both the short and the long term, of *not* spending on social programs. It unduly reduces the causes of deficit and debt to overspending; it ignores revenue shortfalls caused by unemployment and consistent reductions in corporate taxation over the last twenty years, as well as the effects of high interest rates.[2] It also ignores the costs of cost cutting. Spending cuts mean loss of employment and income to public-sector employees, as well as fewer government purchases of goods and services from private firms. Money is taken out of the economy, resulting in job losses, reduced consumer spending, lower tax revenues, and higher costs relating to unemployment benefits, social assistance, and health care.

More generally, cuts in one area of government programs and services inevitably turn up as costs in other areas. Examples are not hard to find: cuts to unemployment benefits put more people on social assistance; cuts to social assistance put more people in the health care system, as inadequate nutrition and housing cause illness; deteriorating social conditions resulting from cuts to various forms of income support and social housing lead to higher rates of crime and greater public expenditure on police, prisons, and the legal system; overcrowded schools, fewer special programs, and cuts to extracurricular sports, music, art, and other community programs put more children at risk for getting involved in delinquency and crime; cuts to AIDS awareness increases the disease's incidence, thus leading to higher health-care costs for treating a preventable disease; cuts to public transportation mean greater reliance on automobiles, generating more air pollution, which in turn translates into higher health-care costs. Finally, failing to invest in infrastructure reduces economic growth. To take just one example, cuts to education, training, and research, at a time when knowledge and information are increasingly important for the economy, mean fewer options for economic diversification as a hedge against global competition, and thus higher unemployment, with all of its associated costs.

Another fact obscured by the obsession with deficit and debt is that reducing public expenditure on social services does not reduce people's needs for the services provided. If people do not pay for services through government taxation, they will have to pay for the services through prices, user fees, insurance premiums, and so on (Brooks 1996). There are two major drawbacks to private delivery of services and programs. First, many people cannot afford to buy services in the market, and reductions in public services thus exacerbate the suffering caused by economic inequality. Deterioration in publicly provided health care and education services, for example, may present little difficulty for those who can afford to buy services in the market (from private clinics and health insurers or private schools), but those who cannot afford such services end up with inferior publicly provided services. The result is a two- (or, more accurately, several-) tier system. Second, the nature and scope of privately provided services are determined by levels of profitability, not the public good. To take an example from chapter 4, corporate sponsorship, in broadcasting, education, research, or arts, inevitably shapes content in ways that support, directly or indirectly, the sponsors' drive for profit, and this tends to exclude alternative and dissident voices. In other areas, such as health care and transportation, services will be provided only if they are profitable. Expensive medical procedures will not be available in hospitals in low-income communities where clients cannot afford them, and privatized railways, ferry systems, and airlines will be reluctant to serve communities on unprofitable routes. In short, the need for a particular service does not disappear when its funding is cut, and leaving provision of that service to the market generates substantial inequalities.

My purpose in criticizing calls for reductions in government spending is not to suggest that we should be sanguine about debts and deficits, nor is it to imply that measures to reduce them are always inappropriate. Rather, my argument is aimed at the view, all too common among policy makers and pundits, that reducing debt and deficit should be governments' top priority, regardless of social and economic circumstances and consequences. That view is irrational because it fails to consider the actual causes of debts and deficits and the actual costs of reducing them through cuts in government spending. The tendency of governments (at least in North America) to fix arbitrary deadlines and targets for reducing debts and deficits reflects a rigid ideological orthodoxy that is simply bad policy because it ignores the ever-varying relationship between government finances and social and economic conditions.[3]

III

Let me conclude this chapter by observing that deregulation, privatization, and reduced social spending, the fundamentals of neoliberalism, are rooted in the same liberal ideologies – anti-statism and atomism – as are dominant discourses of rights; they therefore embody narrow and formal conceptions of equality, freedom, and democracy, and it is necessary (though not sufficient) that programs for progressive social change challenge them.

In conclusion to the book as a whole, I reiterate my central claim that Charter litigation and rights discourse are blunt tools for redressing social injustice. This is a sceptical conclusion, but it is neither pessimistic nor cynical about progressive social change. The struggle for social justice is much larger than constitutional rights; it is waged through political parties and movements, demonstrations, protests, boycotts, strikes, civil disobedience, grassroots activism, and critical commentary and art. In Canada today we must use all of these measures to combat the vast disparities of welfare and power among us and to ensure that all people have an effective voice in determining the conditions of their lives. I hope that this book makes a contribution to the struggle for social justice by shedding some light on the question of how we might get from where we are now to a better world.

Notes

Chapter 1: Introduction

1 This is paraphrased from the original quotation.

2 My method is qualitative, not quantitative. Statistical analyses of Charter law address similar questions to those posed in this book and also adopt an external perspective, but their method is quantitative. They are complementary to this book's project. See, for example, Morton, Russell, and Withey 1992; Russell 1992.

3 The extra-litigation effects of rights discourse are a subject deserving a book of their own. That is not the main focus of this book, however; outside of chapters 8 and 9 I concentrate on litigation itself. For an excellent study of rights discourse outside the courts, see Herman 1994.

4 See, for overview, any text on sociology of law. Good examples are Cotterrell 1992 and Hunt 1993.

5 This is not surprising, given that legal academics are lawyers, train lawyers, and produce knowledge typically aimed at and consumed by lawyers (Arthurs 1983). For the most part, they adopt an internal perspective, eschewing analysis of law's social constitution and effects and often condemning such analysis as inappropriate. Historically, construction of law as an autonomous and closed system has served as a form of 'eulogy and of defence (apology)' (Goodrich 1992, 19–20), representing 'a kind of superstitious veneration of [the law] beyond what is just and reasonable' (Goodrich 1992, 7, quoting Hale). Notably, some jurists recognize the importance of social scientific knowledge for deepening the factual basis of making and applying law, but not for understanding law itself as a social phenomenon (Pound 1912, Dickson 1986). Still other academics focus on law's discursive contradictions, incoherence, political slant, and progressive possibilities but do not necessarily relate these to the constraints of wider social structures (for discussion of this phenomenon, see, for example, critiques of critical legal studies in Sargent 1991 and Cotterrell 1992, 414).

6 One definition of an ideological process, according to D. Smith (1990), is a 'method of reasoning about and interpreting society and history [that] obstructs inquiry by giving primacy to concepts and their speculative manipulation' (34–5). Internal analysis of law is such a process (Kerruish 1991, 143).

7 The point is illustrated by responses to recent equality decisions by the Supreme Court of Canada (*Andrews* 1989; *Brooks* 1989; *Janzen* 1989; *Turpin* 1989; *Hess* 1990; *Schacter* 1992). In these cases, the Court accepted an approach to equality that requires analyses of the effects of laws in their social context (substantive equality), rather than focusing exclusively on whether or not laws formally treat actors differently (formal equality). The limitations of these cases in actually advancing social justice are discussed below. Analyses of them usually do not get much beyond legal language and particular results. L. Smith's (1994) response is typical; she concludes, after reviewing the Court's jurisprudence on equality rights, that these rights have 'led to a small number of positive outcomes, either through litigation or through law reform initiatives' (71), fostered 'a number of promising statements' (60), and influenced interpretations of other rights in positive ways (72–4). On balance, she concludes, 'the equality rights have done more good than harm, and show clear potential for further development' (76), though she does not analyse the likelihood of courts' engaging in this development, the probable consequences if they did, and the actual effect on people's lives of the Court's decisions to this point. See also C. Sheppard 1989; Orton 1990; McAllister 1992; Mahoney 1992.

8 There is a close link between law and religion. 'Both [jurisprudence and theology] draw their knowledge from specific books, both develop a dogmatics and both, because of their dogmatics, are antagonistic towards sociology and philosophy' and primarily concerned with 'arguments about words' (Kraft 1993, 117–19). Lawyers 'are presumed to share the faith' when arguing, teaching, writing, or learning law. Their inquiry can range freely, so long as it remains within the canon (Levinson 1988, 156). Parallels between law and religion exist in legal procedures as well. Hay (1975), for example, notes in his study of eighteenth-century English criminal law the 'elaborate ritual of the irrational' (11) accompanying assizes in a country town: 'In its ritual, its judgements and its channelling of emotion the criminal law echoed many of the most powerful psychic components of religion' (13). Ritual is as much a part of law today as it was in the eighteenth century. In a trial (and, perhaps more important, its dramatized television versions), 'the participants are brought before a judge in a black robe who sits elevated from the rest, near a flag ...; the architecture of the court room is awesome in its severity and in its evocation of history and tradition; the language spoken is highly technical and intelligible only to a select few who have been "admitted to the Bar". This spectacle of symbols is both frightening and perversely exciting. It signifies to people that those in power deserve to be there by virtue of their very majesty and learning' (Gabel and Harris 1982/83).

In Canada, as in the United States, the ritualistic foundation of judicial authority is further deepened through constitutional rights themselves. The judiciary has assumed the role of final guardian of the Charter, understood as a semi-sacred text, embodying 'the cardinal values of society' (*Oakes* 1986, 119). This role only reinforces the religious imagery of courts as temples of justice. Such symbolism is nicely illustrated in a decision by the Supreme Court upholding an injunction against picketing of a courthouse: according to the Court, in the absence of access to courts, 'Charter protections would become merely illusory, the entire Charter undermined' (*BCGEU* 1988, 229). Though an exercise of freedom of expression by the employees, the picketing threatened the Charter, including its guarantee of freedom of expression, the Court held. 'Without the public right to have absolute, free and unrestricted access to the courts, the individual and private right to freedom of expression [and other Charter rights] would be lost' (247–8). The courts are thus elevated to new symbolic heights by the Charter. Like priests, judges are seen as the link between the sacred word (of the Charter) and the profane world of social life.

9 Some other external progressive Charter scholars are William Bogart, Judy Fudge, Harry Glasbeek, Didi Herman, Allan Hutchinson, Hester Lessard, Michael Mandel, and Andrew Petter. Constitutional rights scholars in the United States whose approaches are similar include Kim Crenshaw, Gerald Rosenberg, Stuart Scheingold, and Mark Tushnet.

10 The anti-democracy critique of the Charter can be found on the right as well as on the left, in academic work (Knopf and Morton 1992; 1996), and in Reform party debates (Canadian Press, 'Reformers Propose Charter Changes,' *Globe and Mail*, 4 June 1996, A6).

11 Governments, Parliament, and legislatures, for example, created social welfare programs, universal access to health care and education, and unemployment insurance.

12 As I stated in an earlier piece (Bakan 1992c), 'Judicial activism in aid of civil liberties in the face of excessive national security legislation in South Africa (or in Canada or Britain) is entirely different than that in aid of restricting progressive social policy in another context (or in South Africa); and such differences must be accounted for in any defence of judicial deference to legislatures' (511).

13 According to Dworkin (1986), legal scholarship must 'grasp the argumentative character of our legal practice by joining that practice and struggling with the issues of soundness and truth participants face' (13) and 'impose order over doctrine, not ... discover order in the [historical and social] forces that created it' (14). Though he nominally acknowledges that 'both perspectives on law, the internal and external, are essential, and each must embrace or take account of the other' (14), he then collapses the external perspective into the internal one: 'The participant's [internal] point of view envelops the historian's [external one] when some claim of law depends on a matter of historical fact: when the question whether segregation is illegal, for example, turns on the motives either of the statesman who wrote the constitution or of those who segregated the

school' (14). In other words, the external perspective's use is limited to answering questions raised within the internal perspective, not those about law itself. See Fiss 1981–82 and Langille 1988 for explicit critiques of the external approach; see Brest 1981–2, Coombe 1989, and Hutchinson 1989, for critiques of those critiques.

Chapter 2: Constitutional Interpretation and the Legitimacy of Judicial Review

1 In relation to constitutional law, legitimation arguments normally take the form of theories of interpretation, which 'attempt to govern interpretations of particular texts by appealing to an account of interpretation in general' (Knapp and Michaels 1985, 11; see also Fish 1985, 106–8).

2 Appeals to the Judicial Committee of the Privy Council in constitutional cases were abolished in 1949.

3 For exposition and discussion of this approach, see Lefroy 1897, 21–40; Clement 1916, 472–92; W.P.M. Kennedy 1932, 71–95; V. MacDonald 1948, 31.

4 For a classic example of this type of reasoning, see *Citizens Insurance* 1881.

5 I am using gender-specific language here because there were no women judges at the time.

6 The Canadian 'new deal' cases include *Reference Re Weekly Rest in Industrial Undertakings Act, Minimum Wages Act and Limitation of Hours of Work Act* 1937; *Reference Re Employment and Social Insurance Act* 1937; and *Reference Re Dominion Trade and Industry Commission Act* 1937.

7 While seemingly oblivious to the contradictions between them.

8 See also McWhinney 1965, 223–4.

9 For a similar view, see Willis 1951.

10 See also McWhinney 1965, 201.

11 See also Cairns 1971, 335.

12 See also Lederman 1964, 185 and 261; McWhinney 1965, 215; and Monahan 1984, 64–6.

13 See *Edwards* 1930, 136; *British Coal Corp.* 1935, 518; *A.-G. Ontario v. A.-G. Canada* 1947, 154. See also McWhinney 1965, 66–7.

14 See also McWhinney 1965, 234; and Snell and Vaughan 1985, chaps. 8 and 9.

15 For discussion of the Court's approach to the Canadian Bill of Rights, 1960, see Tarnopolsky 1975, and Snell and Vaughan 1985, 214–32.

16 For similar arguments, see Lyon and Atkey 1970, 68–70.

17 See also Klare 1978, 280.

18 Section 1 states: 'The Canadian Charter of Rights and Freedoms guarantees the rights and Freedoms set out in it subject only to such reasonable limits prescribed by law as can be demonstrably justified in a free and democratic society.'

19 Scholars differed, however, on what sources the courts should look to in determining the

purpose of a right or freedom – history, fundamental values and traditions, or the principles underlying conventional sources of constitutional law. See, for examples, Roman
1982–83, 190, 193, 198 (arguing that judges must turn to political and legal history to
give meaning to rights and freedoms); Monahan 1983, 436 (in order to apply section 1,
judges need to have background theories of the nature and requirements of the democratic polity); Lyon 1983, 242 (judges must move away from the text of the Charter and
to the political tradition that the Charter is meant to reflect); Finkelstein 1983–4, 143–
5 (the Charter directs courts to examine the underlying basis of modern society, which is
that 'people still enter into society for the limited purpose of self preservation'); Beckton
1983, 122–3 (courts must develop theories that are not premised solely on the judge's
perception of which societal values are important); Gold 1982, 131–4 (judicial power is
limited by the duty to take into consideration certain basic principles that inform the
enterprise on which the Court is embarked); and Rogers 1986, 183–7 (judicial choice
can be constrained by a principle that requires judges to make sure that judicial power is
used to strike down statutes that infringe substantive equality).

20 Quoting from *Minister of Home Affairs v. Fisher* 1979, 329.

21 While purposive reasoning is the predominant structure of constraint-based arguments
in Charter jurisprudence, members of the Court still sometimes use 'narrow and legalistic' techniques in interpreting the Charter. See, for example, Justice McIntyre's decisions
in the following cases: *Dolphin Delivery* 1986, *Mills v. the Queen* 1986, *Dubois v. the
Queen* 1985, *Reference Re Public Service Employee Relations Act, Labour Relations Act and
Police Officers Collective Bargaining Act* 1987 (hereinafter *Alberta Reference*), and *Morgentaler* 1988.

22 Though only one case, *Edwards* 1930, is cited, and, as suggested above, the 'living tree'
did not really have much life prior to the Charter.

23 Beatty and Kennett (1988) explicitly draw a connection between determinacy and consensus. They postulate that determinacy in constitutional interpretation depends on the
possibility of elaborating definitions of rights and freedoms 'which everyone could
accept' (584). They believe that such definitions can be found and therefore that 'determinate solutions – right answers – do exist' (576) in constitutional law.

24 For a compelling statement of this point, by a judge, see S. Wright 1987, 502.

25 See, for example, the discussions below of the Supreme Court of Canada's decisions on
equality rights (chapter 3) and freedom of expression (chapter 4).

26 See also Braden 1948, 584–9; White 1986; and chapter 7, below.

27 For further discussion of this point, see Unger 1975, 94–8; 1976, 192–200 and 203–
210; 1983, 568–73; and Ely 1980, 63–9.

28 However, the Court held in *Oakes* 1986, there would be times when the elements of the
section 1 analysis are 'obvious or self-evident' (137).

29 Justice LaForest appears to agree with me on this point. In *Jones* (1986) he does not
apply the *Oakes* test (though he refers to *Oakes*), preferring instead simply to balance

competing interests (see further discussion of this in section III of this chapter); and in *RJR-MacDonald* (1995) he holds (in dissent, with three other judges concurring) that the *Oakes* criteria represent only one possible approach to section 1 and he rejected 'the view, unfortunately still held by some commentators, that the proportionality requirements established in Oakes are synonymous with or have even superseded, the requirements set forth in s. 1 itself, which makes it clear that the Court's role in applying that provision is to determine whether an infringement is reasonable and can be demonstrably justified in a "free and democratic society." In Oakes, Justice LaForest continued, this Court established a set of principles, or guidelines, intended to serve as a framework for making this determination. However, these guidelines should not be interpreted as a substitute for s. 1 itself' (243).

30 *Zundel* (1992), where a majority of the Court held that the legislative purpose did not meet the 'sufficient importance' standard, is a notable exception, but that decision turned on the majority's characterization of the purpose in indefensible terms.

31 The final stage of the *Oakes* test is, of course, applied when legislation is upheld under *Oakes* because of the necessity of satisfying each criterion. Even in these situations, however, the Court deals with it very quickly and then moves on. See, for example, *Edwards Books* 1986; *Irwin Toy* 1986; *Prostitution Reference* 1990; *Ross* 1996; *Egan* 1995. However, in a recent decision, *Dagenais* (1994), the Supreme Court makes the final stage of the *Oakes* test more difficult for governments to meet by requiring that the deleterious effects be balanced against the 'salutary effects,' as well as the importance of the objective. It is not yet clear how this will affect its application of the test, though the *Dagenais* (1994) modification was applied by the Court in *RJR-MacDonald* (1995).

32 The Court has moved away from rigid application of the least-restrictive means test in some contexts (see, for example, *McKinney* 1990; *Keegstra* 1990; *Butler* 1992) but not in others (*RJR-MacDonald* 1995).

33 *Jones* is the first of a line of cases in which Justice LaForest advocates, sometimes in dissent (*RJR-MacDonald* 1995), other times in the majority (*McKinney* 1990; *Ross* 1996), avoiding the rigidities of the *Oakes* test in favour of more open and explicit balancing. That is why I analyse the case – it is not because I am sympathetic with Mr Jones's plight. More recently, in *Hill* (1995) the Court explicitly adopted a flexible approach to section 1, which emphasizes balancing competing values rather than applying the *Oakes* test, for challenges to common law rules in private litigation. The points of the following analysis of balancing tests are nicely illustrated by Justice Cory's majority judgment in *Hill*. See note 35.

34 See, for example, Miliband 1973; Griffiths 1981; Petter 1986. For more detailed exploration of this point see chapter 7, below.

35 We can see the importance of how competing interests are articulated by reversing the relative levels of generality and particularity of the government's and the individual's interests in *Jones*. Suppose that the Court had characterized the government's interest as

a particular aspect of its more general interest in education – namely, its interest in ensuring that the applicant (and possibly others similarly situated) complied with the requirement of applying for a certificate to educate children outside the public schools. And suppose that the Court had characterized the appellant's interest in general terms – namely, his interest in freedom of religion. Now we would have to balance the government's 'particular and narrowly conceived claim' in a minor and limited exception to its policy of requiring applications for certificates against the appellant's 'highly generalized and obviously crucial' interest in freedom of religion. The scales would now be weighted in favour of the appellant. Similar points can be made in relation to the way the Court balances the value of defamatory speech (rather than the more general freedom of expression) against the reputation of an individual (rather than an individual's particular interest in not being defamed) and, not surprisingly, finds in favour of the latter (*Hill* 1995).

36 Labour injunctions, whether judicially or legislatively mandated, are, of course, enforced by the police. Injunctions can thus turn peaceful demonstrating and picketing into violent confrontations between police and workers. See Fine and Millar 1985.

37 For examples, see Michelman 1986; 1988; Minow 1987; Perry 1988; Cornell 1988; A. Fraser 1993. For critiques, see Bakan 1989; Hutchinson 1995.

38 It is also probably the reason why mainstream legal scholars are not theatened by this work. Fiss (a chief defender of conventional legal analysis: Fiss 1981–2), for example, not long after writing an article called 'The Death of the Law?' (1986) in response to critical legal studies, wrote 'The Law Regained' (1989). There he argues that the slogan 'law is politics,' which he had equated with nihilism in the earlier piece, is no longer a threat, because, at least when voiced by trust-oriented theorists, it contemplates 'the possibility of a more noble and idealistic politics, one that is more an expression of public values, or of principles, or of rights, than of private preference' (247). Fiss understands that, despite other differences, these theorists agree with him that the 'politics of law' is a politics of principle, not of interest; they may be radicals, but they are not heretics.

39 For more detailed critiques of Beatty, see Bakan 1990; 1991; for other critiques of Beatty, see Mandel 1994, 56; 1989; and Hutchinson 1995.

40 See Bakan 1992 for further discussion of this point.

41 Both Beatty (1987b) and Dyzenhaus (1989) explicitly rely on Ronald Dworkin's work. Dworkin (1986) believes that legal interpreters must be committed to construing law in its 'best light' (52). Legal interpretation is 'a matter of imposing purpose on an object or practice in order to make of it the best possible example of the form or genre to which it is taken to belong' (52).

42 See, for example, Fairley 1982, 231–54; Gold 1982; R.A. MacDonald 1982, 346; LaForest 1983, 25–6; Hogg 1985.

43 Comparing *Egan* 1995 with *RJR-MacDonald* 1995 is particularly instructive. The cases were decided within a couple of months of each other. Though some of the judges were

consistently activist or deferential in the two cases, Chief Justice Lamer and Justices Major and Sopinka, who in *Egan* emphasize the need to defer to legislative judgment in complex social and economic matters, concur, in *RJR-MacDonald*, with Justices Iacobucci and McLachlin, who insist on an activist approach.

44 Whether this occurs will depend on the political and social circumstances at particular times and places. In Canada today, it is rare, for reasons I discuss in the chapters that follow, for the judiciary to play a substantial role in advancing social and economic equality.

45 The view that courts should defer to 'economic' legislation in constitutional adjudication, for example, developed in response to the pro-business, anti-regulatory activity of courts under the u.s. Bill of Rights in the early twentieth century and the BNA Act, 1867, in the 'new deal' decisions and subsequent decisions that struck down regulatory regimes. The restraint argument was thus linked to the substantive politics of particular decisions. That link is, however, absent in much of the restraint rhetoric we find today. The restraint argument is used to legitimate decisions to defer to legislation that is economic in form, regardless of its substance. The Court, for example, seems confused about when deference is appropriate, sometimes arguing that courts should be cautious not to roll back social and economic legislation that protects 'vulnerable groups' (*Edwards Books* 1986; *Irwin Toy* 1989; *Potash* 1994), and other times holding that deference is appropriate for all social and economic legislation (*Egan* 1995, per Justice Sopinka; *McKinney* 1990, per Justice LaForest). See also Monahan (1987, 126–7), who argues that the Court should not intervene in the economy to provide 'minimum levels of income, housing and education.' Such interference would, in his view, be undesirable because of the historical record of the court in blocking social welfare measures. Monahan's argument appears, however, to derive an 'ought' from an 'is.' He is accurate in his description of the historical record, but it is not clear how that description supports a normative (as opposed to strategic) prescription that the Court continue in that mode.

46 I do not mean to suggest that there are no instances of Charter critics prescribing deference, only that this is not always the gist of their critiques, and certainly not mine.

Chapter 3: Equality and the Liberal Form of Rights

1 See also recent cases in the u.s. Supreme Court that have curtailed affirmative action programs in the name of equality (Beltrame 1995).

2 The Legal Education and Action Fund (LEAF) intervened in *Andrews* 1989 and other equality cases. For discussion of LEAF's involvement in Charter litigation, see Razack 1991.

3 See the various judgments in *Egan* 1995 and *Miron* 1995 for the latest word on how members of the Court translate this purpose into doctrine.

4 Moreover, members of the Court appear to be back-pedalling towards a narrower under-

standing of equality. See, in particular, *Egan* 1995, per Justice LaForest; and *Miron* 1995, per Justice Gonthier. See also Philipps and Young 1995; Trakman 1995a.

5 See definition of equality in chapter 1, above.

6 The Charter's scope is defined by section 32: 'This Charter applies to (a) the Parliament and government of Canada in respect of all matters within the authority of Parliament including all matters relating to the Yukon and Northwest Territories; and (b) to the legislature and government of each province in respect of all matters within the authority of the legislature of each province.'

7 This immunity for private actors is further protected by the Court's explicit holding that judicial orders in disputes between private actors are not subject to the Charter: in such cases, according to the Court, courts are not government actors but neutral arbiters of legal conflict: *Dolphin Delivery* (1986). In contrast, where courts perform a 'governmental' role (*BCGEU* 1988; *Dagenais* 1994) or are deciding certain kinds of criminal matters (*Rahey* 1987; *Bernard* 1988; *Swain* 1991), they are subject to the Charter. The Charter also applies to the common law – including, presumably, the law of property and contract – and courts are thus obliged to 'develop the principles of the common law in a manner consistent with the fundamental values enshrined in the Constitution' (*Dolphin Delivery* 1986, 603). The Court has interpreted this latter statement as requiring it to reformulate common law rules so as to reflect the principles of the Charter even in private litigation, thus creating an indirect, but not very effective, way to subject private action to the Charter (*Hill* 1995).

8 Except where a Charter provision explicitly creates a positive right, such as section 23, which guarantees rights to minority-language education, and section 14, which grants a right to have an interpreter in a trial.

9 Justice Wilson explicitly uses the fence metaphor to describe the Charter in her judgment in *Morgentaler* 1988.

10 Examples can be found in Sheppard 1989; Clark 1990, 391; Orton 1990, 298–9; Trackman 1994.

11 A group of hearing-impaired plaintiffs claimed that section 15(1) requires the BC government to provide them (through the BC Medical Services Plan) with sign-language interpreters when they receive medical treatment. The Court rejected this argument, holding, among other things, that section 15 could be used only to attack legal restrictions, not to impose an obligation on government to provide a service.

12 Brodsky and Day (1989) argue, correctly in my view, that this approach imposes a substantial limitation on the potential of the Charter to address gender inequality (280). The unwillingness of courts to recognize positive obligations extends beyond section 15 to other provisions that raise equality concerns. The majority judgments in *Morgentaler* 1988, for example, make it clear that 'security of the person' (section 7) is breached only by direct state interference with women's choice to have (or not) abortions, not by the absence of state action. Justice Beetz was explicit on this point: 'Generally speaking, the

constitutional right to security of the person must include some protection from state interference when a person's life or health is in danger. The Charter does not, needless to say, protect men and women from even the most serious misfortunes of nature. Section 7 cannot be invoked simply because a person's life or health is in danger. The state can obviously not be said to have violated, for example, a pregnant woman's security of the person simply on the basis that her pregnancy in and of itself represents a danger to her life or health. There must be state intervention for 'security of the person' in s. 7 to be violated' (90).

Thus, only if the state prohibits an individual who is sick or in need of an abortion from getting treatment will there be a violation of that individual's security of the person under section 7. The state would not be required by section 7 to take positive action that ensured women access to safe abortions and, more generally, all people access to health care. See also *Haig* 1992 and *Native Women's Association of Canada* 1994 for discussions of positive rights in the context of freedom of expression. As I argue in chapter 5, despite the rhetoric in these cases about the importance of positive rights, the idea does not get beyond rhetoric; see also Bakan et al. 1995 and Trakman 1995.

13 Because of the size of the benefit and the size of the group seeking it, according to the Court, 'the ensuing financial shake-up' of granting it constitutional protection would be too great and 'could mean that other benefits to other disadvantaged groups would have to be done away with to pay for the extension' (*Schacter* 1992, 723).

14 The Court compromised by 'declar[ing] the provision invalid but ... suspend[ing] that declaration to allow the legislative body in question to weigh all relevant factors in amending the legislation to meet constitutional requirements' (723–4).

15 According to the Court, this remedy was consistent with the purposes behind human rights legislation, and the case could be distinguished from *Schacter* (1992) because the financial implications of 'reading in' were not as substantial as they would have been in that case. The minority judges in *Egan* (1995) adopt a similar approach.

16 Recent decisions, such as *Egan* 1995, *Miron* 1995, and *Thibadeau* 1995, suggest that the Court is moving in the opposite direction. As well, outside equality rights, the Court has not been enthusiastic about positive rights: *Native Women's Association of Canada* 1994 (freedom of expression); *Prosper* 1994 (right to counsel). See also Trakman 1995b.

17 This is true, at least, of dominant conceptions of rights. Below I discuss scholars who have reconceived rights in non-dyadic terms. See section III of this chapter.

18 Poverty is defined by the National Council of Welfare (NCW) as the income at which a person must spend 54.7 per cent of income or more on the necessities of life – food, shelter, and clothing (NCW 1995). According to the NCW, 17.4 per cent of all Canadians lived in poverty in 1994. Breaking this figure down reveals some more disturbing features of poverty. The gender ratio of poverty rates (women:men) is 1.33; for children under eighteen the poverty rate is 20.8 per cent; for single-parent mothers with children under eighteen (and their children) it is 59.8 per cent (NCW 1995); it is 78 per cent for

single-parent families where the parent (almost always the mother) is under thirty (Little 1996). For unattached women over sixty-five years old it is 47.3 per cent (compared to 32.1 per cent for men in this category); the poverty rates among renters and immigrants (who arrived after 1979) are at least double the national rate. Finally, most impoverished people (roughly 60 per cent) are employed on either a full- or part-time basis.

19 Economic and class inequality extends far beyond those who live below officially determined poverty lines. The almost exclusive focus on poverty in mainstream discourses about economic 'class' can serve to obscure more pervasive problems. According to Westergaard and Resler (1975, 124): 'Even when not intended that way, preoccupation with "poverty" runs a constant risk of encouraging a distorted image of society. In that image "the poor" – or a series of separate categories of poor – are singled out from the mass of wage earners from which they are recruited. And the division is ignored between the wage-earning class – in or out of poverty – and the secure though differentiated ranks of the "middle and upper" classes.'

20 A relatively small minority of Canadians own the vast majority of general wealth and almost all productive wealth, and income distribution is also seriously skewed (see, for example, Calvert 1984, table 63; Statistics Canada 1984). The reality of substantial inequality in income and wealth distribution provides the empirical basis for the theoretical account of property, power, and dependence developed here.

21 Hutton (1996) is characterizing this argument in order to criticize it. He develops a theory of 'stakeholder capitalism' which rejects the accepted view that capitalism and equality are at odds. His is a latter-day version of Keynsian economics and has had great influence on the British Labour party.

22 The operation of this logic has been softened by welfare measures introduced since 1945. As those measures are rolled back, the harsh effects of capitalist logic are becoming apparent in increasing levels of 'social insecurity.'

23 See above, note 18. Also, for discussion of gender/class intersections see Bakker 1994; Brodie 1995.

24 Poverty and unemployment rates among First Nations peoples in Canada are notoriously high (Statistics Canada 1993). For immigrants who arrived after 1979, poverty rates are double those of the general population (38.8 per cent for heads of families; 65.5 per cent for unattached individuals) (National Council of Welfare 1995).

25 More generally, women are subject to violence and harassment from men, tendencies not reducible to but exacerbated by, and operating in conjunction with, financial dependence. To take just one example, Dr Jonathan Mann (1995), chair of Harvard's Global AIDS Policy Coalition, argues that women's vulnerability to AIDS is related to a convergence of forces, including financial dependence: 'In marriage, the pervasive threat of physical violence or divorce without legal recourse or legal rights to property may totally disempower a woman even if she knows about AIDS, even if condoms are available and even if she knows her husband is HIV-infected.'

26 A related critique of equality rights can be found in Iyer (1992), who has criticized what she calls the categorical approach to equality in Charter and human rights jurisprudence. Couching claims in terms of particular categories of discrimination ('sex,' 'race,' 'sexual orientation,' and so on), she argues, ignores the 'existing web of social relations' (204) and dangerously oversimplifies the reality of discrimination. Individuals and groups are defined in terms of one category, with two kinds of effects – the group is treated as autonomous of all others, and it is presumed to be homogeneous. Gender discrimination is thus treated as separate from racism and the oppression of class relations, leading to claims 'falling through the cracks' of the discrete categories; and within the category of 'sex' all women are presumptively similarly situated, leading to essentialist constructions of gender relations. The realities of intersecting and overlapping social relations around gender are thus obscured, and 'law and legal actors remain conveniently innocent of the injustices entailed by legal doctrine and legal cases' (204).

Another helpful analysis of the limits of rights discourse can be found in Trakman's critique of affirmative action (1994, 31–3). He argues that, while affirmative action provides access to institutions for groups that have historically been excluded, it alters neither the 'substantive conditions' responsible for social disadvantage nor the 'racial, economic and social conditions' of the institution that has now been forced to open its doors a bit wider. For example, programs designed to compel white schools to admit African Americans change neither the institutional and structural conditions of racial inequality in the United States nor the racialized nature of education itself (for example, the cultural values imbedded in curricula). Trakman states: 'To redefine privilege to include excluded groups, without modifying the substantive content of privilege, is to arrive at false equality. The mere sharing of privilege fails to redress the social structure that perpetuates a falsely equal market in which everyone starts off, somewhat doubtfully, with equal capacities to succeed' (37).

27 Here are some examples of the types of claims made (see M. Jackman 1988 and 1993 for detailed discussion of the cases in which these claims were made): in housing – to require three months' notice of a rent increase or termination for subsidized tenants (which non-subsidized tenants were entitled to); to nullify zoning by-laws prohibiting use of land for neighborhood rehabilitation homes or low-income housing; in social assistance – to strike down legislation reducing social assistance payments for single, employable persons between eighteen and thirty years old unless they participate in a 'workfare' program; to increase social assistance payments to enable persons with certain physical disabilities to live at home rather than in a hospital; and in employment – to extend minimum-wage provisions to patients in psychiatric institutions.

28 Brodsky (1992a, 51–2) argues, correctly in my view, that the latter are unlikely to succeed.

29 See chapter 9, below, for development of this argument in the context of social rights.

30 This does not mean that such claims should not be pursued, only that they have limits,

which may – depending on the context – be more or less constraining than those of other strategies.

31 This does not mean that economic inequality and poverty cannot be fought while the structure of society remains capitalist, nor do I want to suggest that economic inequality and poverty are unique to capitalist systems. Analysing the structural features of capitalist economic relations does, however, provide a starting point for thinking about what kind of tactics might be necessary for combating poverty and economic inequality and, in particular, for assessing the utility of rights tactics such as those discussed above. See E.O. Wright 1994 and chapter 10, below, for further discussion.

32 barb findlay has suggested that about 25 per cent of British Columbia's 483 statutes discriminate against lesbians and gays (Griffin 1995).

33 Such concessions were made in *Veysey* 1990; *Knodel* 1991; *Haig* 1992.

34 Most important, the Supreme Court of Canada, in *Egan* 1995. See chapter 7, below, for further discussion of *Egan*.

35 The majority judgments in *Egan* 1995, while accepting that section 15 of the Charter includes protection for lesbians and gays, establishes high hurdles for lesbian and gay litigants within section 15 (Justice LaForest) and section 1 (Justice Sopinka).

36 *Egan* 1995 casts some doubt on the viability of this approach. Four of the five majority judges held that limiting 'spouse' to heterosexual arrangements is not discriminatory, and the fifth majority judge adopted a very deferential approach under section 1 to legislation that discriminates against lesbians and gays. See chapter 7 for further discussion.

37 Many women are forced to have abortions for economic reasons – they cannot afford to have a child. See *Globe and Mail*, 4 Oct. 1994. See also Mandel 1994, 434 and 437.

38 The legislative amendments that created these changes (Bill C-21, *An Act to amend the Unemployment Insurance Act* and the *Employment and Immigration Department and Commission Act*) were introduced in the House of Commons by the minister of employment and immigration, Barbara MacDougall, as necessary 'to make [the Unemployment Insurance Act] more equitable, so that it reflects the changing work patterns of Canadians and responds to the Charter of Rights and Freedoms' (House of Commons Debates, Official Reports, Second Session, Thirty-fourth Parliament, Vol. I, 1989, 11 April, p. 318). Schacter commented: 'I am happy the government is moving to address the points of my case. Benefits will be available to fathers and not at the expense of mothers' (Canadian Press, Toronto, 12 April 1989, 2.09 EDT).

39 Moreover, women's role as primary care-givers to children itself inhibits entry and re-entry into the labour force, a difficulty that is exacerbated by the UI amendments.

40 Examples of this line of argument are: Minow 1990; Nedelsky and Scott 1992; Nedelsky 1993; and Trakman 1994.

41 For similar critiques, see Bakan 1989b; Hutchinson 1994, 165–72.

Chapter 4: Freedom of Expression and the Politics of Communication

1 Though the Court may be willing to apply the Charter indirectly to private action by reviewing common law rules that allegedly infringe freedom of expression (*Hill* 1995). For a fuller discussion of the limits on the Charter's scope, and exceptions to these limits, see chapter 3, above.

2 This is true even of communications that appear to fly in the face of the values underlying freedom of expression, such as hate or holocaust-denial literature. The reason for not excluding these from the scope of freedom of expression, according to the Court, is 'to ensure that expression more compatible with these values is never unjustifiably limited' (*Keegstra* 1990, 766; cited in *Zundel* 1992, 759). However, violence as a form of expression is not protected – 'a murderer or rapist cannot invoke freedom of expression in justification of the form of expression he has chosen' (*Irwin* 1989, 970). In less extreme circumstances, an expression of anger at someone who has just stolen a parking spot that involves driving into that person's car would not be considered expression for the purpose of the Charter. Violence as the substance of communication, including 'threats of violence' (*Keegstra* 1990, 732–3), is constitutionally protected, so long as the form of communication is not violent. What is true of violence is also true of sex. The Court has rejected the argument that, because pornography involves depiction of 'physical activity,' it is not expression. The content may be physical, but the form is communication, and it is therefore protected (*Butler* 1992, 487).

3 There are two further situations where the Court may consider the content of a particular expressive act in determining whether restricting that act limits section 2(b), where the restriction relates to government-owned property (such as an airport or utility pole) (*Committee for the Commonwealth* 1991; *Peterborough* 1993), and where the purpose of the impugned legislation is not to restrict any particular content of expression, but it none the less has the effect of restricting expression (for example, a noise or littering by-law). Here the complainant may have to prove that what she is saying advances one of the values underlying freedom of expression (*Irwin* 1989; *Peterborough* 1993; Bakan et al. 1995, 109–10).

4 Though the Court has also regularly struck down laws designed to protect people from harm on the ground that such laws are too broad: see, for example, *Rocket* 1990; *Zundel* 1992; *RJR-MacDonald* 1995. See chaps. 7 and 8, below.

5 Compare, for example, Justices McLachlin and LaForest in *RJR-MacDonald* 1995.

6 For analyses developing similar themes, see Fiss 1986; Hutchinson 1995, c. 7.

7 Seventeen per cent of those surveyed by Angus Reid in 1995 said that they could log onto the information superhighway; 74 per cent of these were male, and half of these men were under thirty-five years of age (CP News 1995). A 1996 survey by Statistics Canada reports that only 7.4 per cent of Canadian households use the Internet from their home computers (Mitchell 1996).

8 In 1984 the CBC's operating budget was reduced by $75 million. Between 1988 and 1990 its operating capacity has decreased by about 15 per cent because of government cuts. Prior to that, operating capacity was maintained only by increases to advertising revenue. Since then, further and very deep cuts have been made and proposed by Jean Chrétien's government. Not surprisingly, the CBC has relied on more advertising and direct corporate sponsorship – in other words, further privatization of funding – to deal with government cuts. From 1994 to 1995 advertising revenue increased by $8.6 million (2.9 per cent). Advertising now represents 22.6 per cent of revenue (CBC 1994–5; see also Godfrey 1995). See also *Globe and Mail*, 16 Nov. 1994. The final stage of a $414-million cut (imposed by Ottawa between 1994–5 and 1997–8), representing approximately one-third of the CBC's federal funding allowance, was recently announced. These cuts will require elimination of four thousand CBC positions and substantial changes to programming (C. Harris 1996). See also Windsor and Harris (1996). Deep cuts have been made as well in the funding of First Nations public broadcasting – for example, the Northern Native Access Program and the Native Communications Program (*Windspeaker* 1995).

9 Such programs are, of course, controversial. Conservative groups such as REAL Women and the NCC have argued that they represent a bias towards support of 'radicals,' while those on the left are uncomfortable with the potential for cooptation represented by state support and concerned about potential fragmentation of social movements that may result from the structure of funding (Phillips 1991).

10 The most important programs are administered by the Secretary of State. The five major groups receiving support from these two departments are official-language minorities, First Nations groups, women's groups, disabled persons, and multicultural groups. Over the last decade there has been a discernible trend of cutting back Secretary of State funding for women's and First Nations advocacy groups. As well, there is a move away from core funding of groups – which allows for greater autonomy – towards project-based grants (*Windspeaker* 1993; 1994; 1995; *Canadian Women's Studies* 1994; *Canadian Dimension* 1995).

11 Government funding of arts has been steadily dropping (Statistics Canada 1994b; 1995a; 1995b). 'Every time the government makes a statement about cutting, that leaves only one option: for the corporate sector to take a leadership role. I would hope that other companies would follow Ford's leadership and step in to fill an obvious void,' states Garth Drabinsky, head of Live Entertainment of Canada, defending an arrangement under which Ford paid millions of dollars towards the cost of a new downtown theatre in Vancouver in exchange for having the theatre named the Ford Centre for the Performing Arts (Cernetig 1994). Drabinsky would probably agree with the Continental Bank's comments: 'Today's corporate sector ... does have a powerful, though subtle, influence on the arts and on all other facets of humanistic services ... simply by supporting some activities and ignoring others. On the cultural scene, this gives an obvious edge

to those performances that: (a) promise to be well attended; (b) appeal to the main-stream of the general public; and (c) contain a minimum of material that migh be considered offensive' (cited in Moore 1985, 101). See, generally, Moore 1985; Canada 1986; Gates 1990.

12 An exhibition on the history of Coca-Cola at the Royal Ontario Museum and corporate logos on library cards in Vancouver are examples of the steps that publicly funded institutions are taking to compensate for cutbacks in public funding. See, generally, Schiller's (1989) discussion of museum and library funding. The *Globe and Mail* reports: 'Canada's largest public library soon could be known as the Burger King Reference Library. Or perhaps the Labatt's Blue Reference Library, or maybe even the Nintendo Reference Library. The Metropolitan Toronto Reference Library, which holds the country's largest non-academic reference collection, is seeking companies to help underwrite its operations. In exchange, the library building at the corner of Yonge and Bloor will bear the company's name' (Saunders 1996).

13 They point out further that government funding agencies, including the SSHRC, are altering their policies to encourage more 'practical' research, which will 'aid private sector development and technological innovation' (83). For discussion of the trend to privatization in universities, see Lewington (1995). Even the *Globe and Mail* (1995) seems worried about the extent to which universities have tied their activities to the immediate needs of corporate Canada.

14 The research for this book, a piece of critical knowledge, was supported by several SSHRC grants, and its production was subsidized by a grant of SSHRC funds from the Canadian Federation of Social Sciences (see Acknowledgments); as well, I have been gainfully employed while writing it by the University of British Columbia and York University. Take away all that public funding, and this book would not exist (unless I could find a corporate sponsor for the project – an unlikely prospect).

15 'There are no demonstrations in Disneyland,' Sorkin (1992, xv) states, because the Disney corporation has an absolute right to demand that demonstrators leave the premises (and would be assisted by the full coercive apparatus of the state – police, courts, prisons – to ensure that they did). On public property, people have at least some (albeit few) expression rights (*Peterborough* 1993). However, as one commentator states: 'Precisely because downtown streets are the last preserve of something approaching a mixing of all sectors of society, their replacement by the sealed realm overhead and underground has enormous implications for all aspects of political life. Constitutional guarantees of free speech and of freedom of association and assembly mean much less if there is literally no peopled public place to serve as a forum in which to act out these rights. Only the myopic magnifying lens of the television camera maintains the demonstration, march, and picketing as a modality of political expression' (Boddy 1992, 125).

16 Many mall owners post signs explaining that they are not public ways but places for tenants and customers to transact business and requiring groups wishing to make public

statements to get permission from management. As Schiller (1989) points out: 'To the extent that private-property owners legally can decide what kind of activity is permissible in their malls, a vast and still expanding terrain is withdrawn from serving as a site of public expression' (100).

17 This message is reinforced by the ubiquitous presence in most malls of private security forces and sophisticated surveillance equipment, as well as decor, design, 'muzak,' and other cues designed to create a welcome environment for the middle-class consumer and exclude others (Crawford 1992, 27; Davis 1992, 179).

18 As one commentator states: 'Raised pedestrian bridges connect dispersed new towers into a linked system; mazes of tunnels lead from public transit to workplace without recourse to conventional streets; people-mover transit systems glide above the scuffling passions of street bound cities ... eliminating the most fundamental of urban activities – people walking along the streets' (Boddy 1992, 124).

19 Zoning laws or city policies limiting height or width on new projects are sometimes waived by officials in exchange for promises by developers and architects to include 'public' squares, parks, or gardens at the street level of their developments. These are always presented as reflecting the beneficence of the developers and the fact that development and public space are not at odds with another. The current development of the Expo '86 lands in Vancouver (which involves construction of forty high-rise condominium buildings on land sold by the provincial government to a private developer for a price that most agree was ridiculously and suspiciously low) is a prime example of this phenomenon.

20 Some have argued recently that the internet is a new form of public space, where people can express opinions to a wide audience, enter dialogues, and so on. See, for a critique of this position, the above discussion of the limits of the internet: note 7 and accompanying text.

21 As Cooper (1994) notes: 'In the case of discursive technologies of power such as knowledge, not only is there not equal access but the production of narratives (discourse) from the perspective of the subjugated [is] likely to hold at best a marginal position. Thus, we need to consider not only who has access to the production of discourse, but also the gendered or raced nature of the discourses they deploy, and of the hierarchy within which they operate' (450).

22 There is certainly respectable academic opinion supporting Rosenbluth's position; see, for example, Philipps 1995; and Brooks 1996. See also McQuaig 1995 for a study of anti-deficit rhetoric that became a bestseller; it is perhaps an even better example than Rosenbluth's of how, even when an author has access to an audience, if her ideas run counter to dominant ideological discourses, their effects will be limited.

23 Feminist writers have argued, for example, that the idea of 'family,' which is capable of bearing many meanings in the abstract, is frozen into a nuclear and heterosexual form in familial ideology, thus reflecting and sustaining gendered and heterosexist

structures of power (Boyd 1991; 1993; Gavigan 1993; Kline 1993; and see chapter 4, above).

24 For analysis of the ideological (consumerist, pro-corporate, sexist) content of advertising, and the effect of reliance on it on the content of non-advertising media, see, for example, Ewen 1976, 43, 108. See also Smythe 1980; R. Williams 1980, 185; Parenti 1986; Ohman 1987; Herman and Chomsky 1988; Jhally 1989; Inglis 1990; Curran and Seaton 1991; Keane 1991, 88; Goldman 1992.

25 It is important not to fall into the trap of assuming that people are 'dupes' to whatever ideological discourses come their way. As Eagleton (1991) and many others have pointed out, the concept of ideology should not be taken to deny that people have agency. The 'audience' does not reflexively accept dominant meanings (Lewis 1991). Hall (1980) elegantly develops this point by noting three levels of engagement by differently situated audience members: preferred (or dominant-hegemonic), negotiated, and oppositional. A 'preferred' reading decodes a message in terms of the 'reference code in which it has been encoded,' including the categories and classifications of dominant ideological discourses. The 'preferred' reading of most media discussions of the deficit, for example, is that the deficit must be eliminated, or at least dramatically reduced, and because tax hikes are unacceptable and would curtail investment and consumer spending, cuts in social spending are inevitable. 'Negotiated' readings also accept dominant definitions, but they incorporate the particular, and often contradictory, concerns of the audience. Many people extol the cutting of government spending while advocating a stronger police presence or more funding for schools in their neighbourhoods. Finally, 'oppositional' readings reject dominant definitions. As we saw above Rosenbluth, for example, reads the call for deficit reduction as a propaganda ploy to legitimate reductions in social spending.

26 Even if the Court is some day prepared to take the quite radical steps of extending obligations to respect freedom of expression to private actors, and requiring governments to take positive action to promote people's access to communications facilities (which I doubt very much), it is unlikely that communicative freedom would be substantially enhanced. The atomistic form of rights would preclude the courts from ordering the kind of transformation of knowledge-producing structures and institutions that would be necessary to ensure that all people could freely and genuinely participate in the so-called marketplace of ideas. In any event, there is no indication that the Court will depart from its negative and anti-statist conception of freedom of expression any time soon.

27 A term popularly used to describe both prior-restraint restrictions and ex post facto criminal liability for certain kinds of speech. I adopt that usage here, even though, technically, censorship means prior restraint.

28 As we see in chapter 7, below, such measures are vulnerable to Charter litigation under section 2(b).

29 I say 'may' to indicate that the point here is analytical, not empirical. Whether restrictions on hate speech actually help or hinder the struggle against cultural imperialism is a difficult sociological question. It is wrong, however, to assume *a priori* that legislative restrictions on speech work against freedom of expression. Analysis should focus on the probable effects of legislative restrictions on wider ideological struggles. Do they help or hinder struggles against racist, sexist, and homophobic ideological processes that denigrate, vilify, and pathologize people's identities? Do they enhance or attenuate the power of dominant groups to shape the discursive environment?

30 Matsuda (1993–4) makes the point thus: 'It is the value of speech I hope to promote by suggesting that we may need to limit some speech. This is indeed a paradox – no easy walk to freedom, no easy civil liberties' (17).

31 See, for judicial examples of this approach, *Keegstra* 1990 and *Butler* 1992. For philosophical explorations, see Feinberg 1984 and Bakan 1985. In the latter, I developed a position from which I depart in the analysis below.

32 More recently, the term seems to have been further generalized to ridicule any and every expression of a view that challenges mainstream public opinion. It has become a dominant ideological discourse with important (and I think regressive) effects.

Chapter 5: Freedom of Association and the Dissociation of Workers

1 Another example: the International Labour Organisation (ILO) has recently criticized Nova Scotia's government for unilaterally reducing public-sector salaries. According to the ILO, these rollbacks violate the Freedom of Association and Right to Organize Convention, 1948, to which Canada is a signatory: the measures 'cannot be defined as exceptional measures and clearly go beyond what the [ILO] has found to be permissible restrictions on collective bargaining, especially as regards the duration of the period covered' (reported in *Canadian Association of University Teachers Bulletin* 1995).

2 The labour-law changes of the first NDP government in British Columbia (1972–5) were repealed by subsequent Social Credit governments. The changes introduced by the NDP government elected in 1991 are safe for now, as the party was re-elected in May 1996; the BC Liberal party, which was only narrowly defeated, had promised if elected to repeal the NDP's labour code. The changes of the first NDP government in Ontario were repealed, along with pro-union measures introduced by previous governments (such as card rather than vote certification), by the subsequent Progressive Conservative government in November 1995 (see Bill 7: An Act to Restore Balance and Stability to Labour Relations and Promote Economic Prosperity).

3 The cases, *Dolphin Delivery* 1986, *Alberta Reference* 1987, *PSAC* 1987, *Saskatchewan Dairy Workers* 1987, *BCGEU* 1988, *Professional Institute* 1990, *ILO* 1994 – all unsuccessful for the unions – are a source of considerable academic debate not only about the relationship between the Charter and labour but more generally about the Charter's

potential for bringing about progressive social change. Criticism of the Supreme Court's rejection of union claims often focuses on the historical antipathy of courts towards unions (see, for example, Petter 1986; 1987; Fudge 1987; 1988; Mandel 1989; 1994; Bakan 1990; 1991; Glasbeek 1990; 1993; Fudge and Glasbeek 1992); on the incoherence of its reasoning (Beatty and Kennet 1988; Beatty 1991), and on the fact that a constitutional right to strike and bargain collectively would have been effectively undermined by the Court's deference to government under section 1 of the Charter (as it was in the minority judgments – see Panitch and Swartz 1988, 62–6; Mandel 1994).

4   On 'reasonable limits' under section 1 the minority split, with Chief Justice Dickson easily finding that most of the legislative measures could be sustained, and Justice Wilson reaching the opposite conclusion. See *Alberta Reference* 1987, *PSAC* 1987, *Saskatchewan Dairy Workers* 1987.

5   In *Professional Institute* (1990), Justice Cory tried unsuccessfully to expand the recognized right to form and join trade unions to include protection of the right of trade unions to engage in their essential activities, including collective bargaining. The majority, including Chief Justice Dickson, rejected this approach, insisting that freedom of association prohibited only state interference with individuals who want to form or join a trade union.

6   Widespread support of Poland's Solidarity movement in the mid-1980s is a good example of how people in the West can be moved by the need for trade unionism when it is not in their own countries.

7   Chief Justice Dickson's judgment is replete with this kind of social-democratic vision of labour relations. The purposes of constitutional protection of freedom of association are, according to him, to enable 'those who would otherwise be vulnerable and ineffective to meet on more equal terms the power and strength of those with whom their interests interact, and, perhaps, conflict' (366) and, relatedly, 'to protect the individual from State-enforced isolation in the pursuit of his or her ends' as part of a recognition of 'the profoundly social nature of human endeavours' (365). Understood in this way, freedom of association is a 'vital ... means of protecting the essential needs and interests of working people' (368) and the 'cornerstone of modern labour relations' (334). The interests protected by collective bargaining are not 'merely pecuniary in nature' (371) because work is central to a person's 'sense of identity, self-worth and emotional well-being' and working conditions are thereby 'highly significant in shaping the whole compendium of psychological, emotional and physical elements of a person's dignity and self-respect' (368). Finally, according to Chief Justice Dickson, effective protection of collective bargaining requires protection of the freedom to strike (371).

8   The 'victory' of the sceptics must, in his view, be 'hollow,' 'pyrrhic,' and 'bittersweet' (1991, 860), because it means that it is factually correct that the Charter, as understood by Canadian courts, does not protect unions and that the Supreme Court is unlikely to 'correct its mistakes' and overturn its anti-union decisions (861).

9 Though fragmentation is not per se undesirable from labour's perspective (Hirst and Zeitlin 1991, 6), it has served, at least in North America and Britain, to centralize further the power of capital (Harvey 1991).

10 In 1993 61 per cent of Canadians worked 35–40 hours a week (though not necessarily in the same job). Part-time jobs accounted for a quarter of all jobs, and 35 per cent of these were held by people who said that they were unable to find full-time employment (Canada 1995). Seventy percent of part-time employees are women (Shalla 1995); 35 per cent of female employees held part-time jobs in 1994, compared to just over 10 per cent of males (Statistics Canada 1995c).

11 The constantly changing composition of the workforce at a particular worksite is often referred to as 'numerical flexibility.' The employer's advantage is obvious. The size of the workforce can expand and contract to meet the employer's immediate production needs, thus promoting efficiencies.

12 Home work is common in the garment industry, and increasingly in the service sector in areas, such as telephone sales and ticket booking, that rely on computer networks. One commentator notes: 'The work site – as we have come to know it – may no longer be a work site. The workforce may be scattered and strewn, many workers never leaving their homes if they so choose, many of them paying only casual visits to the workplace. Even those who have a fixed job at a fixed place are not likely to stay there for any great portion of a lifetime' (Tyler 1986, 384).

13 Unless the legal structure of collective bargaining is significantly changed (perhaps through the introduction of sectoral bargaining: O'Grady 1992, 159–61).

14 Again, just as fragmentation of the worksite is not inherently bad for workers, so too is there a theoretically positive side to workers' having more creative involvement in the production process through such mechanisms as quality circles. There is thus a surface believability to the claim made by business interests that such measures are humanistic, but their actual operation often belies such lofty statements.

15 1992 was the first time in five years that there was a decrease in overall union density, down 0.1 per cent to 34.9 per cent. In the private sector, union density declined from 25.7 per cent to 20.7 per cent in the period 1975–85. Projections suggest that rates will be around 16 or 17 per cent by the end of this decade: O'Grady 1992, 153.

16 According to a recent report of the Public Service Commission, the number of full-time permanent employees in the federal public service has dropped from 209,000 to 194,000, and rates of hiring have steadily dropped to their lowest point since the Second World War. Use of casual, term, and temporary workers, in contrast, is at an all-time high (May 1995; see also Statistics Canada 1995d).

17 Nestle plants in the United States had no weekend overtime, and the union representing workers in a Nestle plant in Manitoba had recently agreed not to have it. The president of the union local representing workers at the Manitoba plant noted that Nestle has 'no commitments to regions, provinces or countries.'

18 To take one example, a BC sawmill closed down in 1983, with 654 employees laid off because of low demand for its products. It reopened in 1985 on a different site, with computer-controlled automation. Only 145 workers were rehired, sixty of them employed by the original mill. (The employer, MacMillan Bloedel, was able to do this by waiting until the two-year term of a hire-back clause in the collective agreement had expired before reopening.) See also Leach and Shutt 1984, 90–1. The point was made by Michael Decter, then Ontario's deputy minister of health, when justifying impending cuts in public employees: 'In an era when my [electronic] mail connects me to 2200 people in the Ministry, do we need as many levels as when people had a much-less-effective technology?' (*Globe and Mail,* 17 April 1993).

Chapter 6: Power to the Powerful

1 As I have argued elsewhere: 'The purpose of much modern legislative regulation is to provide at least some limited safeguards against the more egregious abuses by individuals and corporations of the power they derive from their property rights' (Bakan 1992a, 119). Regulatory regimes impose restrictions on private actors, most importantly business corporations, to contain the harm that they may cause in pursuing their economic interests. There is great pressure from the economic right to reverse such legislation (in areas such as labour, environmental protection, anti-monopoly, consumer standards, and so on) because it increases production costs and precludes new avenues of profit making. Regulatory legislation, in the words of one Supreme Court judge, is designed 'to protect the public or broad segments of the public (such as employees, consumers and motorists, to name a few) from potentially adverse effects of otherwise lawful activity' (*Wholesale Travel* 1991, 219, per Justice Cory).
2 See chapter 2, above, for discussion of these cases.
3 The leading case is *Lochner* 1905, and the years during which the u.s. Supreme Court blocked social welfare and regulatory legislation in the name of constitutional rights have come to be known as the Lochner era. The gist of the court's reasoning during this period is represented by Justice Peckham's judgment in *Lochner*: 'The general right to make a contract in relation to his business is part of the liberty of the individual protected by [the right to life, liberty, or property in] the 14th Amendment. The right to purchase or sell labour is part of the liberty protected by this amendment, unless there are circumstances which exclude the right ... It is unfortunately true that labour ... may possibly carry with it the seeds of unhealthiness. But are we all, on that account, at the mercy of legislative majorities? ... This interference on the part of the legislatures of the several states with the ordinary trades and occupations of the people seems to be on the increase. [It] is impossible for us to shut our eyes to the fact that many of the laws of this character, while passed under what is claimed to be the police power for the purpose of protecting the public health or welfare, are, in reality, passed for other motives.' Given

the work of the court during the Lochner era, it is hard to fault historian Charles Beard (1986) for stating, in 1913, his view of the U.S. constitution this way: 'The Constitution was essentially an economic document based upon the concept that the fundamental private rights of property are anterior to government and morally beyond the reach of popular majorities' (324–5).

4 Through the 1980s and 1990s the U.S. Supreme Court has effectively fashioned a new version of its earlier anti-regulatory work, striking down progressive legislation under equality and expropriation provisions of the Bill of Rights. For some recent discussions, see Beltrame 1995; G. Fraser 1995.

5 Even federal Justice Minister Kim Campbell was concerned that 'courts would [use the Charter to] strike down progressive legislation' (though her real concern was probably that courts would strike down Progressive Conservative legislation) (cited in Bakan 1991a, 123).

6 The Court was unwilling to apply the same logic to Irwin Toy's application for a declaration that a law restricting advertising aimed at children was unconstitutional under section 7. The fact that Irwin Toy was not defending a charge meant that the *Big M* (1985) route was not available (*Irwin Toy* 1989; see also *Dywidag Systems* 1990). Nor would the logic apply if the law under which the corporation was charged applied only to corporations, since, as we have seen, it depends on the possibility of there being a human being whose rights are restricted by the law (*Wholesale Travel* 1991, 179–83). In neither *Big M* (1985), nor *Wholesale Travel* (1991), which (as we see below) followed *Big M* (1985) on this point, did the Court consider 'reading down' the legislation in issue to apply only to corporations instead of striking it down altogether, a route clearly open to it, given the language in section 52, that a law is of no force or effect only 'to the extent of the inconsistency' with a Charter right. Reading down was suggested by the attorney general of Manitoba, who intervened in *Wholesale Travel* (1991, 180, per Chief Justice Lamer); see Tollefson 1992, 377.

7 Especially when corporate decision making is geographically and hierarchically dispersed and not all decisions are recorded in the company documents.

8 The reason for placing the onus on the accused to prove due diligence is that requiring the Crown to prove facts demonstrating negligence would 'leave the Crown the legal burden of proving facts largely within the peculiar knowledge of the accused ... mak[ing] it virtually impossible for the Crown to prove public welfare offences ... [and] prevent[ing] governments from seeking to implement public policy through prosecution' (*Wholesale Travel* 1991, 258, per Justice Iacobucci). Where regulatory legislation does not state explicitly the nature of the liability that attaches to an offence, courts presume that it is strict liability (*Sault Ste. Marie* 1978).

9 In *Wholesale Travel* (1991), a corporation was charged with false and misleading advertising under the Competition Act. A statutory defence of due diligence was available, but only if the accused had made a prompt correction or retraction. The latter require-

ment was treated by the majority as creating an absolute-liability offence, since failure to meet it would mean that no defence was available and an accused could be convicted without there having been any fault on its part. Since imprisonment of officers of the corporation was a possible sanction, the prompt-retraction or -correction requirement effectively combined absolute liability with the possibility of imprisonment, and a unanimous Court thus held, following its earlier decision in the *Motor Vehicle Reference* (1985), that it violated section 7 and should not be upheld under section 1. The reasons of the Court make it clear that it will be a rare case indeed where absolute liability combined with the possibility of imprisonment will be constitutionally permissible. By their reliance on the *Big M* (1985) approach to standing (179–83 per Chief Justice Lamer), members of the Court implied that section 11(b), like sections 2(a) and 7, is a right that does not directly protect corporate interests.

10 In *Wholesale Travel* (1991) itself, seven of nine members of the Court found that imposition of a burden on the accused to establish that it was duly diligent violated the right to be presumed innocent in section 11(b). Four of the seven held that this 'reverse onus' should not be upheld under section 1, and the other three that it should. Because the remaining two judges on the Court did not find a violation of section 11(b), the provision was upheld by a narrow, five-to-four margin. It is hard to imagine a more precarious basis for the constitutionality of a provision, and taken together, the judgments of various members of the Court suggest that regulators should be concerned about the fate of due-diligence, reverse-onus provisions in future decisions.

11 For now the Court appears to be treating its decision in *Wholesale Travel* (1991) as standing for the proposition that strict-liability, reverse-onus clauses generally meet section 1 criteria (see *Ellis Don* 1992). Lower courts appear to be treating *Wholesale Travel* (1991) similarly (attaching substantial importance to the distinction between strict and absolute liability, since there is a strong constitutional presumption against the latter): see *Consolidated Maybrun Mines* 1993; *Nickel City Transport* 1993. The potential remains, however, for *Wholesale Travel* (1991) to restrict the use of strict-liability in regulatory offences. See discussion in section IV.

12 Again, see discussion in section IV. *Wholesale Travel* (1991) represents just one opening through which corporations might challenge regulatory legislation under the Charter. In addition, if they can successfully argue that legislation creating a regulatory offence (which might impose liability on humans as well as corporations) is too vague, it might be found to contravene section 7. *Ontario v. Canadian Pacific* (1995) develops this doctrine but finds that its criteria are not met by CP's challenge to provisions of the Environmental Protection Act, RSO, 1980, c. 141.

13 This point is made explicitly in Justice Stevenson's discussion of *Slaight Communications* (1989) in *CIP Inc.* (1992, 852–3).

14 Recent decisions of the Court have developed a more nuanced approach to section 8's protection of privacy interests in the corporate context than that of *Hunter* (1994), but

the premise that corporations have such interests has not been seriously questioned (*McKinley Transport* 1990, *Thomson Newspapers* 1990, and *Potash* 1994). These cases, each involving a corporate complainant alleging that a legislatively authorized search or seizure violated section 8, suggest that a person has less of a reasonable expectation of privacy in the context of searches or seizures under administrative or regulatory legislation than when criminal or quasi-criminal legislation is involved, and when business records and documents, as opposed to personal ones, are the subject of the search or seizure. The reasons for these glosses on *Hunter* (1984) appear to be related both to the moral stigma that attaches to criminal conviction (per Justice LaForest in *Thomson* 1990 and *Potash* 1994) and to the role of regulatory legislation in protecting important social and economic values and interests (per Justice L'Heureux-Dubé in *Thomson* 1990 and *Potash* 1994). Throughout the Court's jurisprudence in this area, however, the premise from *Hunter* (1984), that corporations have a privacy interest that is protected by section 8, is not questioned. The only suggestion in this direction is by Justice L'Heureux-Dubé (in *Potash* 1994), who notes that less protection of business documents is especially germane when corporations are involved.

15 See, again, *CIP* 1992 for an explicit statement of this point.

16 The BC Court of Appeal's decision in *Wilson* (1988) illustrates this point. Under new legislation and regulations, the commission responsible for granting billing numbers to medical practitioners could attach conditions to such grants restricting the place, time, and nature of practice for which a doctor could bill the insurance plan. The regime was challenged successfully under section 7 of the Charter by a group of doctors, some of whom had been denied permanent numbers and others of whom were granted numbers with conditions that restricted their practices to particular geographic areas. The Court understood the plight of the doctors as more than economic: 'The trial judge [incorrectly] characterized the issue as "right to work" (a purely economic question), when he should have directed his attention to a more important aspect of liberty, the right to pursue a livelihood or profession (a matter concerning one's dignity and sense of self-worth) ... The rights being asserted in this case are personal rights affecting the freedom and quality of life of individual doctors. The effect upon them of the alleged deprivations is personal, and has far-reaching implications. It is not a purely business interest which is affected' (184, 187–8). The reasoning appears to be limited to professionals and not to extend to workers in general. Consistent with this, the rights of the former have received substantial protection under sections of the Charter other than section 7 (thereby implying that they entail something more than purely economic interests) (*Mia* 1985; *Black* 1986; *Andrews* 1989; *Rocket* 1990; *Island Equine Clinic* 1991), while the rights of workers have received little protection and have explicitly been deemed purely economic (*Alberta Reference*, per Justice McIntyre – see chapter 8, below).

17 Consistent with the Court's general approach, however, the closer particular expression

is to being purely commercial, in the Court's view, the less likely it will be protected by the Charter (*Prostitution Reference* 1990; *Rocket* 1990).

18 The fallacy in this reasoning, as Justice LaForest points out in dissent, is two-fold: first, it presumes that some cigarettes are healthier than others – a point not supported by scientific evidence; and, second, it presumes that some cigarette companies will relate accurate information in their advertisements.

19 Sections 70.1(1) and 72(1), Canada Elections Act, RSC 1970, c. 14, as amended.

20 There was, according to the Court, no 'actual demonstration of harm to a society value' as a consequence of allowing third-party electoral spending, and mere 'fears or concerns' (at 496) that such harm would occur were insufficient to sustain the limit.

21 The Turner government decided not to appeal the decision, and the chief electoral officer indicated in his 1984 report that, because of the decision, he did not prosecute people (in relation to the 1984 election) under the provisions that had been declared unconstitutional by the Alberta court. The same held true in 1988.

22 Third-party expenses thus exceeded the cap on a political party's election expenses – $8 million. The substantial bulk of these expenses were incurred in support of free trade and hence the Tories. The umbrella group for third parties against free trade, Pro-Canada Network, spent only $750,000 during the election period.

23 Presented, debated, and passed in the House of Commons and Senate, and assented to in May 1993 as an amendment to the Canada Elections Act, SC 1993, c. 19.

24 The restrictions did not, according to the Court, satisfy the first criterion of the *Oakes* (1986) test: they were not sufficiently pressing and substantial as to outweigh free expression (paragraph 24). Several reasons were offered by the Court in support of this conclusion: the chief electoral officer was not concerned about the absence of third-party limits and did not see fit to investigate whether third-party advertising affected election results; the expert witnesses for the attorney-general did not address the fact that some provincial jurisdictions did not have third-party limits; and those witnesses did not address quantitative studies that concluded that third-party advertising had no such effects. In short, the judge was not persuaded that third-party advertising had any affect, let alone any harmful effect, on the electoral process. Thus, in his view, the limits could not be sustained under section 1 (paragraphs 24–33). The decision was upheld in the Alberta Court of Appeal (Somerville 1996).

25 Though the challenge is brought by Robert Foret, it is being supported by the NCC. According to the NCC's president, David Somerville, in an interview on the case: 'We're determined to strike down the gag law of NDP Premier Mike Harcourt as well [as the federal one]' (Pemberton 1995).

26 Commonly known as an 'agency shop,' or Rand formula (named after Justice Ivan Rand, who conceived of it).

27 Because, according to Justice LaForest, of the unworkability of alternatives and the

importance of unions and the labour movement in Canada's social and political life (*Lavigne* 1991, 333–9).

28 The three minority judges argued that Lavigne's freedom of association was not affected by the agency shop because that freedom protects people only from prohibitions on association, not from requirements to associate.

29 This argument was rejected, however, in one lower court decision on the ground that the majority in *Lavigne* (1991) held that there was no freedom not to associate (a questionable interpretation of *Lavigne* 1991) and that judges should defer to government agencies in the labour context (*Strickland* 1992).

30 This case was approved of and followed in a Canadian case, *Beck* (1993). In that case an independent taxi owner-operator successfully challenged an Edmonton by-law requiring him to affiliate with a registered broker in order to use his vehicle as a taxi cab. The acknowledged purpose of this law was to ensure, for public safety reasons, that taxis were available in Edmonton twenty-four hours a day and to provide safe working conditions for drivers. The Court followed *Lavigne* (1991) in reaching its conclusion that the by-law violated individual drivers' freedom of association and held that it was not a justifiable limit under section 1.

31 The Crown prosecuted Zundel under this provision rather than the hate-literature provisions because the latter require proof of wilful promotion of hatred against an identifiable group, and holocaust-denial literature has been judicially determined (wrongly, in my view) not to meet that standard.

32 She goes on to point out: 'One possible reason for the astounding number of successful challenges initiated by men is that of the few remaining ... explicit uses of gender-based classification in the statute books most benefit women' (529).

33 Ninety-nine per cent of offenders in sexual-assault cases are men; 90 per cent of the victims are women (*Canada* 1992, 13).

34 Though if the accused is married to her, that is a defence under the provision.

35 The offence is thus currently one of strict liability.

36 Section 276(1) Criminal Code is commonly referred to as the 'rape shield' provision.

37 Though the Court did recognize some of the concerns expressed about the operation of the old common law rules. According to the Court, these rules, which would become operative again with striking down of the legislation, had to be modified because they were too permissive in their unrestricted admission of evidence of past sexual conduct. The Court therefore stated that such evidence could not be admitted to support the inference that a complainant is either more likely to have consented to sexual activity or less worthy of belief; however, it was admissible for other purposes where it had probative value and where that value was not outweighed by its potential of unfair prejudice to the complainant. These modifications to the common law rules were codified by Parliament shortly after the *Seaboyer* decision: Bill C-49, An Act to Amend the Criminal Code (Sexual Assault), SC 1992, c. 38, s. 276.

38 Perhaps it was in recognition of this that Parliament used the opportunity of this bill to strengthen the substantive protection offered women by sexual assault law. The common law rule that an honest but mistaken belief in consent is a full defence to a charge of sexual assault was modified in the following way: the accused's belief in consent would not afford him a defence if he 'did not take reasonable steps, in the circumstances known to him at the time, to ascertain that the complainant was consenting' (section 273.2). This new provision is vulnerable to a Charter challenge, though recent decisions of the Supreme Court of Canada may provide support for its constitutionality (Stuart 1993, 7; McInnes and Boyle 1994, 350–1).

39 The Court appears now to have endorsed an approach to section 1 that requires that the actual positive effects, rather than only the purpose, of legislation be balanced against the deleterious effects in the third stage of the proportionality test (*Dagenais* 1994). Arguments that legislation does not in fact protect vulnerable groups – such as those made by Justice McLachlin in *Keegstra* (1990), *Rocket* (1990), and *Zundel* (1992) – will now have mandatory doctrinal footings (*Dagenais* 1994). The overall effect will be to make it more difficult for governments to meet the criteria of the *Oakes* (1986) test. See, for discussion and application of this new approach, *Egan* 1995, per Justice L'Heureux-Dubé, and *RJR-MacDonald* 1995, per Justice McLachlin.

40 The reason to defer to Parliament or the legislature is sometimes stated by judges in the more traditional terms of legislative supremacy in relation to social and economic policy, rather than concerns that the courts not reverse progressive legislation. See *Egan* 1995, per Justice Sopinka.

41 Historical swings in the U.S. Supreme Court, including the most recent to the right, support this point. See notes 3 and 4, above, and accompanying text.

42 Though I wrote this line prior to the Court's decision in *RJR-MacDonald* 1995, that case provides chilling support for my prediction. Justice McLachlin, in her majority judgment, departs explicitly from the spirit of earlier decisions, such as *Edwards Books* (1986) and *Irwin* (1989), which call for deference to social and economic policy that protects vulnerable groups. Chief Justice Lamer and Justices Major and Sopinka depart from their strong insistence on deference to Parliament, voiced only a couple of months earlier in *Egan* (1995) and *Thibodeau* (1995).

Chapter 7: Judges and Dominant Ideology

1 Criticism of judges can be found in popular, professional, and academic forums for, among other things, their sexism in the way they deal with sexual assault cases, their racism in the way they approach First Nations and other peoples, and, more generally, their conservative, sometimes reactionary, perspective. Governments, governing bodies of the legal profession, and professional associations have responded by commissioning reports on systemic bias among judges and lawyers and supporting attempts to ensure greater

gender and racial diversity in judicial appointments, and judges have themselves supported initiatives to deal with these issues (see, for example, Brockman and Chunn 1993; Wilson 1993; Lamer 1996). There continue, however, to be strong voices among the judiciary and legal profession that do not support, and even condemn, such initiatives, arguing that they politicize the judicial process, undermine judicial independence, and represent enforcement of 'political correctness' (see Peacock 1996, xii, for an academic version of this critique). Advocates of this view are usually quick to point out that criticism of the judiciary is per se unfair because judges are unable to respond to such criticism, and that the proper role of the legal profession is therefore to come to the judiciary's defence.

2 There is a vast literature in the field of sociology of law that deals with the relationship between law and dominant ideologies in the context of adjudication. See, for example, Cotterrell 1984; Hunt 1985; Gavigan 1988; Kline 1993; 1994.

3 The Canadian Bar Association's (CBA's) membership database showed that 15 per cent of provincially and federally appointed judges are women (Albert 1996). Breakdown by jurisdiction of federally appointed women judges in 1990: federal courts (14 per cent), Alberta (12 per cent), British Columbia (9 per cent), Manitoba (12.5 per cent), New Brunswick (3 per cent), Newfoundland (7 per cent), Northwest Territories (0 per cent), Nova Scotia (7 per cent), Ontario (8 per cent), Prince Edward Island (12.5 per cent), Quebec (8 per cent), Saskatchewan (9.5 per cent), Yukon (0 per cent). For the country as a whole, there were seventy-five women among 854 federally appointed judges (information as of 1 April 1990, provided by the constituency office of Minister of Justice Kim Campbell).

4 On the basis of interviews with chief justices' secretaries in the provincial and superior courts of the four western provinces, there were seven provincial and superior court judges in these jurisdictions who were members of visible minority groups as of 30 April 1990.

5 The proportion of appointments by the first Mulroney government (1984–8) of persons with known connections to the Progressive Conservative party range from a high of 88 per cent in Manitoba to a low of 31 per cent in British Columbia. Altogether, 48 per cent of 225 federal judicial appointments were of such persons (Russell and Ziegel 1989). The CBA has reported that 'political favouritism has played no part in appointments' of provincial court judges in Alberta, British Columbia, Newfoundland, Saskatchewan, and Northwest Territories. However, the CBA compiled its data from statements made by judges and politicians (Canadian Bar Association 1985, 37–8 and 57–8).

6 A 1989 study by the Canadian Financial Aid Project found that 65 per cent of the 1,718 law students surveyed indicated that their parents earned over $45,000 annually. The greatest proportion of students' parents (37.1 per cent) earned over $75,000 annually. A 1988 survey of incoming students to Osgoode Hall Law School found that 7 per cent reported annual family incomes in excess of $250,000, 37 per cent in excess of

$100,000, and 65 per cent in excess of $60,000; 85 per cent of students were white (survey by Professor Neil Brooks, Osgoode Hall Law School, York University). In a 1992 survey, 12 per cent of law students identified themselves as members of a visible minority, and 18 per cent said that their parents income was below average; the remainder were split equally between average and above average (Meredith and Pasquette 1992).

7 The large majority of law professors are white and male. By one estimate there were only ten non-white law professors in Canada (*Vancouver Sun* 1994).

8 As noted in Arthurs (1983, 19): 'Law study and law practice are effectively beyond the reach of many able but disadvantaged groups.' This problem has been partly addressed by what are often referred to as 'discretionary' programs, which usually involve a certain percentage of spots being devoted to individuals who may not meet the general requirements for admission but who have other life experience that compensates for this (see Special Advisory Committee 1992).

9 Part-time law programs are rare, and those that exist are limited in scope. Half-time LLB programs for applicants demonstrating family, financial, or health hardship and, in exceptional circumstances, are available in several universities: British Columbia, Saskatchewan, Toronto, Victoria, and Windsor.

10 Also see chapter 1, above. This is reflected not only in the content of legal education but also in the narrow and hierarchical case method through which most areas of law are taught; most courses do not venture beyond detailed dissection of one appellant case after another. Duncan Kennedy (1985) argues that this method is in itself a form of 'training for hierarchy,' helping socialize students for an elite profession.

11 Though you would not know this from listening to complaints from the bar and within law faculties that 'political correctness' is taking over legal education. According to Peacock (1996, x): 'The materialists, postmaterialists, and feminists ... constitute the mainstream of legal academic scholarship, a rigid orthodoxy that has had an unparalleled influence on constitutional reform, interpretation and theory in Canada.'

12 The content of such discourses will depend on the particular mix in a given time and place of emerging, fading, sedimented, local, and global elements; this process in turn is shaped by the particular compromises and divisions existing within a dominant social bloc and society as a whole (Eagleton 1991). For an example of conflict among dominant ideologies in legal discourse, see Finkleman's (1987) discussion of conflict in the pre-Civil War United States between local dominant ideologies (relating to slavery) and national ones (relating to capitalist industrialization).

13 Judicial appointments of NDPers are rare, but not unheard of (especially in provinces where the NDP has held power) – David Vickers and Tom Berger, both BC stalwarts of the party, were appointed by Ottawa to the province's Supreme Court (though Berger later left the bench).

14 Examples of the influence of dominant ideological thought of a conservative and reactionary nature on judicial decisions are well documented. The presence and effects of

racist ideological discourses in legal decisions, for example, have been demonstrated in a number of studies. Taken together, these studies suggest that in a wide variety of areas of law stereotypes and derogatory images of racialized groups play an important role in the reasons that judges offer in support of their decisions (see Clamore 1992; Fisher 1993; Kline 1994). Similarly, dominant ideological discourses relating to female sexuality have been shown in a number of analyses to inform the way in which judges explain and justify their decisions in sexual assault cases (Smart 1989; Wilson 1990; M. Smith 1993); and the dominant ideology of motherhood – the 'constellation of ideas and images in western capitalist societies that constitute the dominant ideals of motherhood against which women's lives are judged' (Kline 1993, 310) – is another area where links have been drawn between gender ideologies and judicial discourse (Boyd, 1989; Gavigan 1993; Kline 1993; Mosoff 1995).

15 When asked why CLC President Bob White had never been asked to do a commentary for CBC, producer Peter Hutchinson said: 'We don't have labour do Commentary' (O'Brien 1995). Media enterprises are not, however, the only knowledge-producing institutions that contribute to the dominance of negative discourses about unions. Employers, especially in non-union workplaces, make use of their regular access to employees to propagandize against unions; business and government leaders often blame low productivity, high deficits, and costly goods and services on unions; school curricula do not generally cover the history and operations of the labour movement; and so on (Freedman and Medoff 1984; Puette 1992).

16 Survey data suggests that negative images of unions are widespread and seem to be stronger when unions are weaker (Puette 1992). A more subtle, sophisticated, and increasingly apparent variation of anti-union themes can be found in the notion that unions, though perhaps necessary in the industrial economies of the past, have no place in a post-industrial age. More than being anachronistic, the argument goes, they stand in the way of moving towards more efficient, and even more enlightened, modes of workplace organization (see chapter 5). Unions' attempts to establish stable, protective regimes for their members are viewed as self-interested and as contrary to the public's interest in development of more flexible production.

17 The presence of business sections in newspapers, business reports on television and radio, business panels on CBC's *Morningside*, and so on implies that business's interests are inseparable from those of the more general public – a construction that contrasts sharply with the constructions of other groups, such as labour, the women's movement, and environmentalists.

18 The apparent influence of dominant ideological thought in these areas is, however, neither new nor unique to Charter law. The anti-union orientation of courts' historical treatment of organized labour is notorious (Griffiths 1981; Schneider 1982; Arthurs 1983; Holt 1984; Fudge 1989; Glasbeek 1990; Macklem 1992). Courts have consistently portrayed unions as pursuing the narrow interests of their membership at the

expense of society as a whole, represented strikes as harmful because they interrupt production, and constructed picketing as coercive, violent, and irrational. Recognition of the difficulties posed by these kinds of attitudes for the administration of collective-bargaining legislation provided much of the impetus in the postwar period for creating specialized administrative tribunals to interpret and apply collective bargaining laws (Manwarring 1982; Arthurs 1983). Judicial attitudes towards labour were viewed as strongly informed and reinforced by more general ideologies in law – particularly those of private property rights, individualism, and anti-collectivism – and it was thought best to take the bulk of labour-relations issues out of the hands of judges altogether. Such attitudes are not mere relics of the past. Chief Justice Lamer noted on his appointment as chief justice that he considers himself a 'libertarian' and that because 'it's usually collectivities that are despotic ... Whenever in doubt, I'll come down on the side of the individual' (*Vancouver Sun*, 27 June 1990).

   Just as judicial attitudes towards labour in Charter cases can be traced to pre-Charter jurisprudence, so too can those about corporations. Many studies have demonstrated that courts have a tendency to favour corporate parties and to equate their interests with those of society as a whole (Glasbeek 1984; Bakan and Blomley 1992). In relation to advertising, the area of corporate activity being analysed here, there is a long history of judicial interpretations of common law and legislation that reveals a favourable attitude towards advertising (Preston 1975; Black 1988).

19 The Court has held that both picketing and advertising are forms of expression and thus protected by the Charter's guarantee of freedom of expression. With respect to picketing, the Court has noted: 'There is involved at least some element of expression. The picketers would be conveying a message which at a very minimum could be classed as persuasion, aimed at deterring customers from doing business with the respondent' (*Dolphin Delivery* 1986, 586). About advertising, the Court has stated: 'Surely it aims to convey a meaning, and cannot be excluded as having no expressive content. Nor is there any basis for excluding the form of expression chosen from the sphere of protected activity' (*Irwin Toy* 1989, 971).

20 According to the Court, the 'action' element of picketing does not necessarily deny it an expressive element. The Court adds, however, that 'freedom [of expression], of course would not extend to protect threats of violence or acts of violence. It would not protect the destruction of property, or assaults, or other clearly unlawful conduct' (*Dolphin Delivery* 1986, 588; also see *BCGEU* 1988, per Justice McIntyre). The message is clear: while the expressive element of picketing must be acknowledged, one must always be wary of the potential for, even if there is not actual, violence. This point is reinforced by the way in which the Court lumps together its discussion of picketing in *Irwin Toy* (1989) with its observation that murder and rape do not count as forms of expression (970).

21 This latter quote, taken by Chief Justice Dickson from *Heather Hill* (1966), is followed

in the original case with some xenophobic comments by the judge: 'In discussing the conduct of union members it may not be amiss to recognize that a high percentage of unions are dominated by persons from another State whose basic concepts of law, order, good conduct and labour relations are not necessarily ours, but whose control seems almost to be absolute. The fundamental (and it may be entirely proper) view held by one country may be entirely inappropriate to another' (13–14, per Justice Stewart).

22 The Court, in *Dolphin Delivery* (1986) and *BCGEU* (1988), was so convinced of picketing's coercive nature that it failed to give due weight to the character of the actual picketing at issue in each case. Indeed, in *Dolphin Delivery* no picketing had even occurred, as the case concerned an application for prior restraint of picketing. In *BCGEU* there were no facts on the record suggesting that the picketing was violent or coercive, and what facts there were (an affidavit of a lawyer) suggested that pickets in no way impeded access to the courts. Nobody was prevented from entering the courthouse; even those individuals who wished to respect the picket line but who had urgent business in the courthouse were provided a means for crossing the line and salving their conscience.

23 *Rocket* (1990) and *RJR-MacDonald* (1995) are discussed above, in chapter 6. Legal analysts other than Supreme Court judges also are a bit sanguine about the positive potential of advertising. A leading constitutional commentator, Robert Sharpe (1987, 235) (now an Ontario judge), said: 'There is nothing in the marketplace of ideas analysis which calls for its restriction to the subjects of politics or art. There is an interest in having the *truth* about material goods and services, and some advertising provides consumers with information needed to assess the *truth* about available products and their prices. It is not unimportant to many to know which car goes fastest, uses least fuel or lasts longest. Commercial speech provides consumers with that kind of information, and to the extent that it provides the information needed to make accurate choices, I suggest that if one accepts the market-place of ideas analysis, there is a strong case that commercial speech should be protected as a form of expression ... The purpose of protecting expression in the commercial sphere, I suggest, is to ensure that consumers have the information they need to make choices' (235).

The contrast between the Court's reasoning about advertising, as performing a public service, and the notion in the labour cases that unions are involved in purely economic activities, is not a result of the judges' not being exposed to alternative arguments. In *Ford* (1988), the first commercial-expression case, for example, the attorney general of Quebec's factum stated: 'A guarantee of freedom of expression which embraces commercial advertising would be the protection of an economic right ... This court, in refusing to constitutionalize the right to strike, has recognized that the Canadian Charter does not extend to economic rights or freedoms' (763).

The Court's fondness for commercial expression appears confined to mainstream business concerns. When sex workers argued that restrictions on communicating for the purpose of selling sexual services violate freedom of expression, the Court easily found that the limitation could be justified under section 1. Soliciting for sex, the majority held, was purely economic and not at the core of section 2(b)'s protection, and it caused a nuisance and harmed the interests of mainstream business concerns (*Prostitution Reference* 1990).

24 Technically, in the picketing cases, the burden of proof under section 1 is on those asserting that picketing causes harm (*Oakes* 1986). However, because the Court presumes that picketing is per se harmful, no evidence is required to make the case in favour of restricting it, and the burden is close to meaningless (*Dolphin Delivery* 1986; *BCGEU* 1988). In sharp contrast, the cases on commercial expression are notable for the high hurdles set under section 1 for justifying restrictions and the abundance of argument and social scientific evidence that the Court considers. Even with this, in only one of the four major commercial-expression cases (*Ford* 1988; *Irwin Toy* 1989; *Rocket* 1990; *RJR-MacDonald* 1995) – *Irwin Toy* (1989) – did the Court uphold such a restriction, and there it was because the social-scientific evidence overwhelmingly supported the proposition that television advertising directed at children is manipulative (implying, at least in the way the Court interpreted it, that regular advertising is not). *RJR-MacDonald* (1995) reveals how substantial the burden is for a government seeking to justify restrictions on advertising. The majority in that case refused to uphold a ban on cigarette advertising on the ground that 'logic and reason' suggest that not all such advertising increases cigarette consumption, and no evidence is offered by the government to refute this presumption. At the same time, the majority appears to accept the view that no evidence could refute the presumption, given the difficulties in proving definitively a link between advertising and consumption, and thus implies that its sense of 'logic and reason' is superior to that of Parliament.

25 The blatant unfairness of bringing in replacement workers, which substantially undermines striking workers' bargaining power, is often what generates emotion and sometimes violence on a picket line. Recognition of this has led to legislative bans on using replacement workers during a strike in British Columbia, Ontario (repealed), and Quebec.

26 The Court's uncritical acceptance of the 'signal' conception of union members' unwillingness to cross a picket line presumes that it is irrational to make a decision on the basis of a pre-existing political or moral belief: if generalized, this view would lead to characterizations of most political actions and positions as irrational – it would be irrational for Jewish people to be against anti-semitism; or for women to challenge sexism; or for Liberals to vote for the Liberal party.

Workers who risk being disciplined by their union if they cross a picket line are, arguably, not making an entirely free choice. But here it is not the picket line that constrains them, but the union's constitution. This is not, in other words, a basis for dubbing picket lines coercive. The picket line informs employees that a strike is on, but it has no authority to discipline employees who choose to break a strike – that authority remains with the union and employer. While crossing a picket line is 'the classic example of strike breaking' (Adams 1993, 786), it is not the crossing of the picket line per se that is the breach; rather, it is the employee's returning to work during a strike. An employee would be just as much a strikebreaker if she were brought onto the employer's property to resume work at a time when no pickets were up (because of, say, a snowstorm) as if she physically crossed the picket line to return to work.

27 See discussion of *Dolphin Delivery* (1986), above, chapter 2. Moreover, according to a far-reaching study of trade unions, unions have a positive effect on the economic system as a whole in that they contribute to efficiency, equality in the workplace, and political and economic freedom (Freedman and Medhoff 1984). This is not to deny that strikes cause inconvenience and that members of society not immediately involved in a dispute might be negatively affected; it is only to suggest that rights to strike and picket, and the exercise of those rights, also serve the interests of members of the public in providing measures through which unionized employees can achieve decent benefits and working conditions, with indirect benefits to non-union employees. See *Lavigne* 1991, per Justice LaForest, for a discussion of the benefits of unionism to workers and democracy in general (and an example of the way in which contradictory ideological elements influence judicial discourse).

28 According to Goldsen (1980, as cited in Parenti 1986): 'Commercials do not announce [a product's price] nor accurately represent its size, weight and dimensions. On the contrary, such features are intentionally distorted by tricks of staging, such as special camera angles and lighting, and by tricks of wording, such as "family size" or "economy size." Product descriptions are vague and ambiguous. Ingredients, for example, are rarely mentioned, certainly not by generic name. On the contrary, they are often deliberately disguised by invented terms: "painreliever," "antiwetness spray product," "cough suppressant," "sleep remedy," "germ-chaser," and so on. Food and candy are described as "chocolaty" or "peanuty" glossing over how much real chocolate or real peanuts are used, if any. Breakfast foods are described as "yummy," never as "sugary." Who it is that produces products advertised on television often remains a mystery. Brand names are stressed, but not corporate ownerships or affiliations; it is a rare television watcher who knows that the company producing Twinkies and Wonderbread is owned by General Mills, that Creative Playthings is owned by CBS, Inc., that White Cloud and Charmin – toilet paper rivals on the air – are both made by companies which Proctor and Gamble owns. For what reason does General Mills, a food and agricultural conglomerate, sell toys, while ITT, an international conglomerate that once specialized in communications, sells food? Commercials do not tell.' See, for similar analyses, Black 1988.

29 He states further: 'Rationality plays only a small part in our total motivational makeup ... Human beings use two modes of expressive thought, not just one. The process of analytical, logical, common sense thinking is entirely different from that used in creative imagination and intuition ... The creative person in advertising uses both modes of

expression. But many of the symbols which he uses to convey meanings, often more important than the rational meanings, are just not expressible in literal terms, because they are connected with a different process of thought' (Martineau 1957, 200).

Research on the brain demonstrates that the rational/emotive dichotomy may be reflected in brain organization, with rational thought being more associated with the left hemisphere of the brain and emotive thought with the right (Paul Bakan 1977–8). The advertising industry has been quick to incorporate this research into its strategies, with one firm advising advertisers that perfume and beer ads should be pitched to the right side of the brain, and car and insurance ads to the left. In a similar vein, the manager of public opinion research for General Electric commented that 'much of response to advertising is right brain' (cited in Bagdikian 1987, 185).

30 A concise summary of the critique can be found in a report prepared by UNESCO on advertising. 'Regarded as a form of communication, it (advertising) has been criticized for playing on emotions, simplifying real human situations into stereotypes, exploiting anxieties, and employing techniques of intensive persuasion that amount to manipulation. Many social critics have stated that advertising is essentially concerned with exalting the materialistic virtues of consumption by exploiting achievement drives and emulative anxieties, employing tactics of hidden manipulation, playing on emotions, maximizing appeal and minimizing information, trivializing, eliminating objective considerations, contriving illogical situations, and generally reducing man, women and children to the role of irrational consumer' (cited in Pollay 1986, 21).

31 For an excellent description and analysis of the various devices used by advertisers to achieve this, see Black 1988, 546–56.

32 For further discussion of lesbians' and gays' engagement with the Charter, see chapter 3.

33 The argument for toleration is bolstered in the view of these judges by the historical fact that 'homosexuals, whether as individuals or couples, form an identifiable minority who have suffered and continue to suffer serious social, political and economic disadvantage' (600–1).

34 Herman (1994) makes this point in relation to the immutability approach, but I believe her insight applies as well to the 'choice approach' as developed by the judges in *Egan* (1995).

35 Though Justice LaForest uses the gender-neutral terminology of 'single parents' in the relevant passage, one can infer that he means single mothers, since most single parents are women.

Chapter 8: Rights as Political Discourse

1 The Charlottetown Accord (Canada 1992a) was an agreement to amend the Canadian constitution reached by federal, provincial (including Quebec), and First Nations leaders in Charlottetown, Prince Edward Island, in August 1992. It was the culmination of

a two-year process of public consultations and intensive negotiations that followed
failure of an earlier package of constitutional amendments in 1990 (the Meech Lake
Accord) (see Canada 1991a; 1992c). Amending the constitution normally requires
agreement by Parliament and legislatures of most or all of the provinces, depending on
the issue. The holding of a referendum on the Charlottetown Accord was viewed as a
political necessity (the process surrounding the Meech Lake Accord had been criticized
for its elitism), but it was not legally required. For more general discussions of the
events leading to the referendum, see Bakan and Pinard 1989; Bakan and Schneiderman 1992.

2 It is, however, questionable whether rights strategies can ever be fully separated from law
and litigation, especially where, as in Canada, abstract rights are part of the constitution
and justiciable (see Scheingold 1989; Fudge and Glasbeek 1992b). In relation to the
Charlottetown Accord, for example, rights claims were made primarily in forums other
than courts and did not centre around a particular litigation (though NWAC at one
point challenged the constitutional amendment process in court: NWAC 1994). But the
claims concerned potential legal effects of entrenching the accord in the constitution.

3 I mean here the set of rights discourses that constitutes the prevailing and generally
unquestioned 'common sense' about what rights are; helps sustain the dominant order
of social relations by allowing that order to be presented as natural and legitimate, mask-
ing social facts that reveal its nastier sides, and universalizing the interests of dominant
groups; and embodies elements sufficiently attractive and believable to command popular support. Dominant rights ideology is thus a particular set of rights discourses. Its elements, identified by the above-noted characteristics, are drawn from a much wider range
of discursive possibilities and vary across history and geography. However, because these
elements constitute the 'common sense' understanding of what rights are in Canadian
society, such contingency is masked (Michael Smith 1993; and see above, chapter 3, on
dominant rights ideology, and chapters 5 and 7, on other ideological phenomena and
processes).

4 The accord dealt as well with a whole range of issues in addition to recognizing Quebec
as a distinct society and creating a structure for First Nations self-government. Among
these were a social rights regime (see Bakan and Schneiderman 1992 and chapter 9,
below), proposals to promote 'free trade' among the provinces, restrictions on the power
of the federal government to spend money in areas outside its legislative jurisdiction,
explicit recognition of provincial jurisdiction in certain areas, and creation of an elected
Senate (see Canada 1991; 1992a; 1992b; and 1992c). In the referendum, voters had to
approve or reject the whole package.

5 Federalism as a political structure primarily governs relations among social collectivities,
usually, but not necessarily, with a territorial base. Federalism poses questions about
what kinds of collectivities – which socio-political units – should have the status of coor-
dinate (as opposed to subordinate) levels of government and thus exclusive political

authority within their constitutionally defined jurisdictions. In Canada, there are currently two kinds of political units so recognized: federal and provincial.

6 Other provinces, too, had concerns about the Charter. The social-democratic NDP government of Saskatchewan was worried about potential constraints on progressive state activism, while the Conservative government in Manitoba condemned the Charter on the basis of right-wing concerns about liberal rights.

7 The Reform party, for example, encapsulated its opposition to the accord in the slogan: 'Equal rights for all, special rights for none' (Cernetig 1992; McFeely 1992; Mel Smith 1992).

8 This presumes, of course, that political divisions exist within social movements – a point too often neglected in social theory. 'Left pluralism' (McClure 1992), for example, discusses social movements as comprised of 'new' identities, such as race and gender, with 'old' political divisions, particularly those of class, no longer relevant (Laclau and Mouffe 1985). Socialist critiques of left-pluralism apparently accept this empirical claim – that social movements lack class politics (Miliband 1991; Fudge and Glasbeek 1992b) – thus denying the presence of socialist groupings within various social movements. Mainstream political theory often portrays social movements as representing particular and narrowly defined interests, in contrast to allegedly universal ones, such as constitutional order (Cairns 1990), quasi-national communities (Taylor 1993), and the 'moral majority' (Knopf and Morton 1992).

9 The issue of their acceptance of non-Charter rights may be another matter.

Chapter 9: What's Wrong with Social Rights?

1 See chapter 4, above, concerning the Court's general refusal to interpret section 15 as including protection of positive rights.

2 I use this term to describe the kind of abstract formulations of rights characteristic of current social charter proposals and instruments, and constitutional discourse more generally. I do not mean to include the more concrete and particular kinds of rights found in social and economic legislation and regulation. As becomes clear below, many of the difficulties with 'social rights' flow from their abstract articulation, not from any problem inherent to regulating social relations through law.

3 The idea of a social charter was first officially proposed in Ontario's (1991) discussion paper of September 1991, though its impetus came from various community and anti-poverty groups. The federal NDP came up with its own proposal as well.

4 As I argue in the chapters above, the fact that a right is broad enough to include reasonably a progressive interpretation indicates only that such an interpretation is possible, not that it is probable.

5 These formulations are taken from the various draft proposals, official and unofficial, that were in circulation before the referendum.

6 The general conservative argument under the social charter will be, as Glasbeek (1992) points out, that the surest route to better health, education, and welfare is economic growth, which is achieved through deregulation and cuts in spending and taxation. Supporters of a social charter seem to forget that the 'right' is not (openly) against a social charter's values. Conservative governments and business groups defend their calls for deregulation, privatization, and low taxes not by saying, 'We want to make more money,' but rather by arguing that such moves will increase competitiveness and, eventually, social welfare.

7 Arguments about the negative effects of strikes and wage increases on consumers of public services are made by governments during public-sector labour disputes. Social rights would give these arguments added bite by grounding them in the language of legal rights.

8 This is a problem under the Charter as well. Interpretations of Charter rights may directly or indirectly require governments to spend money; see discussion of *Schacter* 1992 in chapter 3, above.

9 The most common formulation of social rights in the official and unofficial drafts and proposals of social charters or covenants is in this form. It imposes duties on, or establishes commitments by, governments to provide some service. This is true of the proposal in the legal draft of the Charlottetown Accord.

10 Ross and Shillington (1986) state: 'The overall distributional impact of the income security system ... tends to be rather proportional. The bottom two, and top two quintiles each receive almost 40% of the total benefits, which is identical to their populations. The middle quintile receives a 20% share, also identical to its population share.' This is not surprising. Programs that provide a flat amount regardless of income (Old Age Security, Family Allowance), or provide benefits proportional to income (pension plans, unemployment insurance, tax exemptions) do not have a redistributive effect. The only truly redistributive programs are those that target low-income people (such as Guaranteed Income Supplement, Social Assistance, and a child tax credit) (34–57).

11 The very attraction of rights, and the factor most apparent in popular discourses about them, is that in having a right one has something. A right is 'something to stand on.' It becomes the 'thing,' rather than the basis of a claim to it. In discussing 'rights fetishism,' Kerruish (1991, 4) says: 'What seems to happen is that these general rules somehow cast loose of their moorings as deliberately formulated standards for human action and float off to constitute a realm of the sacred.' This kind of dynamic may be useful for mobilization of political struggle (on both the right and the left), or it may be coopting and promote complacency (see, above, chapter 8).

Chapter 10: Conclusion

1 Though, as I noted in chapter 1, there is much in Mandel and Hutchinson's works with which I do agree.

2 With respect to the latter, for example, it has been suggested by the Dominion Bond Rating Service that 93 per cent of federal debt since 1984, and the more than five-fold increase in federal debt since that time, resulted primarily from compounding interest on a relatively modest program-expenditure deficiency (Cameron and Finn 1996, 3).

3 Professor Vickery, recent recipient of the Nobel Prize in economics, argued that balancing the U.S. federal budget would send the U.S. economy into a tailspin, with 15 per cent unemployment and a stock market crash. He proposed that tripling the deficit over a period of time would boost purchasing power and bring unemployment down to 1 per cent (*Globe and Mail* 1996).

References

Adams, George. 1993. *Canadian Labour Law*. Aurora, Ont.: Canada Law Book.

Albert, Alain. 1996. Electronic mail communication. On file with author. Communications, Canadian Bar Association. Ottawa. 3 April.

Angus, Ian, and Sut Jhally. 1989. 'Introduction.' In Ian Angus and Sut Jhally, eds., *Cultural Politics in Contemporary America*. New York: Routledge.

Anthias, Pleya, and Nira Yuval-Davis. 1992. *Racialized Boundaries: Race, Nation, Gender, Color and Class and the Anti-Racist Struggle*. New York: Routledge.

Arthurs, Harry. 1983. *Law and Learning: Report to the Social Sciences and Humanties Research Council of Canada by the Consultative Group on Research in Education in Law*. Ottawa: Minister of Supply and Services.

– 1988. 'The Right to Golf.' *Queen's Law Journal*, 13, 17.

Asch, M., and P. Macklem. 1991. 'Aboriginal Rights and Canadian Sovereignty: An Essay on *R. v. Sparrow*.' *Alberta Law Review*, 29, 498.

Bagdikian, Ben. 1987. *The Media Monopoly*. 2nd ed. Boston: Beacon Press.

Bakan, Joel. 1985. 'Pornography, Law and Moral Theory.' *Ottawa Law Review*, 17, 1.

– 1989. 'Partiality and Legitimacy in Constitutional Theory.' Legal Theory Workshop, Series 4, Faculty of Law, University of Toronto.

– 1990. 'Strange Expectations: A Review of Two Theories of Judicial Review.' *McGill Law Journal*, 35, 439.

– 1991. 'Constitutional Interpretation and Social Change: You Can't Always Get What You Want (Nor What You Need).' *Canadian Bar Review*, 70, 307.

– 1992a. 'Against Constitutional Property Rights.' In Duncan Cameron and Miriam Smith, eds., *Constitutional Politics*. Toronto: Lorimer.

– 1992b. 'Some Hard Questions about the Hard Cases Question.' *University of Toronto Law Journal*, 42, 504.

– 1995. 'Why B.C. Abortion-Protest Limits Will Likely Endure.' *Vancouver Sun*, 21 June, A11.

Bakan, Joel, and Nick Blomley. 1992. 'Spatial Boundaries, Legal Categories and the Judicial Mapping of the Worker.' *Environment and Planning*, 24, 629.

Bakan, Joel, Bruce Ryder, David Schneiderman, and Margot Young. 1995. 'Developments in Constitutional Law: The 1993–94 Term.' *Supreme Court Law Review*, 6, 67.

Bakan, Joel, and D. Pinard. 1989. 'Getting to the Bottom of Meech Lake.' *Ottawa Law Review*, 21, 247.

Bakan, Joel, and David Schneiderman. 1992. 'Introduction.' In Joel Bakan and David Schneiderman, eds., *Social Justice and the Constitution: Perspectives on a Social Union for Canada*. Ottawa: Carleton University Press.

Bakan, Paul. 1977–8. 'Dreaming, REM Sleep and the Right Hemisphere: A Theoretical Integration.' *Journal of Altered States of Consciousness*, 3, 285.

Bakker, Isabella, ed. 1994. *The Strategic Silence: Gender and Economic Policy*. London: Zed.

Barlow, John. 1995. 'Is There a There in Cyberspace?' *UTNE Reader* (March–April), 52.

Barlow, Maude, and Heather-Jane Robertson. 1994. *Class Warfare: The Assault on Canada's Schools*. Toronto: Key Porter Books.

Barrett, Michele. 1991. *The Politics of Truth: From Marx to Foucault*. Stanford, Calif.: Stanford University Press.

Bartholomew, Amy, and Alan Hunt. 1990. 'What's Wrong with Rights?' *Journal of Law and Inequality*, 9, 1.

Baumeister, A.F., J. Kupstas, and L. Klindworth. 1991. 'The New Morbidity.' *American Behavioral Scientist*, 34, 468.

Beard, Charles. 1986. *An Economic Interpretation of the Constitution of the United States*. Reprint. New York: Free Press.

Beatty, David. 1987. 'Constitutional Conceits: The Coercive Authority of Courts.' *University of Toronto Law Journal*, 37, 183.

– 1987b. *Putting the Charter to Work: Designing a Constitutional Labour Code*. Montreal: McGill-Queen's University Press.

– 1991. 'Labouring Outside the Charter.' *Osgoode Hall Law Journal*, 29, 839.

Beatty, David, and S. Kennet. 1988. 'Striking Back: Fighting Words, Social Protest and Political Participation in Free and Democratic Societies.' *Canadian Bar Review*, 67, 573.

Beaudoin, G.A., and D. Dobbie. 1992. Report of the Special Joint Committee on a Renewed Canada. 28 Feb. Ottawa.

Beckton, C. 1983. 'Freedom of Expression: Access to the Courts.' *Canadian Bar Review*, 61, 101.

Beltrame, Julian. 1995. 'Top U.S. Judges Turn Back Clock.' *Vancouver Sun*, 6 July, A11.

Bennet, Tony. 1990. *Outside Literature*. London: Routledge.

Besser, H. 1995. 'From Internet to Information Superhighway.' In J. Brook and I.A. Boal, eds., *Resisting the Virtual Life*. San Francisco: City Lights.

Black, Vaughan. 1988. 'A Brief Word about Advertising.' *Ottawa Law Review*, 20, 509.

Boddy, Trevor. 1992. 'Underground and Overhead: Building the Analogous City.' In Michael Sorkin, ed., *Variations on a Theme Park*. New York: Noonday Press.

Bogart, William. 1994. *Courts and Country: The Limits of Litigation and the Political and Social Life of Canada*. Toronto: Oxford University Press.

Borrows, John. 1992a. 'A Genealogy of Law: Inherent Sovereignty and First Nations Self-Government.' *Osgoode Hall Law Journal*, 30, 291.

– 1992b. 'Negotiating Treaties and Land Claims: The Impact of Diversity within First Nations Property Interests.' *Windsor Yearbook of Access to Justice*, 12, 79.

– 1996. Fish and Chips: Aboriginal Commercial Fishing and Gambling Rights in the Supreme Court of Canada. Unpublished manuscript on file with the author.

Boyd, Susan. 1991. 'Some Postmodernist Challenges to Feminist Analyses of Law, Family and State: Ideology and Discourse in Child Custody Law.' *Canadian Journal of Family Law*, 10, 79.

– 1993. 'Peculiar Paradoxes: Legal Regulation of Families and Women's Lives.' *Canadian Journal of Law and Society*, 8, 171.

– 1994. '(Re)Placing the State: Family, Law and Oppression.' *Canadian Journal of Law and Society*, 9, 39.

Braden, G. 1948. 'The Search for Objectivity in Constitutional Law.' *Yale Law Journal*, 57, 571.

Brest, P. 1981–2. 'Interpretation and Interest.' *Stanford Law Review*, 34, 765.

Brock, Kathy. 1993. 'Polishing the Halls of Justice: Sections 24(2) and 8 of the Charter of Rights.' *National Journal of Constitutional Law*, 2, 265.

Brockman, Joan, and Dorothy Chunn, eds. 1993. *Investigating Gender Bias: Law, Courts and the Legal Profession*. Toronto: Thompson Educational Publishing.

Brodie, Janine. 1995. *Politics on the Margins: Restructuring and the Canadian Women's Movement*. Halifax: Fernwood.

Brodsky, Gwen. 1992. 'Social Charter Issues.' In Joel Bakan and David Schneiderman, eds., *Social Justice and the Constitution: Perspectives on a Social Union for Canada*. Ottawa: Carleton University Press.

Brodsky, Gwen, and Shelagh Day. 1989. *Canadian Charter Equality Rights for Women: One Step Forward or Two Steps Back?* Ottawa: Canadian Advisory Council on the Status of Women.

Brook, J., and I.A. Boal, eds. 1995. *Resisting the Virtual Life*. San Francisco: City Lights.

Brooks, Neil. 1989. Survey for Canadian Financial Aid Project. Unpublished, on file with author. North York, Ont.: Osgoode Hall Law School.

– 1996a. Attacks by the Right on the Public Sector are Based on Myths the Left Can Puncture. Unpublished manuscript on file with the author.

– 1996b. *Left* vs. *Right*. Ottawa: Centre for Policy Alternatives.

Brown, Wendy. 1995. *States of Injury: Power and Freedom in Late Modernity*. Princeton, NJ: Princeton University Press.

Buber, M. 1951. *Two Types of Faith*. New York: Collier Books.

Cairns, Alan. 1971. 'The Judicial Committee and Its Critics. *Canadian Journal of Political Science*, 4, 301.

– 1990. 'Constitutional Minoritarianism in Canada.' In R.L. Watts, ed., *Canada: The State of the Federation 1990.* Kingston: Institute of International Government Relations.

Calvert, John. 1984. *Government Limited.* Ottawa. Canadian Council for Policy Alternatives.

Cameron, Duncan. 1989. 'Unemployment-Benefit Cuts Legislate Poverty.' *Financial Post,* 12 Oct., 11.

Cameron, D., and E. Finn. 1996. *Ten Deficit Myths.* Ottawa: Centre for Policy Alternatives.

Canada. 1981. *Royal Commission on Newspapers (Kent Commission).* Ottawa: Ministry of Supply and Services.

– 1986. *Funding of the Arts in Canada to the Year 2000.* Ottawa: Task Force on Funding of the Arts.

– 1988. *A Broadcasting Policy for Canada: A Report of the Standing Committee on Communications and Culture.*

– 1988b. *Canadian Voices, Canadian Choices.* Ottawa.

– 1991. *Shaping Canada's Future Together.* Ottawa: Minister of Supply and Services.

– 1992a. *Charlottetown Accord Draft Legal Text.* 8 May. Ottawa: Queen's Printer.

– 1992b. *Consensus Report on the Constitution.* 28 Aug. Ottawa: Canadian Intergovernmental Conference.

– 1992c. *Gender Equality in the Canadian Justice System.* Ottawa: Department of Justice.

– 1992d. *A Renewed Canada: The Report of the Special Joint Committee of the Senate and House of Commons.* Prepared by G.-A. Beaudoin and D. Dobbie. 28 Feb. Ottawa: Queen's Printer.

– 1995. 'Flexible Workstyles: in the future workplace, fewer workers will have full-time, permanent jobs.' *World Backgrounder,* 60 no. 5 (March), 20.

Canadian Association of University Teachers Bulletin. 1995. 42, 7.

Canadian Bar Association. 1985. *The Appointment of Judges in Canada.* Committee Report. Ottawa.

Canadian Broadcasting Corporation. 1994–5. *Annual Report.* Ottawa: CBC.

Canadian Charter of Rights and Freedoms, Constitution Act, 1982, Part I, enacted as Schedule B to the Canada Act, 1982, (U.K.) 1982, c. 11.

Canadian Dimension. 1995. 'NAC: Issues and Strengths, National Action Committee on the Status of Women.' Oct.–Nov., 24 no. 5, 19.

Canadian Press, and Staff. 1992. 'Women's Group Says No.' *Globe and Mail,* 14 Sept., A1.

Canadian Press (CP) News. 1995. 'Survey Suggests Millions of Canadians Have Access to the Internet.' 23 June.

Canadian Women's Studies. 1994. Saying Goodbye to Healthsharing Magazine,' 14 no. 3 (summer), 117.

Carstairs, Sharon. 1992. 'Some Good Reasons for Voting No.' *Winnipeg Free Press,* 27 Sept. A7.

Cernetig, Miro. 1992. 'Reform Attacks Native Self-Rule.' *Globe and Mail*, 5 Oct., A1.

– 1994. 'Mystique Forfeited for Reality of Cash.' *Globe and Mail*, 31 Oct., A5.

– 1996. 'Salmon Plan Devastating, Report Says.' 10 Oct., A8.

Christian, T.J., and K.D. Ewing. 1988. 'Labouring under the Canadian Constitution.' *Industrial Law Journal*, 17, 73.

Clamore, John. 1992. 'Critical Race Theory, Archie Shepp, and Fire Music: Securing an Authentic Intellectual Life in a Multicultural World.' *Southern California Law Review*, 65, 2129.

Clark, Gordon. 1989. *Unions and Communities under Siege: American Communities and the Crisis of Organized Labour*. Cambridge: Cambridge University Press.

Clark, Lorenne. 1990. 'Liberalism and the Living Tree: Women, Equality and the Charter.' *Alberta Law Review*, 28, 384.

Clement, W.H.P. 1916. *The Law of the Canadian Constitution*. 3rd ed. Toronto: Carswell.

Cohen, F. 1935. 'Transcendental Nonsense and the Functional Approach.' *Columbia Law Review*, 35, 809.

Cohen, Margorie. 1987. *Free Trade and the Future of Women's Work*. Toronto: Garamond Press.

Cohen, Morris. 1978. 'Property and Sovereignty.' In C.B. Macpherson, ed., *Property: Mainstream and Critical Positions*. Toronto: University of Toronto Press.

Cohen, Neil. 1993. 'Disciplining Labour – Gutting Unemployment Insurance.' *Canadian Dimension*, (March–April), 38.

Conklin, William. 1989. *Images of a Constitution*. Toronto: University of Toronto Press.

Coombe, Rosemary. 1989. 'Same As It Ever Was: Rethinking the Politics of Legal Interpretation.' *McGill Law Journal*, 34, 603.

Cooper, Davina. 1993. 'The Citizen's Charter and Radical Democracy: Empowerment and Exclusion within Citizenship Discourse.' *Social and Legal Studies*, 2, 149.

– 1994. 'Productive, Relational and Everwhere? Conceptualising Power and Resistance within Foucauldian Feminism.' *Sociology*, 28, 435.

– 1995. *Power in Struggle: Feminism, Sexuality and the State*. Buckingham: Open University Press.

Cooper, Davina, and Didi Herman. 1991. 'Getting the Family "Right": Legislating Heterosexuality in Britain, 1986–1991.' *Canadian Journal of Family Law*, 10, 41.

Cornell, D. 1988. 'Insitutionalization of Meaning, Recollective Imagination and the Potential for Transformative Legal Interpretation.' *University of Pennsylvania Law Review*, 136, 1135.

Cossman, Brenda. 1990. 'Dancing in the Dark.' *Windsor Yearbook: Access to Justice*, 10, 223.

Cotterrell, R. 1984. *The Sociology of Law: An Introduction*. London: Butterworths.

– 1992. 'Realism, Pragmatism and the Appellate Judge.' *Modern Law Review*, 54, 594.

Crawford, Margaret. 1992. 'The World in a Shopping Mall.' In Michael Sorkin, ed., *Variations on a Theme Park*. New York: Noonday Press.

Crenshaw, Kimberle. 1988. 'Race, Reform and Retrenchment: Transformation and Legitimation in Anti-Discrimination Law.' *Harvard Law Review*, 101, 1331.

Curran, James, and Jean Seaton. 1991. *Power without Responsibility: The Press and Broadcasting in Britain*. 4th ed. London: Routledge.

Currie, Dawn H., and Marlee Kline. 1991. 'Challenging Privilege: Women, Knowledge and Feminist Struggles.' *Journal of Human Justice*, 2, 1.

Davies, Kath, Julienne Dickey, and Teresa Stratford, eds. 1987. *Out of Focus: Writings on Women and the Media*. London. Women's Press.

Davis, Mike. 1992. 'Fortress Los Angeles: The Militarization of Urban Space.' In Michael Sorkin, ed., *Variations on a Theme Park*. New York: Noonday Press.

Day, Shelagh. 1992. 'What's Wrong with the Canada Clause.' *Canadian Forum*, 71 (Oct.), 21.

DeCoste, Ted. 1993. 'Taking Torts Progressively.' In Cooper-Stephenson and E. Gibson, eds., *Tort Theory*. North York, Ont.: Captus University Publications.

Delamothe, T. 1991. 'Social Inequalities in Health.' *British Medical Journal*, 303, 1046.

Dickson, Brian. 1986. 'Legal Education.' *Canadian Bar Review*, 64, 374.

Doyle, L. 1979. *The Political Economy of Health*. London: Pluto.

Drache, Daniel, ed., with John O'Grady. 1992. *Getting on Track: Social Democratic Strategies for Ontario*. Montreal: McGill-Queen's University Press.

Drache, Daniel, and Harry Glasbeek. 1989. 'The New Fordism in Canada: Capital's Offensive, Labour's Opportunity.' *Osgoode Hall Law Journal*, 27, 517.

– 1992. *The Changing Workplace: Reshaping Canada's Industrial Relations System*. Toronto: J. Jormier and Co.

Duclos, Nitya. 1990. 'Lessons of Difference: Feminist Theory on Cultural Diversity.' *Buffalo Law Review*, 38, 325.

Duggan, Lisa. 1992. 'Making It Perfectly Queer.' *Socialist Review*, 22, 11.

Dworkin, R. 1986. *Law's Empire*. Cambridge: Belknap Press.

Dyzenhaus, David. 1989. 'The New Positivists.' *University of Toronto Law Journal*, 39, 361.

– 1990. *Hard Cases in Wicked Legal Systems: South African Laws in the Perspective of Legal Philosophy*. Oxford: Oxford University Press.

Eagleton, Terry. 1990. *The Significance of Theory*. Oxford: Basil Blackwell.

– 1991. *Ideology: An Introduction*. London: New York: Verso.

Ebert, Theresa. 1993. 'Ludic Feminism – the Body, Performance and Labour: Bringing Materialism Back into Feminist Cultural Studies.' *Cultural Critique*, 24, 5.

Economist. 1996. 'Life with More Agreeable Unions.' *Globe and Mail*, 19 Oct., D3.

Elliot, Robin. 1993. 'Scope of the Charter's Application.' *Advocate's Quarterly*, 15, 204.

Elliot, Robin, and Robert Grant. 1989. 'The Charter's Application in Private Litigation.' *University of British Columbia Law Review*, 23, 459.

Ely, J.H. 1980. *Democracy and Distrust: A Theory of Judicial Review*. Cambridge, Mass.: Harvard University Press.

End Legislated Poverty. 1990. 'Examples of the Effects of the Proposed UI Changes.' June. 1990.

Ewen, Stuart. 1976. *Captains of Consciousness*. New York: McGraw-Hill.

Ewing, Keith. 1988. 'The Legal Regulation of Campaign Financing in Canadian Federal Elections.' *Public Law* (Winter), 577.

– 1992. *Money, Politics and Law: A Study of Electoral Campaign Reform in Canada*. Oxford: Clarendon Press.

Fairbrother, Peter, and Jeremy Waddington. 1991. 'The Politics of Trade Unionism: Evidence, Policy and Theory.' *Capital and Class*, 41, 15.

Fairley, S. 1982. 'Enforcing the Charter: Some Thoughts on an Appropriate and Just Standard for Judicial Review.' *Supreme Court Law Review*, 4, 217.

Feinberg, Joel. 1984. *The Moral Limits of the Criminal Law*. Volumes I–IV. Oxford: Oxford University Press.

Fine, S., and R. Millar, eds. 1985. *Policing the Miners' Strike*. London: Lawrence and Wishart.

Finkelman, Paul. 1987. 'Slaves as Fellow Servants: Ideology, Law, and Industrialization.' *American Journal of Legal History*, 31, 69.

Finkelstein, N. 1983–84. 'Section 1: The Standard for Assessing Restrictive Government Actions and the Charter's Code of Procedure and Evidence.' *Queen's Law Journal*, 9, 143.

Fiorito, Jack, Christopher Lowman, and Forrest D. Nelson. 1987. 'The Impact of Human Resource Policies on Union Organizing.' *Industrial Relations*, 26, 113.

Fischl, Richard M. 1993. 'The Question That Killed Critical Legal Studies.' *Law and Social Inquiry*, 779.

Fish, Stanley. 1985. 'Consequences.' In W.J.T. Mitchell, ed., *Against Theory*. Chicago: University of Chicago Press.

– 1994. *There Is No Such Thing as Free Speech*. Oxford: Oxford University Press.

Fisher, William W., III. 1993. 'Ideology and Imagery in the Law of Slavery.' *Chicago-Kent Law Review*, 68, 1051.

Fiss, Owen. 1981–2. 'Objectivity and Interpretation.' *Stanford Law Review*, 34, 739.

– 1986. 'The Death of the Law.' *Cornell Law Review*, 72, 1.

– 1988. 'Free Speech and Social Structure.' In J. Lobel, ed., *A Less Than Perfect Union*. New York: Monthly Review Press.

– 1989. 'The Law Regained.' *Cornell Law Review*, 74, 245.

Fitzpatrick, Peter. 1987. 'Racism and the Innocence of Law.' *British Journal of Law and Society*, 14, 119.

– 1992. *The Mythology of Modern Law*. London: Routledge.

Forbath, William E. 1989. 'The Shaping of the American Labor Movement.' *Harvard Law Review*, 102, 1109.

Foster, John, and Charles Woolfson. 1989. 'Corporate Reconstruction and Business Unionism: The Lessons of Caterpillar and Ford.' *New Left Review*, 174, 51.

Fowler, Roger. 1991. *Language in the News: Discourse and Ideology in the Press*. London: Routledge.

Frank, J.A. 1983. 'The "Ingredients" in Violent Labour Conflict: Patterns in Four Case Studies.' *Labour/Le Travailleur*, 12, 87ff.

Frankel, Boris. 1994. 'Class, Environmental and Social Movements.' In A. Giddens, D. Held, D. Hubert, D. Seymour, and J. Thompson, eds., *The Polity Reader in Social Theory*. Cambridge: Polity Press.

Fraser, Andrew. 1993. 'Beyond the Charter Debate: Republicanism, Rights and Civic Virtue in the Civil Constitution of Canadian Society.' *Review of Constitutional Studies*, 1, 27.

Fraser, Graham. 1995. 'U.S. Supreme Court Drops Role as Minority Advocate.' *Globe and Mail*, 14 June, A7.

Freedman, Richard, and James Medo. 1984. *What Do Unions Do?* New York: Basic Books.

Fried, C. 1963. 'Two Concepts of Interests: Some Reflections on the Supreme Courts Balancing Test.' *Harvard Law Review*, 76, 755.

Friedman, W. 1951. 'Judges, Politics and the Law.' *Canadian Bar Review*, 29, 811.

Fudge, Judy. 1987. 'The Public/Private Distinction: The Possibilities and Limits to the Use of Charter Litigation to Further Feminist Struggle.' *Osgoode Hall Law Journal*, 25, 485.

– 1988. 'Labour, the New Constitution and Old-Style Liberalism.' *Queen's Law Journal*, 13, 61.

– 1989. 'The Privatization of the Costs of Reproduction: Some Recent Charter Cases.' *Canadian Journal of Women and Law*, 3, 246.

– 1991. 'Reconceiving Employment Standards Legislation: Labour's Little Sister and the Feminization of Labour.' *Journal of Law and Social Policy*, 7, 73.

Fudge, Judy, and Harry Glasbeek. 1992a. 'Alberta Nurses v. a Contemptuous Supreme Court of Canada.' *Constitutional Forum Constitutionnel*, 4, 1.

– 1992b. 'The Politics of Rights: A Politics with Little Class.' *Social and Legal Studies*, 1, 45.

Gabel, Peter, and Paul Harris. 1982–3. 'Building Power, Breaking Images: Critical Theory and the Practice of Law.' *New York University Review of Law and Social Change*. 11, 369.

Gabel, Peter. 1984. 'The Phenomenology of Rights Consciousness and the Pact of the Withdrawn Selves.' *Texas Law Review*, 62, 1563.

Gabriel, John. 1994. *Racism, Culture, Markets*. New York: Routledge.

Gates, Bruce. 1990a. 'Corporations Cry Bigger Load.' *Financial Post*. 14 May, 15.

– 1990b. 'Why Companies Tread Sponsorship Stage.' *Financial Post*. 14 May, 16.

Gavigan, S. 1988. 'Law, Gender and Ideology.' In A.F. Bayefsky, ed., *Legal Theory Meets Legal Practice*. Edmonton: Academic Printing and Publishing.

– 1993. 'Paradise Lost, Paradise Revisited: The Implications of Familial Ideology for Feminist, Lesbian and Gay Engagement to Law.' *Osgoode Hall Law Journal*, 31, 589.

Geary, R. 1985. *Policing Industrial Disputes: 1893–1985.* Cambridge: Cambridge University Press.

Gerbner, G., et al. 1987. 'Charting the Mainstream: Television's Contributions to Political Orientations.' In Donald Lazere, ed., *American Media and Mass Culture: Left Perspectives.* Los Angeles: University of California Press.

Getman, Julius. 1984. 'Labour Law and Free Speech: The Curious Policy of Limited Expression.' *Maryland Law Review,* 43, 4.

Glasbeek, Harry, 1984. 'Why Corporate Deviance Is Not Treated as a Crime – The Need to Make "Profits" a Dirty Word.' *Osgoode Hall Law Journal,* 22, 393.

– 1989. 'Some Srategies for an Unlikely Task: The Progressive Use of Law.' *Ottawa Law Review,* 21, 387.

– 1990a. 'Contempt for Workers.' *Osgoode Hall Law Journal,* 28, 1.

– 1990b. 'From Constitutional Rights to "Real" Rights.' *Windsor Yearbook of Access to Justice,* 10, 468.

– 1992. 'Social Charter.' In Joel Bakan and David Schneiderman, eds., *The Constitution and Social Justice.* Ottawa: Carleton University Press.

– 1993. 'Agenda for Canadian Labour Law Reform: A Little Liberal Law, Much More Democratic Socialist Politics.' *Osgoode Hall Law Journal,* 31, 233.

Glasbeek, Harry, and Reuben Hasson. 1987. 'Some Reflections on Canadian Legal Education.' *Modern Law Review,* 50, 777.

Glasgow University Media Group. 1976. *Bad News.* London: Routledge.

– 1980. *More Bad News.* London: Routledge.

Glavin, Terry. 1996. 'B.C.'s Remaining Fish Stocks Merely Zoo Population.' 13–20 June, 17.

Globe and Mail. 1989. 'UIC Changes Will Violate Rights of Women Workers, MPs Warned.' 9 Sept.

– 1990. 'NCC Urges No Limits on Spending for Elections.' 9 May.

– 1995. 'Basic Research Is a Wise Investment (Editorial).' 2 Oct., A18.

– 1996. 'B.C.-born Nobel Winner Dies.' 12 Oct., A10.

Godfrey, John, chair. 1995. *The Future of the CBC in the Multichannel Universe: Report of the Standing Committee of Canadian Heritage.* June. Ottawa.

Gold, M. 1982. 'A Principled Approach to Equality Rights: A Preliminary Inquiry.' *Supreme Court Law Review,* 4, 131.

Goldman, Robert. 1992. *Reading Ads Socially.* London: Routledge.

Goldsen, Rose. 1980. 'The Great Consciousness Machine.' *Journal of Social Reconstruction,* 1, 98.

Goodrich, Peter. 1992. 'Poor Illiterate Reason: History, Nationalism and Common Law.' *Social and Legal Studies,* 1, 7.

Graham, Patricia. 1992. 'Native Women Sidelined.' *Vancouver Sun,* 22 Oct., A15.

Gray, Charlotte. 1989. 'Purchasing Power.' *Canadian Forum,* 68 (March), 15.

Greenwalt, Kent. 1995. *Fighting Words: Individuals, Communities, and Liberties of Speech.* Princeton, NJ: Princeton University Press.

Grenier, Guillermo. 1988. *Inhuman Relations: Quality Circles and Anti-Unionism in American Industry.* Philadelphia: Temple University Press.

Greschner, Donna. 1992. 'Aboriginal Women, the Constitution and Criminal Justice.' *University of British Columbia Law Review*, special ed., 338.

Griffin, Kevin. 1995. 'Legal Battles to Keep on Coming.' *Vancouver Sun*, 1 Aug., A12.

Griffiths, J.A.G. 1981. *The Politics of the Judiciary.* Glasgow: Fontana Press.

Haggerty, R.J. 1985. 'The Limits of Medical Care.' *New England Journal of Medicine*, 313 no. 6, 383.

Hall, Stuart. 1980. 'Encoding/Decoding.' In Stuart Hall, Dorothy Hobson, Andrew Lowe, and Paul Willis, eds., *Culture, Media, Language.* London: Hutchinson.

– 1984. 'The State in Question.' In G. McLennan et al., eds., *The Idea of the Modern State.* Philadelphia: Open University Press.

– 1986. 'On Postmodernism and Articulation.' *Journal of Communication Inquiry*, 10, 45.

– 1988a. *The Hard Road to Renewal: Thatcherism and the Crisis of the Left.* London: Verso.

– 1988b. 'The Toad in the Garden: Thatcherism among the Theorists.' In Cary Nelson and Lawrence Grossberg, eds., *Marxism and the Interpretation of Culture.* Urbana: University of Illinois Press.

– 1990. 'The Whites of Their Eyes: Racist Ideologies and the Media.' In Manuel Alvarado and J. Thompson, eds., *The Media Reader.* London: British Film Institute Publishing.

– 1992. 'Cultural Studies and Its Theoretical Legacies.' In Lawrence Grossberg, Cary Nelson, and Paula Treichler, eds., *Cultural Studies.* New York: Routledge.

Harmer, Lily. 1989. 'The Right to Strike: Charter Implications and Interpretations.' *University of Toronto Faculty of Law Review*, 47, 420.

Harrington, Michael. 1989. *Socialism: Past and Future.* New York: Arcade.

Harris, C. 'CBC Considers Radio Show Reruns.' *Globe and Mail*, 23 Oct., 1996, A16.

Harris, Mark. 1994. 'Enigmatic Director Quits on Top.' *Georgia Straight*, 2–9 Dec., 41.

Hart, H.L.A. 1977. 'Problems of Legal Reasoning.' In Joel Feinberg, and H. Gross, eds., *Law in Philosophical Perspective.* Belmont, Calif.: Wadsworth Publishing Company.

Harvey, David. 1991. 'Flexibility: Threat or Opportunity?' *Socialist Review*, 21, 73.

– 1993. 'Class Relations, Social Justice and the Politics of Difference.' In Judith Squires, ed., *Principled Positions: Postmodernism and the Rediscovery of Value.* London: Lawrence & Wishart.

Harvey, Miles. 1993. 'Politically Correct Is Politically Suspect.' In P. Aufderheide, ed., *Beyond P.C.* St Paul, Minn.: Graywolf.

Hasson, R.A. 1989. 'What's Your Favourite Right? The Charter and Income Maintenance Legislation.' *Journal of Law and Social Policy*, 4, 1.

Hay, Douglas. 1975. 'Property, Authority and the Criminal Law.' In Douglas Hay et al., eds., *Albion's Fatal Tree: Crime and Society in Eighteenth Century England*. London: Pantheon Books.

Herman, Didi. 1990. 'Are We Family? Lesbian Rights and Women's Liberation.' *Osgoode Hall Law Journal*, 28, 789.

– 1992. 'Reforming Rights: Lesbian and Gay Struggle for Legal Equality in Canada.' PhD thesis, Deptartment of Sociology, University of Warwick.

– 1993. 'Beyond the Rights Debate.' *Social and Legal Studies*, 2, 25.

– 1994a. 'The Good, the Bad and the Smugly: Perspectives on the Canadian Charter of Rights and Freedoms.' *Oxford Journal of Legal Studies*, 14, 589.

– 1994b. *Rights of Passage: Struggles for Lesbian and Gay Equality*. Toronto: University of Toronto Press.

Herman, Didi, and Carl Stychin. 1995. *Legal Inversions: Lesbians, Gay Men, and the Politics of Law*. Philadelphia: Temple University Press.

Herman, Edward S., and Noam Chomsky. 1988. *Manufacturing Consent: The Political Economy of the Mass Media*. New York: Pantheon Books.

Hiebert, Janet. 1993. 'Rights and Public Debate: The Limitations of a "Rights Must Be Paramount" Perspective.' *International Journal of Canadian Studies*, 7–8, 117.

Hirst, Paul, and Jonathan Zeitlin. 1991. 'Flexible Specialization versus Post-Fordism: Theory, Evidence and Policy Implications.' *Economy and Society*, 20, 1.

Hogg, P.W. 1979. 'Is the Supreme Court of Canada Biased in Consitutional Cases?' *Canadian Bar Review*, 57, 721.

– 1985. *Constitutional Law of Canada*. 2nd ed. Toronto: Carswell.

– 1986–7. 'The Dolphin Delivery Case: The Application of the Charter to Private Action.' *Saskatchewan Law Review*, 52, 273.

– 1987. 'The Charter of Rights and American Theories of Interpretation.' *Osgoode Hall Law Journal*, 15, 87.

Holt, Wythe. 1984a. 'Labour Conspiracy Cases in the United States, 1805–1842: Bias and Legitimation in Common Law Adjudication.' *Osgoode Hall Law Journal*, 22, 591.

– 1984b. 'Tilt.' *George Washington Law Review*, 52, 280.

Hopkinson, Richard. 1985. 'Corporate Donations and Sponsorship of the Arts.' In Canada Council, The Arts: Corporations and Foundations, Arts Research Seminar No. 4, 6 Sept.

Hughes, Patricia. 1995. 'Domestic Legal Aid: A Claim to Equality.' *Review of Constitutional Studies*, 2, 203.

Hunt, Alan. 1985. 'The Ideology of Law: Advances and Problems in Recent Applications of the Concept of Ideology to the Analysis of Law.' *Law and Society Review*, 19, 11.

– 1990. 'Rights and Social Movements: Counter-Hegemonic Strategies.' *Journal of Law and Society*, 17, 309.

– 1992. 'Can Marxism Survive?' *Rethinking Marxism*, 5, 45.

– 1993. *Explorations in Law and Society: Toward a Constitutive Theory of Law*. New York: Routledge.

Hunt, Alan, and Amy Bartholomew. 1990. 'What's Wrong with Rights?' *Journal of Law and Inequality* 9, 1.

Hutchinson, A.C. 1989a. 'That's Just the Way It Is: Langille on Law.' *McGill Law Journal*, 33, 451.

– 1989b. 'The Three "Rs": Reading/Rorty/Radically.' *Harvard Law Review*, 103, 555.

– 1995. *Waiting for CORAF: A Critique of Law and Rights*. Toronto: University of Toronto Press.

Hutchinson, A.C., and Andrew Petter. 1988. 'Private Rights/Public Wrongs: The Liberal Lie of the Charter.' *University of Toronto Law Journal*, 38, 278.

Hutton, Will. 1996. *The State We're In*. London: Vintage.

Hyman, Richard. 1989. *The Political Economy of Industrial Relations: Theory and Practice in a Cold Climate*. London: MacMillan Press.

Inglis, Fred. 1990. *Media Theory: An Introduction*. Oxford: Blackwell.

Iyer, Nitya. 1993. 'Categorical Denials: Equality Rights and the Shaping of Social Identity.' *Queen's Law Journal*, 19, 179.

Jackman, Martha. 1988. 'The Protection of Welfare Rights under the Charter.' *Ottawa Law Review*, 20, 257.

– 1992. 'Constitutional Rhetoric and Social Justice: Reflections on the Justiciability Debate.' In Joel Bakan and David Schneiderman, eds., *Social Justice and the Constitution: Perspectives on a Social Union for Canada*. Ottawa: Carleton University Press.

– 1993. 'Poor Rights: Using the Charter to Support Welfare Social Claims.' *Queen's Law Journal*, 19, 65.

Jacobi, Otto, et al., eds. 1986a. *Economic Crisis, Trade Unions and the State*. London: Croom Helm.

– 1986b. 'Trade Unions, Industrial Relations and Structural Economic "Ruptures."' In Otto Jacobi et al., eds., *Economic Crisis, Trade Unions and the State*. London: Croom Helm.

Jensen, Jane. 1994. 'The Federal Electoral Regime Confronts the Charter ... Again: A Comment on Somerville v. Canada (A.-G.).' *Constitutional Forum*, 5, 25.

Jessop, Bob. 1990. *State Theory: Putting the Capitalist State in Its Place*. University Park, Penn.: Pennsylvania State University Press.

Jhally, Sut. 1989. 'Advertising as Religion: The Dialectic of Technology and Magic.' In I. Angus, and S. Jhally, eds., *Cultural Politics in Contemporary America*. New York: Routledge.

Jin, R.L., C.P. Shah, and T.J. Svoboda. 1995. 'The Impact of Unemployment on Health: A Review of the Evidence.' *Canadian Medical Association Journal*, 153, 529.

Johnson, Andrew, Stephen McBride, and Patrick Smith. 1994. *Continuities and Discontinuities: The Political Economy of Social welfare and Labour Market Policy in Canada*. Toronto: University of Toronto Press.

Johnston, William. 1992. 'Accord Fatally Flawed When It Comes to Protecting Rights.' *Montreal Gazette*, 24 Oct., B5.

Kadi, M. 1995. 'Welcome to Cyberia.' *UTNE Reader* (March–April), 57.

Kane, Elimane, and David Marsden. 1988. 'The Future of Trade Unionism in Industrialized Market Economies.' *Labour and Society*, 13, 109.

Katz, Michael. 1989. *The Undeserving Poor: From the War on Poverty to the War on Welfare.* New York: Pantheon Books.

Keane, John. 1991. *The Media and Democracy.* Cambridge: Polity Press.

Kellner, Douglas. 1990. *Television and the Crisis of Democracy.* Boulder, Col.: Westview Press.

Kennedy, Duncan. 1976. 'Form and Substance in Private Law Adjudication.' *Harvard Law Review*, 89, 1685.

– 1985. 'Legal Education and the Reproduction of Hierarchy: A Polemic against the System.' *Louisiana Law Review*, 45, 1329.

Kennedy, W.P.M. 1932. *Some Aspects of the Theories and Workings of Constitutional Law.* New York: MacMillan.

– 1937. 'The British North America Act: Past and Future.' *Canadian Bar Review*, 15, 393.

Kerruish, Valerie. 1991. *Jurisprudence as Ideology.* London: Routledge.

Klare, Karl. 1979. 'Law-Making as Praxis.' *Telos*, 40, 123.

– 1978. 'Judicial Deradicalization of the Wagner Act and the Origins of Modern Legal Consciousness.' *Minnesotta Law Review*, 62, 265.

Kline, Marlee. 1992. 'Child Welfare Law, "Best Interests of the Child" Ideology and First Nations.' *Osgoode Hall Law Journal*, 30, 375.

– 1993. 'Complicating the Ideology of Motherhood: Child Welfare Law and First Nation Women.' *Queen's Law Journal*, 18, 306.

– 1994. 'The Colour of Law: Ideological Representations of First Nations in Legal Discourse.' *Social and Legal Studies*, 3, 451.

Knapp, S., and W.B. Michaels. 1985. 'Against Theory.' In W.J.T. Mitchell, ed., *Against Theory.* Chicago: University of Chicago Press.

Knopff, Rainer, and F.L. Morton. 1992. *The Supreme Court as the Vanguard of the Intelligentsia: The Charter Movement as Postmaterialist Politics.* University of Calgary, Research Unit for Socio-Legal Studies.

– 1996. 'Canada's Court Party.' In Anthony Peacock, ed., *Rethinking the Constitution.* Toronto: Oxford University Press.

Kraft, Julius. 1993. 'On the Methodological Relationship between Jurisprudence and Theology.' *Law and Critique*, 4, 117.

LaBrie, F.E. 1949. 'Canadian Constitutional Interpretation and Legislative Review.' *University of Toronto Law Journal*, 8, 298.

Laclau, Ernesto, and Chantal Mouffe. 1985. *Hegemony and Socialist Strategy: Towards a Radical Democratic Politics.* London: Verso.

LaForest, G. 1983. 'The Canadian Charter of Rights and Freedoms: An Overview.' *Canadian Bar Review*, 61, 19.

Lamer, Antonio. 1996. 'Remarks by the Rt. Hon. Antonio Lamer, P.C., Chief Justice of Canada at the Canadian Bar Association Annual Meeting, Vancouver. Aug. 26.'

Landsberg, Michele. 1992. 'Unity Deal Will Rob Native Women of Key Rights.' *Toronto Sun*, 22 Sept., B1.

Langille, B. 1988. 'Revolution without Foundation: The Grammar of Scepticism and Law.' *McGill Law Journal*, 33, 451.

Laskin, B. 1947. 'Peace, Order and Good Government Re-Examined.' *Canadian Bar Review*, 25, 1054.

– 1955. 'Tests for the Validity of Legislation: What's the "Matter"?' *University of Toronto Law Journal*, 11, 114.

– 1973. 'The Function of Law.' *Alberta Law Review*, 11, 118.

Laxer, James. 1993. *False God: How the Globalization Myth Has Impoverished Canada*. Toronto: Lester Publishing.

Lazarus, Neil. 1990. 'Imperialism, Cultural Theory, and Radical Intellectualism Today: A Critical Assessment.' *Rethinking Marxism*, 3, 156.

Leach, Bernard, and John Shutt. 1984. 'Crisps and Chips: The Impact of New Technology on Food Processing Jobs in Greater Manchester.' In Pauline Marstrand, ed., *New Technology and the Future of Work and Skills*. London: Frances Pinter.

Lederman, William Ralph. 1964. 'Classifications of Laws and the British North America Act.' In William R. Lederman, ed., *The Courts and the Canadian Constitution*. Toronto: McClelland and Stewart.

– 1976. 'The Independence of the Judiciary.' In A. Linden, ed., *The Canadian Judiciary*. Toronto: Osgoode Hall Law School.

– 1980. *Continuing Constitutional Dilemmas: Essays on the Constitutional History, Public Law and Federal System of Canada*. Toronto: Butterworths.

Lefroy, A.H.F. 1897. *The Law of Legislative Power in Canada*. Toronto: Toronto Law Book and Publishing Company.

Lessard, Hester. 1991. 'Relationship, Particularity, and Change: Reflections on R. v. Morgentaler and Feminist Approaches to Liberty.' *McGill Law Journal*, 36, 363.

Levinson, Sanford. 1988. *Constitutional Faith*. Princeton, NJ: Princeton University Press.

Lewington, Jennifer. 1995. 'Universities Gearing for Change.' *Globe and Mail*, 9 Oct., A6.

Lewis, Justin. 1991. *The Ideological Octopus: An Exploration of Television and Its Audience*. London: Routledge.

Lipstadt, Deborah. 1993. *Denying the Holocaust: The Growing Assault on Truth and Memory*. Toronto: Maxwell Macmillan Canada.

Little, Bruce. 1996. 'The Changing Face of Poverty in Canada.' *Globe and Mail*, 1 July, A5.

Lynd, Staughton. 1984. 'Communal Rights.' *Texas Law Review*, 62, 1563.

Lyon, N. 1982. 'The Teleological Mandate of the Fundamental Freedoms Guarantee: What to Do with Vague but Meaningful Generalities.' *Supreme Court Law Review*, 4, 57.

– 1983. 'The Charter As a Mandate for New Ways of Thinking about Law.' *Queen's Law Journal*, 9, 241.

Lyon, N., and R.G. Atkey. 1970. *Canadian Constitutional Law in a Modern Perspective*. Toronto: University of Toronto Press.

McAllister, Debra. 1992. 'Butler: A Triumph for Equality Rights.' *NJCL* 2, 118.

McClure, Kirstie. 1992. 'On the Subject of Rights: Pluralism, Plurality and Political Identity.' In C. Mouffe, ed., *Dimensions of Radical Democracy*. London: Verso.

MacDonald, Martha. 1991. 'Post-Fordism and the Flexibility Debate.' *Studies in Political Economy*, 36, 177.

MacDonald, R.A. 1982. 'Postscript and Prelude – the Jurisprudence of the Charter: Eight Theses.' *Supreme Court Law Review*, 4, 321.

MacDonald, Vincent. 1937. 'The Canadian Constitution Seventy Years After.' *Canadian Bar Review*, 15, 401.

– 1948. 'The Constitution in a Changing World.' *Canadian Bar Review*, 6, 31.

McFeely, Tom. 1992. 'An Uprising against the Charlottetown Native Deal.' *Western Report*, 19 Oct., 14.

McInnes, John, and Christine Boyle. 1995. 'Judging Sexual Assaualt Law Against a Standard of Equality.' *University of British Columbia Law Review*, 29, 341.

McLachlin, Beverly. 1991. 'The Charter: A New Role for the Judiciary.' *Alberta Law Review*, 29, 540.

McQuaig, Linda. 1995. *Shooting the Hippo: Death by Deficit and Other Canadian Myths*. Toronto: Penguin.

McWhinney, E. 1965. *Judicial Review in the English Speaking World*. 3rd. ed. Toronto: University of Toronto Press.

Macklem Patrick. 1988. 'Constitutional Ideologies.' *Ottawa Law Review*, 20, 117.

– 1990. 'Property, Status and Workplace Organization.' *University of Toronto Law Journal*, 40, 74.

– 1991. 'First Nations Self-Government and the Borders of the Canadian Legal Imagination.' *McGill Law Journal*, 36, 382.

– 1992. 'Developments in Employment Law: The 1990–91 Term.' *Supreme Court Law Review*, 3, 227.

Macpherson, C.B. 1977. *The Life and Times of Liberal Democracy*. Oxford: Oxford University Press.

– 1985. *The Rise and Fall of Economic Justice and Other Papers*. Oxford: Oxford University Press.

Mahoney, Kathleen. 1992. 'The Constituional Law of Canada.' *Maine Law Review*, 44, 229.

Mahoney, Kathleen, and Sheilah Martin. 1985. *Broadcasting and the Canadian Charter of Rights: Justifications for Restricting Freedom of Expression*. Canada. Task Force on Broadcasting Policy.

Mandel, Michael. 1989. *The Charter of Rights and the Legalization of Politics in Canada.* Toronto: Wall & Thompson.

– 1994. *The Charter of Rights and the Legalization of Politics in Canada.* Toronto: Thompson Educational Publishing.

Mann, Jonathan. 1995. 'Rising Rates of AIDS in Women Linked to Male Domination.' *Vancouver Sun,* 25 May, A8.

Manning, M. 1983. *How Capitalism Underdeveloped Black America.* Boston, Mass.: South End Press.

Manwarring, J.A. 1982. 'Legitimacy in Labour Relations: The Courts, the British Columbia Labour Relations Board and Secondary Picketing.' *Osgoode Hall Law Journal,* 20, 274.

– 1987. 'Bringing the Common Law to the Bar of Justice.' *Ottawa Law Review,* 19, 413.

Martineau, Pierre. 1957. *Motivation in Advertising.* New York: McGraw-Hill Book Company.

Marx, Karl. 1967. 'On the Jewish Question.' In Loyd D. Easton, and Kurt H. Guddat, eds. and trans., *Writings of the Young Marx on Philosophy and Society.* Garden City, NY: Anchor Books.

Marx, Karl, and Frederick Engels. 1981. *The German Ideology.* New York: International Publishers.

– 1988. 'The Communist Manifesto.' In David McLellan, ed., *Karl Marx: Selected Writings.* Oxford: Oxford University Press.

Matsuda, M. 1993–4. 'Progressive Civil Liberties.' *Temple Political and Civil Rights Law Review,* 3, 9.

Matsuda, Mari, et al. 1993. *Words That Wound: Critical Race Theory, Assaultative Speech and the First Amendment.* Boulder, Col.: Westview Press.

Mattiasson, I., F. Lindgarde, J.A. Nilsson, and T. Theorell. 1990. 'Threat of Unemployment and Cardiovascular Risk Factors: Longitudinal Study of Quality of Sleep and Serum Cholesterol Concentrations in Men Threatened with Redundancy.' *British Medical Journal,* 301, 461.

May, K. 1995. 'Temporary Workers Replacing Full-time Civil Servants, Report Finds.' *Vancouver Sun,* 20 Sept., A6.

Meikins Wood, Ellen. 1986. *The Retreat from Class: A New 'True' Socialism.* London, Verso.

– 1995. *Democracy against Capitalism: Renewing Historical Materialism.* Cambridge: Cambridge University Press.

Meredith, Colin, and Chantal Pasquette. 1992. Survey of Students at Ten Law Schools in Canada. March.

Michelman, F. 1986. 'Forward: Traces of Self-Government.' *Harvard Law Review,* 100, 4.

– 1988. 'Law's Republic.' *Yale Law Journal,* 97, 1493.

– 1992. 'Universities, Racist Speech and Democracy in America: An Essay for the ACLU.' *Harvard Civil Rights-Civil Liberties Law Review,* 27, 339.

Miliband, Ralph. 1973. *The State in Capitalist Society.* London: Quartet Books.

– 1991. *Divided Societies: Class Struggle in Contemporary Capitalism*. Oxford: Oxford University Press.

Millbank, J. 1994. 'What Do Lesbians Do? Motherhood Ideology, Lesbian Mothers and Family Law.' LLM thesis, Faculty of Law, University of British Columbia.

Minow, Martha. 1987. 'Forward: Justice Engendered.' *Harvard Law Review*, 101, 10.

– 1990. *Making All the Difference: Inclusion, Exclusion and American Law*. Ithaca, NY: Cornell University Press.

Mitchell, A. 1996. 'Few Succumbing to Internet's Allure.' *Globe and Mail*. 24 Oct., A1.

Monahan, P. 1983. 'Book Review.' *Canadian Bar Review*, 61, 434.

– 1984. 'At Doctrine's Twilight: The Structure of Canadian Federalism.' *University of Toronto Law Journal*, 34, 47.

– 1987. *Politics and the Constitution: The Charter, Federalism and the Supreme Court of Canada*. Toronto: Carswell.

Monahan, Patrick, and Andrew Petter. 1987. 'Developments in Constitutional Law: The 1985–86 Term.' *Supreme Court Law Review*, 10, 61.

Monture, Patricia. 1990. 'Now That the Door is Open: First Nations and the Law School Experience.' *Queen's Law Journal*, 15, 179.

Moody, Kim. 1988. *An Injury to All*. London: Verso.

Moore, Heather. 1985. 'The Effects of Corporate Sponsorship on Canadian Orchestras.' In Canada Council, Arts Research Seminar No. 4, 6 Sept.

Morton, F.L., Peter Russell, and Michael Withey. 1992. 'The Supreme Court's First One Hundred Charter of Rights Decisions: A Statistical Analysis.' *Osgoode Hall Law Journal*, 30, 1.

Mosoff, Judith. 1995. 'Motherhood, Madness, and Law.' *University of Toronto Law Journal*, 45, 107.

Mossman, M.J. 1985. 'The Charter and Legal Aid.' *Journal of Law and Social Policy*, 1, 21.

Mouffe, Chantal. 1993. *The Return of the Political*. London: Verso.

Musqueam Indian Band. 1992. Charter Equality Rights and Self-Government. Unpublished document on file with the author.

Myles, John. 1992. 'Constitutionalizing Social Rights.' In H. Echenbgergy, A. Milner, J. Myles, L. Osberg, S. Phipps, J. Richards, and W.B.P. Robson, eds., *A Social Charter for Canada: Perspectives on the Constitutional Entrenchment of Social Rights*. Toronto: C.D. Howe Institute.

National Anti-Poverty Organization. 1992. Draft Social Charter. 27 March.

National Council of Welfare (NCW). 1990. *Health, Health Care and Medicare*. Ottawa: Ministry of Supply and Services.

– 1994. *Poverty Profile 1992*. Ottawa: Ministry of Supply and Services.

– 1995. *Poverty Profile 1993*. Ottawa: Ministry of Supply and Services.

Native Women's Association of Canada (NWAC). 1992. 'Statement on the Canada Package.' Prepared by Gail Stacey-Moore, speaker. Ottawa: NWAC.

Nedelsky, Jennifer. 1993. 'Reconceiving Rights as Relationship.' *Review of Constitutional Studies*, 1, 1.

Nedelsky, Jennifer, and Craig Scott. 1992. 'Constitutional Dialogue.' In Joel Bakan and D. Schneiderman, eds., *Social Justice and the Constitution: Perspectives on a Social Union for Canada*. Ottawa: Carleton University Press.

Newson, Janice, and Howard Buchbinder. 1988. *The University Means Business: Universities, Corporations and Academic Work*. Toronto: Garamond Press.

O'Brien, Tom. 1995. 'Biased against Labour (Letter to the Editor).' *Globe and Mail*, 29 May, A20.

O'Grady, John. 1992. 'Beyond the Wagner Act, What Then?' In Daniel Drache, ed., *Getting on Track*. Montreal: McGill-Queen's University Press.

Ohman, Richard. 1987. 'Doublespeak and Ideology in Ads: A Kit for Teachers.' In Donald Lazere, ed., *American Media and Mass Culture: Left Perspectives*. Los Angeles: University of California Press.

Olsen, D. 1977. 'The State Elites.' In Leo Panitch, ed., *The Canadian State: Political Economy and Political Power*. Toronto: University of Toronto Press.

Ontario, Ministry of Intergovernmental Affairs. 1991. 'A Canadian Social Charter: Making Our Shared Values Stronger.' Toronto: Ministry of Intergovernmental Affairs.

Orton, Helena. 1990. 'Section 15, Benefits Programs and Other Benefits at Law: The Interpretation of Section 15 of the Charter since Andrews.' *Manitoba Law Review*, 19, 288.

Panitch, L., and D. Swartz. 1988. *The Assault on Trade Union Freedoms*. Toronto: Garamond Press.

− 1993. *The Assault on Trade Union Freedoms*. 2nd ed. Toronto: Garamond Press.

Parekh, Bhikhu. 1993. 'The Cultural Particularity of Liberal Democracy.' In David Held, ed., *Prospects for Democracy*. Stanford, Calif.: Stanford University Press.

Parenti, M. 1986. *Inventing Reality: The Politics of the Mass Media*. New York: St Martin's Press Inc.

Parkdale Community Legal Services. 1988. 'Homelessness and the Right to Shelter.' *Journal of Law and Social Policy*, 4, 3.

Pashukanis, E.B. 1978. *Law and Marxism*. London.

Peacock, Anthony. 1996. 'Introduction: The Necessity of Rethinking the Constitution.' In Anthony Peacock, ed., *Rethinking the Constitution*. Toronto: Oxford University Press.

Peller, Gary. 1985. 'The Metaphysics of American Law.' *California Law Review*, 73, 1152.

Pemberton, Kim. 1995. 'Election "Gag Law" Faces Court Challenge.' *Vancouver Sun*, 18 July, B4.

Perry, M. 1988. *Politics and Law: A Bicentennial Essay*. New York: Oxford University Press.

Petter, Andrew. 1986. 'The Politics of the Charter.' *Supreme Court Law Review*, 8, 473.

− 1987. 'Immaculate Deception: The Charter's Hidden Agenda.' *Advocate*, 45, 857.

− 1989. 'Legitimating Sexual Inequality: Three Early Charter Cases.' *McGill Law Review*, 34, 358.

Petter, Andrew, and Allan Hutchinson. 1989. 'Rights in Conflict: The Dilemma of Charter Legitimacy.' *University of British Columbia Law Review*, 23, 531.

Philipps, Lisa. 1995. 'Discursive Deficits: A Feminist Perspective on the Power of Technical Knowledge in Fiscal Law and Policy.' Unpublished manuscript. Faculty of Law, University of Victoria, Sept.

Philipps, L., and M. Young. 1995. 'Sex, Tax and the Charter: A Review of *Thibadeau v. Canada*.' *Review of Constitutional Studies*, 2, 221.

Phillips, Susan. 1991. 'How Ottawa Blends: Shifting Government Relationships with Interest Groups.' In Francis Abele, ed., *How Ottawa Spends: The Politics of Fragmentation (1991–1992)*. Ottawa: Carleton University Press.

Picciotto, Sol. 1982. 'The Theory of the State, Class Struggle and the Rule of Law.' In Piers Beirne and Richard Quinney, eds., *Marxism and Law*. New York: Wiley.

Pollay, R.W. 1986. 'The Distorted Mirror: Reflections of the Unintended Consequences of Advertising.' *Journal of Marketing*, 50, 18.

Porter, Bruce. 1991. 'Social and Economic Rights and Citizenship: Draft Paper Prepared for the Institute for Research and Public Policy, Victoria, B.C.' 6 Sept.

Postman, Neil. 1992. *Technopoly: The Surrender of Culture to Technology*. New York: Knopf.

Poulantzas, Nicos. 1980. *State, Power, Socialism*. London: Verso.

Pound, Roscoe. 1912. 'The Scope and Purpose of Socio-Legal Jurisprudence.' *Harvard Law Review*. 25, 140, 489.

Preston, Ivan. 1975. *The Great American Blow Up*. Madison: University of Wisconsin Press.

Price, Lee. 1985. 'Growing Problems for American Workers in International Trade.' In Thomas A. Kochan, ed., *Challenges and Choices Facing American Labor*. Cambridge: MIT Press.

Puette, William. 1992. *Through Jaundiced Eyes: How the Media View Organized Labour*. Ithaca, NY: Cornell University Press.

Raboy, Mark. 1990. *Missed Opportunities: The Story of Canada's Broadcasting Policy*. Montreal: McGill-Queen's University Press.

Rachlis, M., and C. Kushner. 1989. *Second Opinion: What's Wrong with Canada's Health Care System*. Toronto: Collins.

Rankin, Thomas Donald. 1990. *New Forms of Work Organization: The Challenge for North American Unions*. Toronto: University of Toronto Press.

Razak, S. 1991. *Canadian Feminism and the Law*. Toronto: Second Story Press.

Readings, Bill. 1996. *The University in Ruins*. Cambridge, Mass.: Harvard University Press.

Rhinehart, James. 1984. 'Appropriating Workers' Knowledge: Quality Control Circles at a General Motors Plant.' *Studies in Political Economy*, 13–15, 75.

Robinson, J. Gregg, and Judith S. McIlwee. 1989. 'Obstacles to Unionization in High-Tech Industries.' *Work and Occupations*, 16, 128.

Robinson, Svend. 1994. Interview with David Beers. *Vancouver Angles*, Sept. 40.

Rodell, R. 1955. *Nine Men: A Political History of the Supreme Court from 1790–1955*. New York: Random House.

Rogers, P. 1986. 'Equality, Efficiency and Judicial Restraint.' *Dalhousie Law Journal*, 10, 139.

Roman. 1982–83. 'The Charter of Rights: Renewing the Social Contract?' *Queen's Law Journal*, 8, 188.

Rose, Joseph, and Gary Chaison. 1990. 'New Measures of Union Organizing Effectiveness.' *Industrial Relations*, 29, 457.

Rosenberg, Gerald. 1991. *The Hollow Hope: Can Courts Bring about Social Change?* Chicago: University of Chicago Press.

Rosenbluth, Gideon. 1992. 'The Political Economy of Deficit Phobia.' In Robert Allen and Rosenbluth, eds., *False Promises: The Failure of Conservative Economics*. Vancouver: New Star.

Ross, D., and R. Shillington. 1986. 'Background Documents on Income Security.' In *WIN: Work and Income in the 90's*. Ottawa: Canadian Council on Social Development.

– 1989. *The Canadian Fact Book on Poverty*. Canadian Council on Social Development.

Royal Commmission on Electoral Reform and Party Financing. 1991. *Reforming Electoral Democracy: The Final Report*. Ottawa: Ministry of Supply and Services.

Russell, Peter. 1983. 'The Political Purposes of the Canadian Charter of Rights and Freedoms.' *Canadian Bar Review*, 61, 30.

– 1988. 'Canada's Charter of Rights and Freedoms: A Political Report.' *Public Law* (Autumn), 385.

– 1992. 'The Supreme Court in the 1980s: A Commentary on the S.C.R. Statistics.' *Osgoode Hall Law Journal*, 30, 771.

– 1994. 'The Political Purposes of the Charter: Have They Been Fulfilled? An Agnostic's Report.' In P. Bryden, S. Davis, and J. Russell, eds., *Protecting Rights and Freedoms: Essays on the Charter's Place in Canada's Political, Legal and Intellectual Life*. Toronto: University of Toronto Press.

Russell, Peter H., and Jacob S. Ziegel. 1989. *Federal Judicial Appointments: An Appraisal of the First Mulroney Government's Appointments*. Toronto: University of Toronto, Faculty of Law.

Rustin, Michael. 1989. 'The Politics of Post-Fordism: Or, the Trouble with "New Times."' *New Left Review*, 175, 54.

Ryder, Bruce. 1991. 'Straight Talk: Male Heterosexual Privilege.' *Queen's Law Journal*, 16, 287.

Saige, Franklin. 1995. 'Mega Buys.' *UTNE Reader* (March–April), 52.

Salutin, Rick. 1996. 'Mainstream Journalism Yields Few Unusual Insights.' *Globe and Mail*, 18 Oct., A12.

Sanders, Douglas. 1994. 'Constructing Lesbian and Gay Rights.' *Canadian Journal of Law and Society*, 9, 99.

Sargent, Neil. 1991. 'Labouring in the Shadows of the Law: A Canadian Perspective on the Possibilities and Perils of Legal Studies.' *Law in Context*, 9, 65.

Saunders, D. 1996. 'Corporate Identity to Cover Library.' *Globe and Mail*, 23 Oct., A1.

Schauer, Frederick. 1992. 'The First Amendment as Ideology.' *William and Mary Law Review*, 33, 853.

Scheingold, Stuart. 1989. 'Constitutional Rights and Social Change: Civil Rights in Perspective.' In Michael McCann and Gerald Houseman, eds., *Judging the Constitution*. Boston: Little Brown.

Schiller, Herbert. 1989. *Culture Inc.: The Corporate Takeover of Public Expression*. New York: Oxford University Press.

– 1995. 'The Global Information Superhighway: Project for an Ungovernable World.' In James Brook and Iain A. Boal, eds., *Resisting the Virtual Life: The Culture and Politics of Information*. San Francisco: City Lights.

Schneider, Elizabeth M. 1986. 'The Dialectic of Rights and Politics: Perspectives from the Women's Movement.' *New York University Law Review*, 61, 589.

Schneider, Mark. 1982. 'Peaceful Labor Picketing and the First Amendment.' *Columbia Law Review*, 82, 1469.

Schudson, M. 1985. 'Advertising: The Uneasy Persuasion.' *Business and Society Review*, 53, 90.

Scott, Craig, and Patrick Macklem. 1992. 'Constitutional Ropes of Sand or Justiciable Guarantees: Social Rights in a New South African Constitution.' *University of Pennsylvania Law Review*, 141, 1.

Scott, F.R. 1937. 'The Consequences of the Privy Council Decisions.' *Canadian Bar Review*, 15, 485.

Shalla, Vivian. 1995. *Poverty in Canada*. Political and Social Affairs Division. Microlog No. 96-01088.

Sharpe, Robert. 1987. 'Commercial Expression and the Charter.' *University of Toronto Law Journal*, 37, 229.

Shaw, George B. 1929. *The Intelligent Woman's Guide to Socialism, Capitalism, Sovietism and Fascism*. London: Constable & Co.

Sheppard, C. 1989. 'The Promise of *Andrews* v. *Law Society of British Columbia*.' *McGill Law Journal*, 35, 207.

Sheppard, N.C. 1986. 'Equality, Ideology and Oppression: Women and the Canadian Charter of Rights and Freedoms.' In Christine Boyle, ed., *Charterwatch: Reflections on Equality*. Toronto: Carswell.

Silva, Edward. 1995. *More Perishable than Lettuce or Tomatoes: Labour Law Reform and Toronto's Newspapers*. Halifax: Fernwood.

Simpson, Jeffrey. 1992. 'Les enfants de Trudeau.' *Le Devoir*, 19 Oct., 14.

Small, Stephen. 1994. *Racialised Barriers: The Black Experience in the United States and England in the 1980s*. New York: Routledge.

Smarden, Bruce. 1992. 'Liberalism, Marxism and the Class Character of Radical Democratic Challenge.' *Studies in Political Economy*, 37, 129.

Smart, Carol. 1989. *Feminism and the Power of Law*. London: Routledge.

Smith, Dorothy. 1990. *The Conceptual Practices of Power: A Feminist Sociology of Knowledge*. Boston: Northeastern University Press.

Smith, Lynn. 1994. 'Have the Equality Rights Made Any Difference?' In P. Bryden, S.

Davis, and J. Russell, eds., *Protecting Rights and Freedoms: Essays on the Charter's Place in Canada's Political, Legal and Intellectual Life*. Toronto: University of Toronto Press.

Smith, Mel. 1992. 'What the Deal Means for the West.' *Western Report*, 5 Oct., 12.

Smith, Michael. 1993. 'Language, Law and Social Power: *Seaboyer* v. *R*; *Gayme* v. *R* and a Critical Theory of Ideology.' *University of Toronto Faculty Law Review*, 51, 118.

Smythe, Dallas. 1980. *Dependency Road*. Norwood, NJ: Ablex.

Snell, J.G., and F.F. Vaughn. 1985. *The Supreme Court of Canada*. Toronto: University of Toronto Press.

Sorkin, Michael. 1992. 'Introduction: Variations on a Theme Park.' In Michael Sorkin, ed., *Variations on a Theme Park*. New York: Noonday Press.

Special Advisory Committee to the Canadian Association of Law Teachers (Alvi, Tariq, et al.). 1992. 'Equality in Legal Education: Sharing a Vision, Creating the Pathways.' *Queen's Law Journal*, 17, 174.

Statistics Canada. 1984. *The Distribution of Wealth in Canada*. Cat. 13-580.

– 1993. *1991 Aboriginal People's Survey: Schooling, Work and Related Activities, Income, Expenses and Mobility*. Ottawa: Minister of Industry, Science and Technology.

– 1994a. *CALURA Labour Unions/Syndicates 1992*. Cat. 7F202. Ottawa: Minister of Industry, Science and Technology.

– 1994b. *Focus on Culture* (spring), 6 no. 1. Cat. 87-004. Ottawa: Minister of Industry, Science and Technology.

– 1995a. *Focus on Culture* (summer), 7 no. 2. Ottawa: Minister of Industry, Science and Technology.

– 1995b. *Focus on Culture* (winter), 7 no. 4. Ottawa: Minister of Industry, Science and Technology.

– 1995c. *Labour Force Annual Averages 1989–1994*. Cat. 71-201. Ottawa: Minister of Industry, Science and Technology.

– 1995d. *Public Sector Employment and Wages and Salaries, 1994*. Ottawa: Minister of Industry, Science and Technology.

Stick, J. 1986. 'Can Nihilism Be Pragmatic?' *Harvard Law Review*, 100, 332.

Stuart, Don. 1993. 'Annotation to *R. v. Olson.*' *Criminal Reports* (4th), 26, 1.

Sumner, Colin. 1979. *Reading Ideologies: An Investigation into the Marxist Theory of Ideology and Law*. London: Academic Press.

Tarnopolsky, W.S. 1975. 'The Supreme Court and the Canadian Bill of Rights.' *Canadian Bar Review*, 53, 649.

Taylor, Charles. 1993. *Reconciling the Solitudes: Essays on Canadian Federalism and Nationalism*. Montreal: McGill-Queen's University Press.

Thompson, Edward Palmer. 1975. *Whigs and Hunters: The Origin of the Black Act*. London: Allen Lane.

Thompson, John B. 1990. *Ideology and Modern Culture: Critical Social Theory in the Era of New Communication*. Stanford, Calif.: Stanford University Press.

– 1994. 'Social Theory and the Media.' In David Crowley and David Mitchell, eds., *Communication Theory Today*. Stanford, Calif.: Stanford University Press.

Thurshen, M. 1988. 'The Struggle for Health.' In R. Cherry et al., eds., *The Imperiled Economy*. New York: Union for Radical Political Economists.

Tollefson, Chris. 1992. 'R. v. Wholesale Travel (Case Comment).' *Canadian Bar Review*, 71, 369.

– 1993. 'Corporate Constitutional Rights and the Supreme Court of Canada.' *Queen's Law Journal*, 19, 309.

Trakman, Leon. 1991. *Reasoning with the Charter*. Toronto: Butterworths.

– 1994. 'Substantive Equality in Constitutional Jurisprudence: Meaning within Meaning.' *Canadian Journal of Jurisprudence*, 7, 27.

– 1995a. 'The Demise of Positive Liberty? *Native Women's Association of Canada v. Canada.*' *Constitutional Forum*, 6, 71.

– 1995b. 'Section 15: Equality? Where?' *Constitutional Forum*, 6, 112.

Turner, Bryan. 1986. *Citizenship and Capitalism: The Debate over Reformism*. London: Allen & Unwin.

Turpel, Mary Ellen. 1991. 'Aboriginal Peoples and the Canadian Charter: Interpretive Monopolies, Cultural Differences.' In Richard Devlin, ed., *Canadian Perspectives on Legal Theory*. Toronto: Emond Montgomery.

Tushnet, Mark. 1985. 'Anti-Formalism in Recent Constitutional Theory.' *Michigan Law Review*, 83, 1502.

– 1987. *The NAACP's Legal Strategy against Segregated Education: 1925–1950*. Chapel Hill: The University of North Carolina Press.

– 1988. *Red, White and Blue: A Critical Analysis of Constitutional Law*. Cambridge, Mass.: Harvard University Press.

Tyler, Gus. 1986. 'Labour at the Crossroads.' In Martin Lipsett, ed., *Unions in Transition: Entering the Second Century*. San Francisco: ICS Press.

Unger, R. 1975. *Knowledge and Politics*. New York: Free Press.

– 1976. *Law in Modern Society*. New York: Free Press.

– 1983. 'The Critical Legal Studies Movement.' *Harvard Law Review*, 96, 56.

Ursel, Jane. 1992. *Private Lives, Public Policy: 100 Years of State Intervention in the Family*. Toronto: Women's Press.

Vancouver Sun 1994. 'Hiring of Minority Law-school Faculty Urged.' 22 Aug., A5.

– 1995. 'Rising HIV Rates in Women Linked to Male Domination.' 25 May, A8.

Van de Wille, P. 1992. 'Trudeau Says Scare Scenerio a "Lie."' Partial text of Pierre Trudeau's speech. *Globe and Mail*, 2 Oct., A4.

Vickers, Jill. 1993. 'The Canadian Women's Movement and a Changing Constitutional Order.' *International Journal of Canadian Studies*, 7–8, 261.

Warrian, Peter. 1987. 'Trade Unions and the New International Division of Labour.' In Robert Argue et al., eds., *Working People and Hard Times: Canadian Perspectives*. Toronto: Garamond Press.

Waters, Malcolm. 1989. 'Citizenship and the Constitution of Structured Social Inequality.' *International Journal of Comparative Sociology*, 30, 159.

Weber, Max. 1954. *Law in Economy and Society (Translation)*. Cambridge, Mass.: Harvard University Press.

Wedderburn, Lord. 1989. 'Freedom of Association and Philosophies of Labour Law.' *Industrial Law Journal*, 19, 1.

Weiler, Paul. 1970. 'Legal Values and Judicial Decision-Making.' *Canadian Bar Review*, 48, 1.

– 1973. 'The Supreme Court and the Law of Canadian Federalism.' *University of Toronto Law Journal*, 23, 307.

– 1974. *In the Last Resort*. Toronto: Carswell Methuen.

– 1984. 'Rights and Judges in a Democracy: A New Canadian Version.' *University of Michigan Journal of Law Review*, 18, 51.

– 1990. 'The Charter at Work: Reflections on the Constitutionalization of Labour Law.' *University of Toronto Law Journal*, 40, 117.

Weinrib, Lorraine. Legal Analysis of Draft Legal Text of October 12, 1992. Unpublished document on file with the author. University of Toronto, 21 Oct. The following indicated their agreement with Weinrib's legal analysis by signing it: P.E. Benson, R.J. Cook, R.J. Daniels, B.M. Dickens, R.E. Fritz, J.P. Humphrey, H.N. Janisch, W.H. McConnell, R. St J. MacDonald, A.N. Stone, C. Valcke, E.J. Weinrib, and G. Triantis.

Weir, Lorna. 1993. 'Limitations of New Social Movement Analysis.' *Studies in Political Economy*, 40, 73.

Weitzer, Ronald. 1980. 'Law and Legal Ideology: Contributions to the Genesis and Reproduction of Capitalism.' *Berkeley Journal of Sociology* 24/25, 137ff.

Westergaard, J., and H. Ressler. 1975. *Class in a Capitalist Society*. London: Heinemann.

Whitaker, Reg. 1989. 'No Laments for the Nation.' *Canadian Forum*, 68 (March), 9.

White, G.E. 1986. 'From Realism to Critical Legal Studies: A Truncated History.' *Southwestern Law Journal*, 40, 819.

Williams, J. 1987. 'Critical Legal Studies: The Death of Transcendence and the Rise of the New Langdells.' *New York University Law Review*, 62, 429.

Williams, Patricia. 1991. *The Alchemy of Race and Rights*. Cambridge, Mass.: Harvard University Press.

– 1993. 'Alchemical Notes: Reconstructing Ideals from Deconstructed Rights.' In D. Kelly Weisberg, ed., *Feminist Legal Theory: Foundations*. Philadelphia: Temple University Press.

Williams, Raymond. 1980. 'Advertising: The Magic System.' In R. Williams, ed., *Problems in Materialism and Culture: Selected Essays*. London: Verso.

Willis, John. 1951. 'Correspondence.' *Canadian Bar Review*, 29, 580.

Wilson, Bertha. 1990. 'Will Women Judges Really Make a Difference?' *Osgoode Hall Law Journal*, 28, 507.

– 1993. *Report of the Gender Equality Task Force*. Toronto: Canadian Bar Association.

Windspeaker. 1993. 'Native Organization Cuts Staff.' 11 no. 15 (11/24 Oct.), 2.

– 1994. 'Funding Cuts Not Fatal: Native Papers Provide Aboriginal Perspective.' 28 March/ 10 April, 12.

– 1995. 'Federal Cuts to Native Broadcasters.' 12 no. 24 (April), 16.

Winsor, H., and C. Harris. 1996a. 'CBC Won't Close Stations.' *Globe and Mail*, 9 Sept., A1.

– 1996b. 'Pro Sport U.S. Soaps to Feel CBC Knife.' *Globe and Mail*, 20 Sept., A1.

Wright, Erik Olin. 1994. *Interrogating Inequality: Essays on Class Analysis, Socialism and Marxism.* London: Verso.

Wright, Skelly. 1987. 'The Judicial Right and the Rhetoric of Restraint: A Defense of Judicial Activism in an Age of Conservative Judges.' *Hastings Constitutional Law Quarterly*, 14, 487.

Young, Claire. 1994. 'Child Care – a Taxing Issue.' *McGill Law Journal*, 39, 540.

– 1994b. 'Child Care and the Charter: Privileging the Privileged.' *Review of Constitutional Studies*, 2, 20.

Young, Iris. 1990. *Justice and the Politics of Difference.* Princeton, NJ: Princeton University Press.

Zhao, Yuezhi. 1993. 'The "End of Ideology" Again? The Concept of Ideology in the Era of Post-Marxian Theory.' *Canadian Journal of Sociology*, 18, 70.

Cases Cited

A & L Investments Ltd. v. Ontario (Minister of Housing) (1993), 13 OR 799 (Gen. Div.).

Action Travail des Femmes v. Canadian National Railway Co. (1987), 40 DLR (4th) 193 (SCC); [1987] 1 SCR 1114.

A.-G. Canada v. Canadian National Transportation Ltd. (1983), 3 DLR (4th) 16 (SCC); [1983] 2 SCR 206.

A.-G. Ontario v. A.-G. Canada (1911), [1912] AC 571 (PC).

A.-G. Ontario v. A.-G. Canada, [1947] AC 127 (PC).

Alberta Reference – (Reference Re Public Sector Employees Relations Act), [1987] 1 SCR 313.

Amway Corp (Regina v.) (1989), 56 DLR (4th) 309; [1989] 1 SCR 21.

Andrews v. Law Society of British Columbia, [1989] 1 SCR 143.

Apsit v. Manitoba Human Rights Commission, [1988] 1 WWR 629 (Man. QB).

Arlington Crane Service Ltd. et al. and Minister of Labour et al. (Re) (1988), 76 DLR (4th) 209 (OCA).

Arrigo and the Queen, (Re) (1986), 29 CCC (3d) 77 (Ont. HCJ).

B.C.G.E.U. v. A.-G. British Columbia, [1988] 2 SCR 214.

Beck v. Edmonton, [1993] AJ No. 657 (Alta QB).

Bernard (R. v.), [1988] 2 SCR 833.

Big M Drug Mart, (R. v.), (1985) [1985] 1 SCR 295.

Black v. Alberta Law Society (1986), 27 DLR (4th) 527 (CA).

Blainey and Ontario Hockey Association (1986), 26 DLR (4th) 728 (CA).

Blair, (R. v.), [1994] AJ No. 807 (QB).

British Coal Corp. v. The King, [1935] AC 500 (PC).

Brooks v. Canada Safeway Ltd., [1989] 1 SCR 1219.

Brown v. Board of Education (1954), 347 U.S. 483.

Butler, (R. v.), [1992] 1 SCR 452.

Byrt v. Government of Saskatchewan, [1987] 2 WWR 475 (QB).

Canadian Newspapers Co. v. A.G. Canada, [1987] 2 SCR 122.

CIP Inc., (R. v.), [1992] 1 SCR 843.

Citizens Insurance Company of Canada v. Parsons (1881), 7 App. Cas. 96 (PC).

Committee for the Commonwealth of Canada v. Canada, [1991] 1 SCR 139.

Consolidated Maybrun Mines Ltd. (R. v.) (1993), 86 CCC (3d) 317 (Ont. Ct General Div.).

Dagenais v. CBC, [1994] 3 SCR 835.

Daviault, (R. v.), [1994] 3 SCR 63.

Delgamuukw v. B.C., [1991] 3 WWR 97 (BCSC).

Dixon v. British Columbia (1989) 59 DLR (4th) 247 (BCSC)

Dolphin Delivery, (RWDSU v.), [1986] 2 SCR 573.

Douglas College, (Douglas/Kwantlen Faculty Assn. v.), [1990] 3 SCR 570.

Dubois v. The Queen, [1985] 2 SCR 350.

Dywidag Systems v. Zutphen Bros., [1990] 1 SCR 705.

Edwards v. A.-G. Canada, [1930] AC 124 (PC).

Edwards Books and Art, (R. v.), [1986] 2 SCR 713.

Egan and Nesbit v. Canada, [1995] 2 SCR 513.

Eldridge v. British Columbia (A.-G.), [1995] BCJ No. 1168.

Ellis Don, (The Queen v.), [1992] 1 SCR 840.

Ertel Ltd. v. Johnson (1986), 25 DLR (4th) 233 (Ont. Div. Ct).

Ford v. Quebec (Attorney-General), [1988] 2 SCR 712.

G. (C.E.), Re. File No. 1995/62. Ont. Fam. Ct (London). 60 ACWS 106, 17 Aug.

Gayme, (R. v.), [1991] 2 SCR 577.

Glad Day Bookshop Inc. v. Canada (1992), 90 DLR (4th) 527 (Ont. Ct Gen. Div.).

Haig v. Canada, [1993] 2 SCR 995.

Haig and Birch v. Canada (Minister of Justice), (1992) 9 OR (3d) 495 (Ont. CA).

Heather Hill 65 CLLC 14083.

Hess, (R. v.), [1990] 2 SCR 906.

Hill v. Church of Scientology, [1995] 2 SLR 1130.

H.S., (R. v.), [1995] OJ No. 1428 (Ont. Ct Prov. Div.)

Hunter v. Southam, [1984] 2 SCR 145.

Hy v. Zel's, [1993] 3 SCR 675.

Imperial Chemical Industries PLC v. Apotex Inc. (1990), 31 CPR (3d) 517 (FCTD).

International Longshoremen's and Warehousemen's Union, Canada Area Local 500 v. Canada, [1994] 1 SCR 150.

Irwin Toy Ltd. v. Attorney-General of Quebec, [1989] 1 SCR 927.

Island Equine Clinic v. P.E.I. (1991), 81 DLR (4th) 350 (PEIAD).

Janzen v. Platy Enterprises, [1989] 1 SCR 1252.

Johnston, (R. v.), [1995] NBJ. No. 557 (NBQBTD)

Jones, (R. v.), [1986] 2 SCR 284.

JPL, (R. v.), [1994] OJ No. 2548 (Ont. CA).

K. and B. (Re) (1995), 125 DLR (4th) 653 (Ont. Ct Prov. Div.).

Keegstra, (R. v.), [1990] 3 SCR 697.

Knodel v. British Columbia, [1991] 6 WWR 728.

Korutz, (R. v.), [1993] 1 SCR 1134.

K (Re) [1995] OJ No. 1425, 24 May.

Lamb v. Bank of Toronto et al. (1887), 12 App. Cas. 575 (PC)

Lavigne v. Ontario Public Service Employees' Union, [1991] 2 SCR 24.

Layland v. Ontario (Minister of Consumer and Commercial Relations), (1993) 14 OR (3d) 658.

Leschner v. Ontario, (1992) 16 CHRR D/184 (Ontario Board of Inquiry).

Levy, (R. v.), (1996) 104 CCC (3d) 423 (Ont. CA)

Lewis, (R. v.), [1996] BCJ No. 3001 (BCSC).

Little Sisters Book and Art Emporium v. Canada, [1996] BCJ No.7 (BCSC).

Lochner v. New York (1905), 198 U.S. 45.

M'Culloch (1819), 17 U.S. 316.

McKinley Transport Ltd. et al. v. The Queen, [1990] 1 SCR 627.

McKinney v. University of Guelph, [1990] 3 SCR 229.

McShane, (R. v.), [1996] O.J. No. 361 (Ont. Ct. Prov. Div.).

Metro Stores (MTS) Ltd. v. Manitoba Food and Commercial Workers, Loc.832, [1988] 5 WWR 544 (Man. QB).

Metropolitan Properties Co. (F.G.C.), Ltd. v. Lannon, [1968] 3 All ER.

Mia v. Medical Services Commission of British Columbia (1985), 61 BCLR 273 (BCSC).

Miles of Music Ltd., (R. v.) (1990), 74 OR (2d) 518 (Ont. CA).

Mills v. The Queen, [1986] 1 SCR 863.

Minister of Home Affairs v. Fisher (1979), [1980] AC 319 (PC).

Miron v. Trudel, [1995] 2 SCR 418.

Misquadis, (R. v.) (1995), 39 CR (4th) 246 (Ont. Ct Prov. Div.).

Morgentaler, (R. v.), [1988] 1 SCR 30.

Mossop, (Canada A.-G. v.), [1993] 1 SCR 554.

Motor Vehicle Act Reference (B.C.) s. 94(2), [1985] 2 SCR 486.

National Citizens' Coalition Inc. v. A.-G. Canada (1984), 11 DLR (4th) 481 (Alta. QB).

Native Women's Association of Canada v. Canada, [1994] 3 SCR 627.

Nguyen, (R. v.), [1990] 2 SCR 906.

Nickel City Transport, (R. v.) (1993), 104 DLR (4th) 340 (Ont. CA).

N.T.C. Smokehouse Ltd., (R. v.), [1996] SCJ No. 78.

O'Flaherty, (R. v.), [1995] OJ No. 1005 (Ont. Ct Prov. Div.).

Operation Dismantle v. The Queen [1985] 1 SCR 441.

Osolin, (R. v.), [1993] 4 SCR 595.

Peterborough v. Ramsden, [1993] 2 SCR 1084.

Potash, (Comité paritaire de l'industrie de la chemise v.), [1994] SCR 406.

Professional Institute of the Public Service of Canada v. N.W.T. (Commissioner), [1990] 2 SCR 367.

Prosper, (R. v.), [1994] 3 SCR 236.

Prostitution Reference Case, [1990] 1 SCR 1123.

Public Service Alliance of Canada v. Canada, [1987] 1 SCR 424.

Rahey, (R. v.), [1987] 1 SCR 588.

Re Griffin and College of Dental Surgeons (1988), 47 DLR (4th) 331 (BCSC).

Re Klein and Law Society of Upper Canada (1985), 16 DLR (4th) 489 (Ont. Div. Ct).

Re PPG Industries Canada and A.-G. Canada (1983), 3 CCC (3d) 97 (BCCA).

Ref Re Dominion Trade and Industry Commission Act, [1936] SCR 379.

Reference Re Employment and Social Insurance Act (1937), [1937] 1 DLR 702 (PC).

Reference Re Weekly Rest in Industrial Undertakings Act, Minimum Wages Act and Limitation of Hours of Work Act (1937), [1937] 1 DLR 673 (PC).

Regina v. Oakes [1986] 1 SCR 103.

RJR-MacDonald v. Canada (Attorney General) [1995] 3 SCR 199.

Rocket and Royal College of Dental Surgeons (Re), (1988), 49 DLR (4th) 641 (Ont. CA); aff'd [1990] 2 SCR 232.

Rodriguez v. British Columbia (A.-G.), [1993] 3 SCR 519.

Roe v. Wade 410 US 113 (1973)

Ross v. New Brunswick School District No. 15, [1996] 1 SCR 825.

Rural Dignity of Canada v. Canada Post Corp. (1992), 88 DLR (4th) 191 (FCA).

RVP Enterprises Ltd. v. British Columbia (Attorney General), [1988] 4 WWR 726 (CA).

Saskatchewan Dairy Workers – RWDSU v. Saskatchewan, [1987] 1 SCR 460.

Sault Ste. Marie, (R. v.), [1978] 2 SCR 1299.

Schachter v. Canada, [1992] 2 SCR 679.

Schiewe, (R. v.), (1992), 72 CCC (3d) 353 (Alta CA).

Seaboyer, (R. v.), [1991] 2 SCR 577.

Sigurjonsson v. Iceland (30 June 1993) *The London Times* 27 July 1993.

Skalbania (Trustee of) v. Wedgewook Village Estates Ltd. (1989), 60 DLR (4th) 43 (BCCA).

Skapinker v. Law Society of Upper Canada, [1984] 1 SCR 357.

Slaight Communications Inc. v. Davidson, [1989] 1 SCR 1038.

Société des Acadiens du Nouveau-Brunswick Inc. v. Association of Parents for Fairness in Education, [1986] 1 SCR 549.

Somerville v. Canada (Attorney General), [1993] AJ No. 504 (Alta. QB).

Somerville v. Canada (1996) 184 AR 241 (CA).

Sparrow, (R.v.), [1990] 1 SCR 1075.

Stoffman v. Vancouver General Hospital, [1990] 3 SCR 483.

Strickland v. Ermel (1992), 91 DLR (4th) 694 (Sask. QB).

Swain, (R. v.), [1991] 1 SCR 933.

Symes v. Canada, [1993] 4 SCR 659.

Tetreault-Gadoury v. Canada (Employment and Immigration), [1991] 2 SCR 22.

Thibadeau v. Canada [1995] 2 SCR 627.

Thomson Newspapers Ltd. et al. v. Director of Investigation & Research et al., [1990] 1 SCR 425.

Turpin, (R. v.), [1989] 1 SCR 1296.

Van der Peet, (R. v.), [1996] SCJ No. 77.

Veysey v. Canada (1990), 109 NR 300 (FCA).

Veysey v. Canada, [1990] 1 FC 321 (TD).

Vriend v. Alberta (1994), 6 WWR 414 (Alta QB).

Weatherall v. Canada (A.-G.), [1993] 2 SCR 872.

Wholesale Travel Group Inc., (R. v.), [1991] 3 SCR 154.

Wilson v. British Columbia (Medical Commission) (1988), 53 DLR (4th) 171 (BCCA).

Young v. Young, [1993] 4 SCR 3.

Zundel, (R. v.), [1992] 2 SCR 731.

Index

abortion, 23, 39, 57–8, 75
academics, role in social change, 144
advertising: general, 92, 107–9, 187–8; of
  tobacco, 75, 90
affirmative action, 46, 164
African Americans, 119, 127
Alberta Reference, 23, 24, 38, 39, 78, 79,
  81, 92, 108, 172
Andrews v. Law Society of BC, 23, 46,
  49–51, 56
anti-semitism, 94–6
*Apsit v. Manitoba Human Rights Commis-
  sion*, 46
Arthurs, Harry, 182
arts funding, 67
Assembly of First Nations, 128

Bakan, Paul, 188
B.C.G.E.U. v. A.-G. British Columbia, 107,
  108, 155, 184, 185, 186
Beatty, David, 36–7, 79–80
Beaudoin-Dobbie Report, 135
Beck v. Edmonton, 179
Big M Drug Mart (Regina v.), 22, 89, 175,
  176
Blomley, Nick, 184
Bogart, William, 155

Borrows, John, 58
Boyd, Susan, 183
Brodsky, Gwen, 138
Brooks, Neil, 169
Brown v. Board of Education, 56
Brown, Wendy, 117
Buber, Martin, 15
Butler, (R. v.), 65, 98, 166, 171

Cairns, Alan, 18
Canadian Bill of Rights, 20, 22
Canadian Broadcasting Corporation, 67
capitalism, 9, 51–5, 60–2, 81–5, 99,
  148–9
censorship, 70–1, 72–6
Charlottetown Accord, 119–20, 117–33,
  135
Charter of Rights and Freedoms: criticism
  of, 6–9, 11, counter-majoritarian critique, 6–7, critical legal studies, 7–9,
  progressive variations of, 5–9, 33, 36–7,
  53–5, 60–2, as scepticism, 11; First
  Nations and, 120–1, 128–9; Quebec
  and, 120–1, 129–30; regressive effects
  of, 59–60, 87–100; section 1, 27–30,
  90, 98–100, 156, 180, 186; section 2(a),
  88–9; section 2(b), 64–5, 90, 93, 94–6,

166, 184; section 2(d), 78–81, 93–4;
section 7, 88–90, 92, 97, 176; section 8,
91; section 11(b), 91; section 11(d), 97;
section 15, 45–62; section 32, 47–50,
161, 166; social rights claims under,
54–5
child-care benefits and the Charter, 59–60
CIP Inc., (R. v.), 89, 91, 92, 176, 177
citizenship, 135, 139–41
class analysis, 9, 51–5, 146–9, 163
collective rights, 25, 79, 121
*Committee for the Commonwealth of
Canada v. Canada*, 64, 90, 166
communications and media, 63–70, 90;
privatization of, 67
Cooper, Davina, 45, 131, 169
corporations: the Charter and, 88–98;
dominant ideological discourses of,
106–7; standing under Charter of,
89–91
Cossman, Brenda, 60
Crenshaw, Kim, 155

Dagenais v. CBC, 158, 161, 180
Daviault, (R. v.), 97
Day, Shelagh, 125
deficit and debt, 69–70, 145–52
democracy, 6–7, 149–52; barriers to realization of, 10–11; definition of, 10–11;
judicial review and, 6–7, 15, 37–40,
98–100, 160
deregulation, 149–50, 174; the Charter
and, 88–98
Dickson, Brian, 25, 26, 27, 29, 38, 79
distinct society clause, 120, 129
Dixon v. British Columbia, 7
Dolphin Delivery v. R.W.D.S.U., 31–2, 64,
107, 108, 161, 184, 185, 186
*Douglas College, (Douglas/Kwantlen Fac.
Assn. v.)*, 49

Dworkin, Ronald, 34–5, 155
Dywidag Systems v. Zutphen Bros., 175
Dyzenhaus, David, 36–7, 40

Eagleton, Terry, 63
economic inequality, 51–5
economic rights, 88–94, 177
education, 67–8
Edwards Books and Art, (R. v.), 29, 38, 98,
180
Egan and Nesbit v. Canada, 23, 105, 159,
160, 165, 180
Eldridge v. British Columbia, 49
election campaign spending, 72, 90, 92–3
Ellis Don, (The Queen v.), 176
equality: administrative, 46; definition,
9–10; economic, 51–5; formal, 46,
64–5; right to, 45–62; sexual, 121,
125–6, 129–30; social, 47; substantive,
46–7

familial ideology, 109, 111–12
family values, 111–12
federalism, 120, 189–90
feminism, 96, 129–30
feudalism, 61
First Nations: Charter and, 120–1, 128–9;
child welfare, 58; collective rights of,
121; fishing rights, 48–9; nationalism,
120; poverty, 53; racism, 53; self-
government, 122–5, 128–9; women,
122–5, 128–9
Fiss, Owen, 34–5, 159
Fitzpatrick, Peter, 129
Ford v. Quebec, 91, 107, 185, 186
free trade, 84, 93
freedom, 10
freedom of association, 24–5, 77–86,
93–4, *see also* labour relations; collective
bargaining and, 83–5; managerial prac-

tices and, 82–5; right to form or join a union, 81–3; strikes and, 83–5; union security and, 93–4

freedom of expression, 63–76, 90, 93, 94–6; harm approach, 73–6; hate speech, 72–6, 94–6; liberal model of, 64–5, 66; oppositional ideas, 67–70, 71–6; picketing, 31, 32–3, 107–9; public space, 68

Friedmann, W., 19, 20

Fudge, Judy, 96, 155

gays and lesbians. *See* lesbians and gays

gender relations, 53, 57–8, 59–60, 96–8

Glad Day Bookshop v. Canada, 75

Glasbeek, Harry, 155, 191

Haig and Birch v. Canada, 50

Haig v. Canada, 64

Hall, Stuart, 131, 170

harm, related to free speech, 73–6

Harvey, David, 77

hate speech, 72–6, 94–6

Hay, Douglas, 154

health, 139–41

Herman, Didi, 110, 118–19, 127, 155, 188

Hess, (R. v.), 96

Hill v. Church of Scientology, 158, 161

Hogg, Peter, 20, 21, 23, 31

Holocaust, 95

homophobia, 71, 72–6

Hunt, Alan, 132

Hunter v. Southam, 22, 23, 26, 38, 91, 92, 176, 177

Hutchinson, Allan, 7–9, 144, 145, 155

ideology, 4, 68–70, 72, 105, 108, 132, 170; and judges, 5, 31, 33, 99, 103–13, 105, 182–3; of law, 4; of rights, 4, 47–8, 60–2, 118–19, 132, 189

internet, 66–7, 166, 169

interpretation of the constitution: formalism, 157; indeterminacy, 14–42, 136; purposive reasoning, Charter, 20–1, 22–7, 30; trust-based approaches, 16–21, 30–3; truth-based approaches, 16–30; weak-constraint approaches, 34–7

Irwin Toy v. Quebec, 65, 89, 91, 92, 98, 107, 166, 175, 184, 186

Iyer, Nitya, 164

Jones, (R. v.), 30–1

Judicial Committee of the Privy Council, 17–19; critics of, 19–21

judges: bias of, 103–4, 180; and dominant ideology, 5, 31–2; personnel, 104

judicial review: deference by judges to democratic bodies, 37–40, 98–100, 160; democracy and, 6–7, 15; history of, 87–8; legitimacy of, 15–42

K. and B. (Re), 57

Keegstra, (R. v.), 65, 75, 94–5, 99, 166, 171, 180

Kennedy, Duncan, 182

Kennedy, W.P.M., 18, 19, 23

Kerruish, Valerie, 191

Kline, Marlee, 104, 183

Knodel v. British Columbia, 57

labour relations, 32–3, 52–5, 77–86, 93–4, 106–8

LaBrie, F.E., 20, 23

Laclau, E., and Mouffe, C., 131, 148

LaForest, Gerald, 110–12, 157–8

Lamer, Antonio, 23, 184

Landsberg, Michele, 123

Langille, Brian, 34–5

Laskin, Bora, 19, 20, 21, 23, 30

Lavigne v. O.P.S.E.U., 93–4, 179
law: external perspective on, 5–6; ideology
    of, 4; internal perspective on, 5–6,
    65, 153; interpretation of, *see* inter-
    pretation of the constituion; religion
    and, 154
legal education, 104–5
Legal Education and Action Fund, 160
lesbian and gay issues, 56–7, 71, 105,
    109–12, 118–19
Leschner v. Ontario, 57
Lessard, Hester, 155
Lewis, (R. v.), 75
L'Heureux-Dubé, Claire, 97, 105
liberalism: discourses of, 4, 47–8, 118–19,
    121–6, anti-statism, 47, 48, 64, 80–1,
    149–52, atomism, 47, 51–5, 57–60, 65,
    80–1, 139–41, 170, formal equality, 46,
    64–5; rights discourse and, 4, 47–8,
    55–62, 64–5, 71–6, 80–1, 87, 98,
    118–19, 139–41, 146
Little Sisters v. Canada, 71, 75
Lochner v. New York, 174

MacDonald, Vincent, 18, 19, 23
McIntyre, William, 22, 23, 25, 79,
    157
McKinley Transport v. The Queen, 177
McKinney v. University of Guelph, 23, 38,
    48, 49, 98
McLachlin, Beverley, 95, 97, 99, 103
Macpherson, C.B., 51
Macklem, Patrick, 58
Mandel, Michael, 6, 146, 155
Marx, Karl, 3, 6, 77, 82
Matsuda, Mari, 171
media. *See* communications and media
Miliband, Ralph, 31, 126
Mills v. The Queen, 91
Miron v. Trudel, 160, 162

Monahan, Patrick, 38, 39, 160
Morgentaler, (R. v.), 7, 23, 39, 57–8,
    161–2
Mossop, (Canada v.), 112
Motor Vehicle Act Reference, 23, 90, 176

National Action Committee on the Status
    of Women, 125–6, 129–30, 131–2
National Association for the Advancement
    of Colored People (U.S.), 127
National Citizens' Coalition, 92–4, 149
National Citizens' Coalition v. Canada,
    92
nationalism: and First Nations, 120; and
    Quebec, 120, 129–30
Native Women's Association of Canada,
    123–5, 128–9, 131–2
*Native Women's Association of Canada v.
    Canada*, 64, 162
neo-conservatism, 99
neo-liberalism, 99, 137
'New Deal' cases, 18
New Democratic Party (NDP), 78, 93, 99,
    134–5
normative premises of book, 9–11
N.T.C. Smokehouse, (R. v.), 58

Oakes, (R. v.), 27–30, 31, 155, 157–8, 180,
    186. *See also* Charter: section 1
Operation Dismantle v. The Queen, 23

Peller, Gary, 23
Peterborough v. Ramsden, 166, 168
Petter, Andrew, 39, 155
Philips, Lisa, 161, 169
Phillips, Susan, 67
picketing, 31, 32–3, 107–9
political correctness, 73–5
Porter, Bruce, 135
postmodernism, 8, 131

Potash, (Comité paritaire de l'industrie de la chemise v.), 98, 177
poverty, 51–5, 139–41, 162–3; First Nations and, 53; women and, 53
privatization, 149–52; of communications, 67
Professional Institute of P.S.C. v. N.W.T., 79, 81, 172
progressive, definition, 9–11
property rights, 51–5, 92, 147
Prosper, (R. v.), 49
Prostitution Reference Case, 178
Public Service Alliance of Canada v. Canada, 78, 172
public space, 68
purposive reasoning. *See* interpretation of the constitution

Quebec: and Charter, 120–1, 129–30; collective rights of, 121; nationalism, 120, 129–30

racism, 53, 72–6, 90, 94–6
Rand formula, 93–4
rape shield provision, 97
Rebick, Judy, 130
Reform party, 122, 149
regulatory law. *See* corporations
rights: collective, 121; critique of, 6–9, 118; economic, 88–94, 177; ideology of, 4, 8, 47–8, 60–2, 118–19, 189; liberalism and, 4, 47–8, 55–62, 64–5, 118–19; negative versions of, 49–51; political discourses of, 117–33, 140–1; positive versions of, 49–51, 64, 124–41; progressive advocacy of, 131; of professionals, 177
RJR-MacDonald v. Canada, 38, 75, 92, 107, 108, 159, 166, 180, 185, 186
Robinson, Svend, 65
Roboy, Mark, 67

Rocket and Royal College of Dental Surgeons, 92, 99, 107, 108, 166, 180, 185, 186
Roosevelt, F.D., 88
Rosenberg, Gerald, 155
Rosenbluth, Gideon, 69
Ross v. New Brunswick School District, 75, 98
Rural Dignity of Canada v. Canada Post, 49
Russell, Peter, 51, 87
Ryder, Bruce, 111

Saskatchewan Dairy Workers case, 78, 172
Schacter v. Canada, 50, 59, 143
Scheingold, Stuart, 155
Schiewe, (R. v.), 49
Schneiderman, David, x
Scott, F.R., 8, 23
Seaboyer, (R. v.), 97
sexism, 72–6, 90, 96–8
sexual assault, 96–8
sexuality, dominant ideological discourses of, 109–11
Shaw, George Bernard, 52
Skapinker v. L.S.U.C., 22
Slaight Communications Inc. v. Davidson, 49, 98, 176
Smart, Carol, 140
social charter, 134–41; indeterminacy of, 136–7; justiciability, 137; regressive potential of, 136–9; symbolism of, 140–1
social democracy, 98, 99
social justice, definition, 9–11
social movements, 126–30, 190
Somerville v. Canada, 93
Sparrow, (R. v.), 58
Stoffman v. Vancouver General Hospital, 49
Strickland v. Ermel, 179
strike, right to, 83–5. *See also* labour relations

Swain, (R. v.), 47
Symes v. Canada, 56, 59–60

Tetrault-Gadoury v. Canada, 59
Thibadeau v. Canada, 162, 180
Thompson, E.P., 6
Thompson, John B., 66
Thomson Newspapers v. Director of Investigation and Research, 177
tobacco advertising, 75, 90
Trakman, Leon, 6, 60, 161, 162, 164, 215
Trudeau, Pierre, 122, 126
Turpin, (R. v.), 54, 56
Tushnet, Mark, 155

unemployment, 52–3, 84
unions. *See* freedom of association; labour relations
universities, 68, 73–4

Van der Peet, (R. v.), 58
vulnerable groups, 98–100

Weatherall v. Canada, 56
Weber, Max, 5
Weiler, Paul, 20, 21, 23
Weinrib, Lorraine, 124, 128
Wholesale Travel, (R. v.), 38, 90, 175, 176
Williams, P., 56
Wilson, 177
Wilson, Bertha, 105

Young, Claire, 59
Young, I.M., 134
Young, Margot, 161

Zundel, (R. v.), 95–6, 166